WRINKLIES'
WIT & WISDOM
~ THE COMPLETE COMPANION ~

Published by Prion
an imprint of the Carlton Publishing Group
20 Mortimer Street, London W1T 3JW

This edition published 2011 for Index Books Ltd

A catalogue record for this book is available from the British Library.

ISBN 978-1-85375-810-2

Typeset by E-Type, Liverpool

Printed and bound in Great Britain by CPI Mackays, Chatham ME5 8TD

1 3 5 7 9 10 8 6 4 2

WRINKLIES'
WIT & WISDOM
~The Complete Companion~

*Humorous stories, funny jokes and amusing
quotes for Wrinklies everywhere*

Mike Haskins & Clive Whichelow

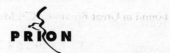

PRION

Contents

Part One: Jokes

Part Two: Your Bedside Companion

Part One: Jokes

You're only young once, but you're older every year. Not fair is it? But then who said life was fair? And who said you're a wrinkly come to that? You're not are you? Of course you're not. Well, you're fairly sure you're not. OK, you may have a few wrinklyist tendencies, but on the whole you're in the prime of life. Aren't you? Apart from the odd laughter line (and some of them are in quite odd places for laughter lines), the odd dodgy joint (and no, we're not talking about your choice of nightspots here) and the occasional senior moment, you're fighting fit.

Yes, we know exactly what's happened: some joker, someone a bit younger than you naturally, has bought you this book for a laugh because you're on the wrong side of 40 and they think it will be amusing to wind you up with jokes about commodes and plastic surgery and forgetfulness, but it'll be like water off a duck's whatsit ("back", dear) because you ain't old. And if anyone says you are you can hit them with your walking stick. Only kidding!

And anyway, in this little volume you will find mini-quizzes to determine if you are in fact a wrinkly. Perhaps you are. Someone has to be. But not you. No, OK, we hear you loud and clear, we've got the message, so now you can sit back and read on in the full knowledge that wrinkliedom is someone else's domain and, hell, you can laugh at them for a change. What's that? You've just got to go and find your reading glasses? You know you left them somewhere, but where....? OK then, whenever you're ready...

Getting Older And Wrinklier

As you get older, you will find you lose interest in sex, your friends drift away and your children often ignore you. There are other advantages, of course, but these are the main ones.

My grandmother is over 80 and still doesn't need glasses. Drinks right out of the bottle.

Henny Youngman

My grandfather will be there tonight. A marvellous old chap – you'd never think he was 104 – he looks much older.

Ronnie Corbett

When I was young I was called a rugged individualist. When I was in my 50s I was considered eccentric. Here I am doing and saying the same things I did then and I'm labelled senile.

George Burns

There are only two things we do with increasing frequency as we get older. One is to urinate and the other is to attend funerals.

Three things happen when you get to my age. First your memory starts to go and I've forgotten the other two.

Denis Healey

A man is only as old as the woman he feels.

Groucho Marx

At 65 you begin to regret the sins you did NOT commit.

I don't feel old. I don't feel anything until noon. Then it's time for my nap.

Bob Hope

The greatest problem about old age is the fear that it might go on too long.

A. J. P. Taylor

I smoke cigars, because at my age if I don't have something to hang on to I might fall down.

George Burns

It's a frightening feeling to wake up one morning and discover that while you were asleep you went out of style.

Erma Bombeck

Of course there's one way the ageing process could be slowed down: by making it work its way through Parliament.

It's scary when you start making the same noises as your coffee maker.

When you're old you think you've developed more patience, but really you're just past caring any more.

A newspaper reporter asks old Alf, "To what do you attribute your old age?" "To the fact I was born a long time ago," says Alf.

There was no respect for youth when I was young and now that I am old there is no respect for age – I missed it coming and going.

J. B. Priestley

Wrinkly's car bumper sticker: Don't worry. I drive far too fast to worry about cholesterol.

A sexagenarian? At his age? That's disgusting.

Gracie Allen

I'm looking forward to being properly old. Really old. So that I can lean over in a restaurant and say to my son, "You know what I just did? I just pissed myself... You deal with it!"

Dylan Moran

I'm going to stay in show business until I'm the last one left.

George Burns

Wrinkly's Bumper Sticker: Too old to care... Too senile to remember.

As we grow older, our bodies get shorter and our anecdotes longer.

Robert Quillen

An old man tells a friend, "I've got good news and bad news. The good news is I've finally discovered the Fountain of Youth." "What's the bad news?" asks his friend. "At my age," says the first old man, "I've forgotten what I wanted it for."

As we grow older year by year, my husband always mourns: the less and less we feel our oats, the more we feel our corns.

At my age flowers scare me.

George Burns

Have you ever thought, in 40 years' time when they're going over all the things they had to do without when they were young, what exactly are the children of today going to moan about?

An old man is being shown round a house by an estate agent. "This house," says the estate agent, "is not only beautifully appointed and in first class decorative order, but it's a fabulous long-term investment." "Long-term?" says the old man. "You're joking aren't you? Blimey, at my time of life I don't even buy green bananas!"

Wrinkly's Bumper Sticker: Young at heart... slightly older in other places.

I don't need you to remind me of my age. I have a bladder to do that for me.

Stephen Fry

Phrases People Use To Indicate That You Are Old – Without Actually Saying So

Past the first flush of youth

Mature

In your third age

Matronly

No spring chicken

Not as young as she/he used to be

And some less polite ones

Past it

Over the hill

Knocking on a bit

Geriatric

Senile

Old fogey

Crone

Coffin-dodger

Old git

Wrinkly

Funny how there's more rude ones than polite ones, isn't it?

Definitions For Wrinklies

Age always corresponds inversely to the size of your multi-vitamin tablets.

Age is not a particularly interesting subject. Anyone can get old. All you have to do is live long enough.

Don Marquis

Dorothy: Age is just a state of mind.
Blanche: Tell that to my thighs.

The Golden Girls

Age seldom arrives smoothly or quickly. It's more often a succession of jerks.

Jean Rhys

Age: that period of life in which we compound for the vices that we still cherish by reviling those that we no longer have the enterprise to commit.

Ambrose Bierce

Age is something that makes wine worth more and people worth less.

Old age is the out-patients' department of purgatory.

Lord Hugh Cecil

Old age is when you resent the swimsuit issue of *Sports Illustrated*, because there are fewer articles to read.

George Burns

To me old age is always 15 years older than I am.

Bernard Baruch

You're not old. You're chronologically challenged.

Welcome To Wrinkly World

It sounds like one of those theme parks doesn't it? Wrinkly World – a mildly enjoyable day out for all the family who are over 40! White-knuckle wheelchair rides! The ghost train – haunted by recent customers! The wall of deaf! Slow food (boiled ham burgers, toffee apples with custard, warmed-up dogs!)

Perhaps some budding entrepreneur should get on to it. Official figures show that by the year 2050, 110% of the population will be over-60, (or something like that), so there's a huge potential market, with wrinklies from John o'Groats to Lands End all raring to go – and have a nice sit down.

But before that happens we have the real world of wrinklies. And wrinklyhood is not just a state of mind or concerned with how your body is refusing to cooperate these days. It's about every aspect of your life, from the clothes you wear to the pets you keep. So, if you want to keep wrinklyhood at bay a bit longer pay careful attention to the following – and avoid behaving like a typical wrinkly.

Wrinkly World: Food And Kitchenware

Examine your kitchen cupboards and fridge. Do you possess any of the following:

Horlicks

Ovaltine

Custard powder

Camp coffee

A brown teapot

A teapot shaped like a country cottage

A tea strainer

A swear box

An apron with a picture of breasts on the front that the man of the house uses to amuse people at barbecues

A grey-looking cloth that is used for cooking spotted dick

A novelty tea towel showing London landmarks

A jokey poster detailing the "rules of the house"

A tea cosy that you or another member of your family has knitted or crocheted

A set of egg cosies

A non-fitted kitchen unit

A china toast rack

An egg coddler

Any sort of butter pat implement

Doggie choc drops

Bird seed for the wild birds in your garden

A recipe book that has actually been used and has not been purchased solely to show your hip affinity to the latest celebrity chef

Sugar tongs

A biscuit barrel

The more of the above you possess the more of a wrinkly you are.

You Know You're Getting Old When...

You come out of a supermarket and spend 15 minutes looking for your car before remembering you gave up driving four years ago.

Even pensioners are looking younger.

You look back at your old love letters and find the stamps on the front have got kings on them.

You're asked to be the "before" face in a Botox ad.

Some children come to visit and you're not sure whether they're grandchildren, great-grandchildren or somebody else's great-grandchildren.

When you bend your knees everyone suddenly ducks because they think there's a sniper on the loose.

You dread one of your household appliances breaking down, because you're not sure whether you can master any more new technology.

You leave the pub before closing time – even on your birthday.

You don't look forward to birthdays any more.

The highlight of your day is putting your feet up.

Your idea of a good time is not having to do anything.

You've given up trying to keep up with the Joneses and even have trouble keeping up with the plotline of *Eastenders*.

Your idea of a workout is trying to chew a toffee.

The local paper rings to ask if you'd help them with a nostalgia piece.

The doctor tries to take your pulse and has trouble finding it.

You start planning who to cut out of your will.

A sexy young thing catches your fancy and your pacemaker opens the garage door.

A strenuous bout of weight-lifting only involves getting out of a chair.

After painting the town red, you have to take a week's rest before applying a second coat.

Middle-age (aka The First Age Of Wrinklydom)

Yes, it's that strange never-never land between being young and being old. You're too old for discos, but a bit young for slipped discs, too old for speed dating, but a bit young for carbon dating. You've still got some of your energy, but frankly you can't be bothered to use it. But it's also the point where you suddenly want to recapture some of your fading youth before it's too late. Men will suddenly buy large motorbikes, because they like to feel something throbbing between their legs, women will think about having a toy boy, because, well, because it makes them feel younger. Luckily it's a very loosely defined concept so no one admits to it. Being middle-aged is something that only happens to other people. Just beware that coming home with a boy's toy or a toy boy is a dead giveaway.

After 30, a body has a mind of its own.

Bette Midler

Thirty-five is when you finally get your head together and your body starts falling apart.

Caryn Leschen

Not only does life begin at 40, it also really begins to show.

Middle-age is a time of life that a man first notices in his wife.

Richard Armour

Middle-age is having a choice of two temptations and choosing the one that will get you home earlier.

Middle-age is the time when a man is always thinking in a week or two he will feel as good as ever.

Don Marquis

Middle-age is when the broadness of your mind and the narrowness of your waist swap places.

It's called middle-age because it's the time when you stop growing at both ends and start to grow in the middle.

Middle-age is when women stop worrying about becoming pregnant and men start worrying about looking like they are.

It may be true that life begins at 40, but everything else starts to wear out, fall out or spread out.

Middle-age is when you choose a cereal because of its fibre content, rather than because of its free plastic toy.

Middle-age is when your glasses and your waistline get thicker. And your hair and your wallet get thinner.

Everyone is sitting in their seats at the theatre waiting for the performance to start when suddenly a middle-aged woman at the back of the stalls stands up and shouts, "Is there a doctor in the house?" Five men stand up and the woman says, "Thank goodness for that, now if any of you are single would you like to marry my beautiful daughter?"

The really frightening thing about middle-age is knowing you'll grow out of it.

Doris Day

Middle-age is when you go to bed at night and hope you feel better in the morning. Old age is when you go to bed at night and hope you wake up in the morning.

Groucho Marx

Lying About Your Age

They say you're only as old as you feel, which is, very well until you get to 60 and you feel 80. But whatever age you are, it can always remain a secret between you and the yellowing parchment of your birth certificate.

Some stars not only look magically younger every year, their age magically decreases annually too. But such devilish chicanery doesn't have to be the sole province of pop stars and actors. You, too, can fool most of the people most of the time with these simple tips on how to be economical with the truth about your advancing years.

Form filling. Next time you are confronted with the dreaded words "date of birth" simply write February 16th or whatever it is. If challenged you can quite correctly point out that they never asked the year and, to be honest, it's far too long ago for you to remember anyway.

Being asked directly. If someone has the effrontery to actually ask the question outright just ask them how old they think you are. Most people are polite enough to knock a few years off what they really think and then you can make *them* feel good by telling them they're spot on. Everyone's happy!

Inadvertent slippage. You know what it's like – someone starts talking about the war and before you can help yourself you're reminiscing about rationing, air raid shelters and all the rest while suddenly realising that everyone else is making rapid mental calculations about your age – "So, you were five when war broke out then?" It is at this point that you suddenly put them straight, "Oh yes, brilliant, wasn't it, that *Band of Brothers*? It almost made you feel like you'd lived through it yourself!" Phew!

The age of your children. One day someone suddenly realizes that your eldest child is almost 40, which puts you at 56 at the absolute minimum and more likely well into your 60s. It's at this point that you quickly say, "Look, I've never told him, but he was adopted." Just don't over-egg it by trying to pretend that he was 32 when you took him on.

A few pitfalls to watch out for:

If you must knock ten years off your age you will have to revise all your anecdotes. It will sound a bit odd if you talk about that time you were thrown out of the pub for fighting at the age of eight.

Do remember to hide those old pictures of you in flares, hot pants or winkle pickers. People will either assume you were extremely tall for your age and had acne at the age of three or work out that you're telling porkies.

You will be paying full fare on the buses long after all your friends are travelling free.

Unless you actually look a lot younger than you really are, people will be whispering behind your back about how old you look and how you've let yourself go, if you're trying to pretend you're 15 years younger than you actually are.

Be consistent. There's nothing worse than someone suddenly turning round and saying, "Hang on, if you were born in 1964 how come you remember where you were when Kennedy was shot? And not only that, a couple of weeks ago you said your earliest memory was watching the Coronation on your gran's telly?"

The Difference Between Quite Old And Wrinkly – And Really Old And Wrinkly

Quite old and wrinkly	Really old and wrinkly
You get puffed out when exerting yourself	You get puffed out doing the crossword
You can't put names to faces so easily these days	You can't even put a name to your own face
You start thinking about plastic surgery	You start thinking about not having any more plastic surgery as that dimpled chin is actually your belly button
You struggle to keep up with fashion	You know that pyjamas and a dressing gown will never go out of fashion
You start getting a bit grumpy now and then	Grumpy is your permanent default mode
Most of the CDs you buy these days are oldies	What's a CD?
You struggle to read small print	The only thing you read these days is the small print on medicine packaging
You feel a bit jealous of young people	You feel a bit jealous of "quite old" people
Your stomach's expanding, but your memory's shrinking	You're shrinking
You've given up worrying about what you eat	You don't care what you eat because it all tastes the same anyway
Even your children are starting to show signs of age	Your children are showing signs of popping their clogs before you do
You wake up feeling a bit achy	You wake feeling a bit surprised

You struggle with new technology	You put up with new technology as it's the only thing that's keeping you alive
You use anti-wrinkle cream	You realize that if you got rid of the wrinkles there wouldn't be much else left
Some of your views would make Alf Garnett proud	Some of your views would make Alf Garnett blush
You often talk about "the good old days"	You are pretty sure there must have been some "good old days" but can't quite remember whether you were involved in them or not
You feel you ought to be doing more exercise	You feel that any exercise at all might just finish you off
You seem to have more little aches and pains every day	You seem to have more little relatives every day
You lie about your age	You boast about your age
You're given stick by people younger than yourself	You're given a stick
You start to wonder where the years went	You start to wonder how you're still here
You're a bit sad that your kids will soon be flying the nest	You're a bit sad that your kids will soon be selling the nest and putting you in a home
You worry about losing some of your faculties	You worry about losing some of your bladder control
It only seems like yesterday when you first had your kids	It only seems like yesterday that it was yesterday
You don't seem to go out so much these days	Your joints are the only things that go out
Your trousers don't fit any more	Your trousers are suddenly loose again

And How Old Are You Really?

The problem with precise ages is that they conjure up images
that somehow take over from the reality. So, if you're a slim,
youthful looking person in fashionable clothes and you let slip
that you're 40, the person you're talking to suddenly sees you
as sad and middle-aged, despite any physical evidence to the
contrary. Similarly, you see a picture of an attractive film star
in the paper then notice that the caption says they're 60. Even
though they look like a million dollars and they probably had
to pay a million dollars to look like a million dollars, they are
immediately less attractive as you scan the picture for wrinkled
hands, cellulite, wig joins and other tell-tale signs of ageing.
So the only answer, without outright lying, is skilful evasion.
So if someone tells you they're "30-something" you can be
pretty damn sure they're not a day under 39 and possibly the
"30-something" they so blithely refer to is 30-12...

You're never too old to become younger.

Mae West

Forty was a difficult age for her. She took eight years to pass it.

I do wish I could tell you my age, but it's impossible. It keeps
changing all the time.

Greer Garson

I refuse to admit I'm more than 52, even if that does make my
sons illegitimate.

Nancy Astor

If a woman tells you she's 20 and looks 16, she's 12. If she tells
you she's 26 and looks 26, she's damn near 40.

Chris Rock

I've known her for many years. In fact, I remember when she and I were the same age.

The woman who tells her age is either too young to have anything to lose or too old to have anything to gain.

Chinese Proverb

Two old men are talking. "You know, you're only as old as you feel," says the first. "Oh," says the second. "In that case how come I'm still alive when I'm 150 years old?"

She admitted she was 40, but she didn't say when.

She said she was approaching 40... I couldn't help wondering from what direction.

Bob Hope

Two women are discussing a mutual friend. "She's not pushing 40," says one. "No," says the other, "she's clinging on to it for dear life."

No woman should ever be quite accurate about her age. It looks so calculating.

Oscar Wilde

How old would you think you were if you didn't know how old you are?

A census taker knocks on an old woman's front door. She answers and goes through all his questions until he asks her how old she is. "I'm sorry," says the old woman, "but I don't believe it's ladylike to tell anyone my age." "Oh dear," says the census taker, "that does make things rather difficult." "All right. Then I'll just tell you this much," says the old woman, "I'm the same age as Mr and Mrs Hill who live next door." "That's fine," says the census taker, "I'll just put down next to your name, 'as old as the hills'."

I never lie about my age. I just tell people I'm as old as my wife. Then I lie about her age.

A traffic policeman pulls over a lady for speeding. "Madam," he says as he goes up to her car window, "when I saw you tearing down the street, I guessed 65 as a minimum." "That's ridiculous, officer," says the woman. "I'm 54. It's these damn glasses – they put ten years on me."

She was a handsome woman of 45 and would remain so for many years.

Anita Brookner

She's approaching middle-age – for something like the third time.

Two women are talking. "I think 30 is a great age to be," says the first. "Yes," says her friend, "particularly when in reality you're 45."

A man asks a friend, "Did my wife tell you her age?" "Partly," says the friend.

In dog years I'm dead!

Through The Ages

From birth to the age of 18, a girl needs good parents. From 18 to 35, she needs good looks. From 35 to 55, she needs a good personality. From 55 on, she needs good cash.

Sophie Tucker

The ages of man in fruit. At 20, a man is like a coconut; he has so much to offer, but so little to give. At 30, he's like a durian; dangerous, but delicious. At 40, he's like a watermelon; big, round and juicy. At 50, he's like a satsuma; he only comes once every year. At 60, he's more like a raisin; dried out, wrinkled and cheap.

When you're three years old, success is not peeing in your pants. When you're eleven, success is having friends. When you're 17, success is having a driving licence. When you're 20, success is having sex. When you're 30, success is having money. When you're 50, success is having money. When you're 60, success is having sex. When you're 70, success is having a driving licence. When you're 75, success is having friends. When you're 80, success is not peeing in your pants.

The ages of woman in balls. At 18, she's a football; 22 men are running after from all directions. At 28, she's a hockey ball; eight men are panting to get her. At 38, she's a golf ball; there's only one man after her now. At 48, she's a table-tennis ball; two guys are doing their damnedest to get rid of her.

The first 50 miles on the go all the way – your sense of direction – bowling along. Get past 60 and everything slows down to a sudden crawl and you realize you're not going anywhere any more. All the things you thought you were going to do that never came to anything. You can't turn the clock back – it's one-way traffic just gradually grinding to a halt.

Victor Meldrew/ One Foot in the Grave

What dominates the thoughts of men at different stages in their lives: Between 0-3 Their bowel movements; 4-10 guns; 11-14 sex; 15-20 sex; 20-40 sex; 40-60 sex; 60-? their bowel movements...

Health Advice For Wrinklies

Most people breeze through their youth without giving their health a second thought – and why should they? They're brimming with it. Their cup runneth over with the stuff. If health were wealth they'd be millionaires. Then one by one those little gremlins start creeping in like bugs on your computer system. One day your knees start giving you a bit of trouble, your back starts playing up, you can't quite remember things you used to – like... well nothing springs to mind right now...

and before you know where you are you're a walking medical dictionary of symptoms, complaints and syndromes. Then you start to take a keen interest in those articles they keep running in the newspapers about IBS, DVT, MRSA and all that other stuff which is too awful to spell out in full. Before you can say, "Nurse, the screens!" you're a fully-fledged hypochondriac – but a hypochondriac with a difference, because in your case, you've actually *got* every ailment going.

The definition of good health: the slowest possible rate at which you can die.

Jack Benny once said after being presented with a show business award, "I don't deserve this. But I have arthritis and I don't deserve that either."

If I'd known I was going to live this long, I'd have taken better care of myself.

Eubie Blake

I've got to watch myself these days. It's too exciting watching anyone else.

Bob Hope

An old boy goes along to his school reunion and because all his old classmates are now in advanced years they spend most of the evening talking about their failing health and comparing grisly notes. "One was on about his heart problems," the old boy tells his wife when he got home. "Another was discussing his kidney transplant, and another was banging on about his liver problems..." "Oh dear," says his wife, "it doesn't sound so much like a school reunion, more like an organ recital."

A little old lady is having a check-up from her doctor who has been treating her for asthma. He examines her, asks a few questions and notes down her croaky replies. Finally he asks, "And what about the wheeze?" "Oh they're fine," says the old lady, "I went three times last night."

A doctor begins his examination of an old man by asking him what brought him to the hospital. "Er," says the old man. "I think it might have been an ambulance."

An old man goes to see his doctor. "Well," says the doctor, "it's a long time since you've been to see me." "I know," says the old man, "I've not been well."

An old man goes for a thorough examination at the doctor's. After it's over, the old man asks, "Well, doctor, how do I stand?" "To be honest," says the doctor, "that's what's puzzling me."

A lady in her late 80s goes to the doctor's for a check-up. The doctor asks her how she's doing and receives in response a litany of complaints about her aches, pains, stiffness, lack of energy and her general increasing difficulty at doing many things. "Now come on, Mrs Siegel," says the doctor. "You have to expect things to start deteriorating at your age. After all, who wants to live to be 100?" The old lady gives him a cold look and replies, "I would have thought anyone who's 99."

An old man goes to a private practice. "I'll examine you for £100," says the doctor. "Go ahead then," says the old man, "and if you find £100, you can keep it."

Elsie goes to the doctor suffering a whole range of aches, pains, and ailments. The doctor examines her and says, "Well, Mrs Cartwright, I know you must be in some discomfort, but there's not a lot I can do. You're 75 years old and, well, I can't make you any younger you know." "I'm not bothered about getting any younger," says Elsie, "I just want to make sure I get a bit older."

Old Harry goes to see his doctor and the doctor has to give him a rectal examination. "Ooh," says Harry, "that was a bit uncomfortable." "I know," says the doctor. "I had to use two fingers rather than just one." "What was that for?" asks Harry. "I thought I better get a second opinion," says the doctor.

Did you hear about the old man whose health was so bad his doctor advised him not to start watching any serials.

A man is at the doctors to hear the results of his tests. "Well, doctor," he says, "is it good news or bad news?" "Bad news I'm afraid," replies the doctor. "You've only got three months to live." "Three months!" exclaims the patient. "Is there nothing I can do?" "Well, you could try having lots of mud baths," says the doctor. "And that'll prolong my life will it?" asks the patient hopefully. "No," replies the doctor, "but at least it'll get you used to lying in dirt."

An old man hasn't been feeling well for a little while so he goes to his doctor for a complete check-over. After a while the doctor calls him in to hear the results of the tests that have been carried out. "I'm afraid I have some bad news. You're dying and you don't have much time," says the doctor. "Oh no," says the old man. "How long have I got?" "Ten," says the doctor. "Ten?" says the old man. "Ten what? Months? Weeks? What exactly?" "... nine... eight... seven... six..."

Old Fred goes to the doctor's. The doctor examines him then says, "I'm afraid I've got some bad news for you, Fred," and hands him a small bottle of pills. "You're going to have to take these pills for the rest of your life." "That's not so bad," says Fred. "Yes it is," says the doctor. "You're not going to need a repeat prescription."

Tom, Dick and Harry are three old friends. Tom is 80, Dick is 90 and Harry is 100 years old. They all go to the doctor's together for a check-up. Tom goes in first and comes out a few minutes later and tells the others, "The doctor says I'm in extremely good health for an 80-year-old. He thinks I could live another 20 years." Dick goes into the consulting room next and emerges a little while later. He tells the others, "The doctor says I'm in fairly good health considering the fact that I'm 90. He says I could live for another ten years." Harry goes in last and comes out an hour later. "What happened?" ask his friends. "The doctor examined me and then asked how old I was," says Harry.

"And what happened when you told him?" asks Tom. "He told me to have a nice day," says Harry.

Two little boys are talking. One says, "My grandmother is suffering from furniture disease." "What's that?" asks his friend. "It's when your chest falls into your drawers," says the first.

An old man goes to the doctor and says he hasn't been feeling well. The doctor gives him an examination, and then goes to his cupboard and brings out three large bottles of different coloured pills. "Now then," says the doctor, "I want you to take the green pill with a big glass of water when you get out of bed. Then I want you to take the blue pill with a big glass of water after your dinner. Then just before you go to bed, I want you to take the red pill with another big glass of water." The old man is surprised that the doctor wants to put him on so much medication so he says, "So, doctor, exactly what it is that I've got wrong with me?" "You're not drinking enough water," says the doctor.

A pharmacist is going over the directions on a prescription bottle with an elderly patient. "Be sure not to take this more often than every four hours," the pharmacist says. "Don't worry about that," replies the patient. "It takes me four hours to get the bloomin' lid off!"

A middle-aged man is due to have an operation and is very worried about it, so just beforehand he tells the surgeon that he's rather nervous and concerned. "You see, doctor," he says, "I've heard that only one in ten people survives this particular operation. Is that true?" "Unfortunately, yes," admits the surgeon. "Your information is correct. But looking on the bright side you've got absolutely nothing to worry about because my last nine patients all died!"

Old Alf has a very understanding doctor. Because Alf couldn't afford to have the operation he needed, the doctor touched up his X-rays for him instead.

Two old ladies are having a natter about their favourite subject, their various medical conditions. The first tells the second, "The doctor says I need another operation, but I can't afford to get it done privately and there's a 12-month waiting list on the NHS." "That's a disgrace," says her friend. "Still, never mind. We'll just have to talk about your old operation for another year."

A posh old woman is talking to her friend. She tells her, "My husband is now so elderly and infirm, I have to watch him all day and night." "But I thought you'd hired a young nurse to take care of him," says her friend. "I have," says the old woman. "That's precisely why I've got to keep an eye on him."

An old man goes to the doctor. "Doctor," he says pointing to different parts of his body, "when I touch my arm it hurts. When I touch my neck it hurts. And when I touch my stomach it hurts. Do I have some rare disease?" "No," says the doctor, "you have a sore finger."

Grandma was having some stomach problems so the doctor told her to drink tepid water with a teaspoon of Epsom salts an hour before breakfast every morning. After a month she was no better so went back to the doctor. "Did you drink the water an hour before breakfast every morning?" he asked. "No, doctor," she replied. "I'm sorry but I couldn't manage more than 20 minutes."

In the waiting room at the surgery a vast crowd of people were waiting for their appointments while the doctor seemed to be working at a snail's pace. After two hours' wait, one old man slowly got up and shuffled towards the door. When everyone stopped talking to look at him, he turned and announced, "Well, I think I'll just have to go home and die a natural death."

A 90-year-old man is snoozing in the chair one day when a life insurance salesman knocks at the door. He gives him the hard sell, but the old man is a bit wary about the cost of the insurance, which at his age isn't cheap. After about 45 minutes of haggling on the doorstep, the salesman finally says, "Look, I'll tell you what, you have a think about it, sleep on it tonight and if you wake up in the morning give me a ring, OK?"

When asked in his late 90s if his doctor knew he still smoked, George Burns said, "No... he's dead."

Signs That Your Body Isn't What It Used To Be

The doctor asks you to "take off that baggy vest" and you're not even wearing one.

When you run for the bus you're too puffed out to tell the driver what fare you want.

Your waist measurement is bigger than your leg measurement.

The last time you "got on down" at a party you couldn't get up again.

When the doctor asks you to stick your tongue out you ask him how far is absolutely necessary.

You have more replacements than original bits.

When you get to the gym the first thing you have to do is have a little sit down.

You insist on measuring your waist in inches because in centimetres it just sounds too depressing.

Combing your hair seems to take less and less time.

You get out of breath coming down the stairs.

Er... What Was This Section About Again?... Wrinkles In The Memory

They say that after a certain age your brain cells start to go. Where to? And can we have them back? Of course it's infuriating when you start to forget those little things like where you left your car keys, whether you left the gas on when you went out or which house is yours when you go home. But memory loss probably has a biological function – when you look in the mirror and see a wrinkled old soul peering back at you myopically, because you can't remember where you left your glasses, you also forget that in your youth you were often mistaken for the young Marlon Brando or Sophia Loren. When you wake up in the morning full of aches and pains, and bursting to go to the loo, you forget that you used to leap out of bed like a spring lamb raring to go (and not just to the toilet). And if you can't remember stuff like that then growing old doesn't seem quite so bad. It's also pretty good news for the rest of your family who won't have to listen to you going on about "the good old days", because you won't even remember having had any.

Old Bill goes to his doctor's and says, "Doctor, my memory is terrible. I can't remember anything." "OK," says the doctor, "tell me all about it." "All about what?" says Bill.

Do you know, for as long as I can remember I've had amnesia.

A very forgetful old man goes to a singles bar and tries to pick up women by going up to them and saying, "Hello. Do I come here often?"

Two old ladies meet for a weekly game of cards. Halfway through their game one week, one of the old ladies says to the other, "I'm terribly sorry. I know we've been friends for over 60 years, but I'm afraid I just can't think what your name is. Would you remind me please?" The other old lady sits staring at her for a few moments. "I've offended you haven't I?" says the first old lady. "No," says the second, "it's just that I can't remember what it is myself at the moment."

A woman notices an old man sitting on a park bench sobbing his eyes out. She goes over and asks what's wrong. "I have a 22-year-old wife," says the old man. "Every single morning she insists on making mad passionate love with me before she gets up and makes breakfast for me." "OK," says the woman. The old man goes on, "She makes my lunch for me, does my washing, my ironing, keeps the house beautiful and still has the energy to make love as soon as I get home in the afternoon." "I see," says the woman. "Every evening she cooks me a delicious gourmet meal, which she serves with wine and my favourite dessert, before doing all the dishes and making love to me again until bedtime." "Fine," says the woman. "So why are you sitting here sobbing?" "I've forgotten where I live," says the old man.

Ageing men first forget names, then they forget faces. Then they forget to pull up their zips after going to the toilet and finally, worst of all, they forget to pull down their zips *before* they go.

Overall my memory is excellent, apart from three things: faces, names and... something else.

You should try and look on the bright side as regards extreme memory loss. At least it means you get to meet new people every day.

Three sisters aged 92, 94 and 96 all live in a house together. One night, the 96-year-old starts a bath. She puts her foot in, pauses and asks, "Was I getting in or out of the bath?" The 94-year-old yells back, "I don't know, but I'll come up and see!" She starts up the stairs and pauses. "Was I going up the stairs or down?" The 92-year-old is sitting at the kitchen table having tea, listening to her sisters. She shakes her head and says, "I sure hope I never get that forgetful." She knocks on wood for good measure. Then she yells to her sisters, "I'll come up and help both of you as soon as I see who's at the door!"

Old Bert's memory is getting worse. Yesterday he put his shoes on the wrong feet. Now he can't remember whose feet he put them on.

An old lady and her husband are always arguing over which of them has the worse memory. "OK," says the old lady, "if you want to prove your memory's not so bad, go and get me a cup of tea." Off goes her husband to the kitchen, only to return ten minutes later with a steaming bowl of porridge. "You idiot!" says the old woman. "Where the hell are my eggs?"

An old man visits his doctor and says, "Oh, doctor. I've got a terrible problem. I seem to have developed an awful memory. I can't remember where I left my car. I can't remember how I got here. I can't even remember where I live or whether I'm married or not. Can you help me, doctor?" "I can," says the doctor, "but you're going to have to pay me in advance."

The funny thing is I never remember being absent-minded.

In a retirement home two old men are eating breakfast one morning. One notices something in the other one's ear. "I say, old man," says the first, "did you know you've got a suppository in your ear?" His friend pulls it out and looks at it. "Thank goodness you noticed that," he says. "I wondered where that had got to. Now if only I could think where I've put my hearing aid..."

Thanks to the latest fertility technology, a 65-year-old woman gives birth to a baby boy. As soon as she gets home from hospital, her sister invites herself round and asks, "Can I see the new arrival?" "Not yet," says the mother. Half an hour passes and the sister asks, "Can I see him now?" "No," says the mother. The sister soon begins to get really impatient and says, "Come on! Please can I see him?" "No," says the mother. "You've got to wait until he cries." "I don't understand," says her sister. "Why have I got to wait until he cries?" "Because," says the 65-year-old, "at the moment I can't remember where I've left him."

These days the easiest way to find something lost around the house is... to buy a replacement.

Three absent-minded professors were talking together in a bus terminal. They got so engrossed in what they were saying that they didn't notice the bus had pulled in. As the driver sang out, "All aboard," they looked up startled and dashed to the bus. Two of them managed to hop on, but the third didn't make it. As he stood sadly watching the bus disappear into the distance, a stranger tried to cheer him up, saying, "You shouldn't feel too bad. Two out of three of you got on, so that's a pretty good average." "It would be," said the professor, "except those two came to see ME off."

Old Sid tells a friend, "My wife has a terrible memory. She never forgets a single thing."

Joyce tells her friend Glenda, "I'm going to divorce Harry." "Why's that?" asks Glenda. "Because," says Joyce, "he has a rotten memory." "OK," says Glenda, "but why divorce him just because he has a bad memory?" "Because," says Joyce, "Every time he sees an attractive young woman he forgets he's married to me!"

I have a memory like an elephant. In fact elephants often consult me.

Noel Coward

Right now I'm having amnesia and *deja vu* at the same time. I think I've forgotten this before.

Steven Wright

Wrinklies' Failing Faculties

And we're not talking about universities giving out Mickey Mouse degrees. No, we're talking about age's unkindest cut of all. Just when you get to the stage where you can't be bothered to go out so much and all you want to do is sit in front of the TV in the evening... you can't hear it properly. Even with the volume knob turned up to 11 you can still only just about hear the neighbours banging on the walls, so you give up and decide to read a book. But the print's a bit fuzzy. When exactly did they start printing books in a typeface called Now You See Me Now You Don't point 0000001? So you decide to go and make a cup of tea, but you can't quite remember which cupboard the teabags are in, and if you have a cup of tea too late in the evening you'll be up and down to the toilet all night, and those biscuits don't taste as good as they used to, and is it cold in here or is just me...?

Wilt! Droop! Crack! Sag! Ever feel like the warranty on some of your parts just expired?

A very old man, almost bent double, hobbles up to an ice-cream seller and asks for a vanilla cornet. "Crushed nuts, granddad?" asks the ice-cream man. "No," says the old man. "It's rheumatism if you must know."

For a long time old Tom's family thought he had become hunchbacked due to his advancing years. Eventually, though, they found out that it was just because he didn't know his braces were adjustable.

An old lady is waiting to go in to see the doctor. When her name is called she gets unsteadily to her feet, with the aid of a walking stick, and one of the other patients notices she is bent almost double. A receptionist helps the old lady into the doctor's room slowly and carefully, and ten minutes later the door opens and the old woman walks out completely upright. "My goodness!" says the other patient. "That's amazing! You went in there bent almost double and now you're walking out like a guardsman! What did the doctor give you, some sort of miracle cure?" "No," says the old lady, "he gave me a longer stick."

An old man tells a friend, "I just bought myself a new hearing aid. It cost me £4,000, but it's state of the art. It's perfect."

"Really," says his friend. "So what kind is it?" "12.30," says the old man.

An elderly gentleman realizes he has been increasingly suffering from hearing problems for a number of years. So he finally decides to go to his doctor to see if he can offer any help. The doctor fits a hearing aid, which allows him to hear extremely well once again. One month later the elderly gentleman comes back to see the doctor. The doctor says, "Yes, your hearing is pretty good once again. Your family must be really pleased at the improvement." "Oh I haven't told them about it yet," says the elderly gentleman. "I just sit around and listen to what they're all saying to each other. So far I've changed my will five times!"

An old man becomes concerned that his wife is losing her hearing. So, he walks up close to her and says loudly into her ear, "Can you hear me?" His wife doesn't answer. So the old man gets a bit closer again and says even more loudly, "Can you hear me?" Again there is no answer, so he tries once more, standing even closer and speaking even more loudly, "I SAID CAN YOU HEAR ME!!!" And his wife replies, "FOR THE THIRD TIME, YES I CAN BLOODY HEAR YOU!!!"

Three old men who are all hard of hearing are playing golf one morning. One says to another, "Windy, isn't it?" "No," says the second man, "it's Thursday." The third man then pipes up, "Yes. So am I! Let's get a beer!"

Two ageing nuns are talking about where they should go for their holidays. Sister Teresa has gone a bit deaf so Sister Rita has to use hand gestures in order to communicate. "I'd like to go to Florida," says Sister Rita. "You know! Florida! Where the oranges are this big and the bananas are this long." "Pardon?" says Sister Teresa. Sister Rita repeats herself, but still Sister Teresa doesn't hear. In the end Sister Teresa speaks very slowly, with very exaggerated hand gestures. "Florida!" she says. "Where the oranges are THIS BIG and the bananas are THIS LONG." "Which priest are you talking about again?" asks Sister Teresa.

A well-known scientific conundrum: if an old lady falls over in her house when there's no one else around, does she make a sound?

An old man is a witness in a burglary case. The defence lawyer asks him, "Did you see my client commit this burglary?" "Oh yes," says the old man. "But this crime took place at night," says the lawyer. "Are you sure you saw my client commit this crime?" "Yes," says the old man, "I saw him do it." So the lawyer says to the old man, "Sir, you are an elderly man now over 80 years old. Are you really going to tell this court that your eyesight was good enough for you to see my client from several feet away? Just how far do you think you are able to see at night?" "Well," says the old man, "I can see the moon. How far is that?"

While it may not be entirely true to say that all the people who live in Bournemouth are getting on a bit, it is one of the few places where the shops on the high street have to have their windows made from bifocal lenses.

An ageing snake goes to see his doctor. "Doctor, I need something for my eyes," says the snake, "I don't seem to be able to see so well these days." The doctor fixes the snake up with a pair of glasses and tells him to return in two weeks. The snake comes back as requested and tells the doctor he's very depressed. The doctor says, "What's the problem? Didn't the glasses help you?" "Oh yes," says the snake. "The glasses are fine. But I just found out I've been living with a garden hose for the past couple of years!"

A man was sitting on a bus chewing gum and staring vacantly into space. Suddenly the old woman sitting opposite him said, "It's no good you talking to me young man, I'm stone deaf."

A flat-chested woman has problems finding a bra small enough in any of the high street chains, so eventually she tries a little backstreet lingerie shop. The woman behind the counter is a bit short-sighted and also a bit deaf, so the customer has a job explaining what she wants. After a while she simply unbuttons

her blouse and shouts, "Have you got anything for these?"
The old woman squints at her and says, "Try Clearasil, my
granddaughter swears by it."

An old couple are sitting at home watching a documentary
programme about healthcare on the television. "I never want to
end up like that," says the old man, pointing at the television. "I
don't want to end up living in a vegetative state, dependent on
some machine and fluids from a bottle. If that ever happens to
me, just pull the plug." At which point, his wife gets up, unplugs
the TV and pours away the old man's bottle of beer.

Two old men are shuffling down the street. The man on the left
is dragging his right foot, the other is dragging his left foot. The
man on the right says to the man on the left, "So what happened
to you?" "War wound," he replies. "Normandy beach 1944. So,"
he says, indicating the other old man's foot, "what about you?" "I
trod in some dog muck a couple of streets back," says the other.

Three old men are playing cards at home one day when they
decide they should get some beer in. They draw straws and old
Norman is given the money to go and buy some beer. Several
hours pass and there's still no sign of Norman. One of the
other old men says, "Do you know what, I'm beginning to
think old Norman's run off with our money." Norman's voice
is then heard from just outside the front door, "Hey! Any more
comments like that and I'm not going to go at all."

At a nursing home, a group of senior citizens is sitting around
talking about their aches and pains. "My arms are so weak I
can hardly lift this cup of coffee," says one. "I know what you
mean," says another. "My cataracts are so bad I can't even see
my coffee." "I can't turn my head because of the arthritis in my
neck," says a third. "I've got all those problems," says another
member of the group, "plus my blood pressure pills make me
dizzy all the time. I suppose that's the price we pay for getting
old." The group sits silently for a few moments before an old
lady pipes up. "Still, look on the bright side," she says. "At least
we're all still able to drive."

Problems Of Ageing For Wrinkly Men

As if losing your hair, teeth, memory and sense of humour weren't bad enough, Mother Nature (it would be a woman wouldn't it?) has another cruel trick up her sleeve – as you get older you'll lose your libido, too. Of course, some men have led such sheltered lives that they think a libido is an open-air swimming pool, but for the rest of us libido loss is just another part of getting old. True, someone (probably a man) has now invented Viagra, but for some men it's so long since they've had sex they need a Viagram to show them where everything is. But a man losing his sex drive is a bit like a computer losing its hard drive – the memory's still there, but you can't do much with it.

Q: What's the difference between a clown and a man going through a mid-life crisis?
A: The clown realizes he's dressed in completely ridiculous clothes.

I'm getting so old that if a girl says no to me, I feel a sense of relief.

An old man sees a little boy sitting at the side of the road crying his eyes out. "What's the matter, little boy?" asks the old codger. "Why are you crying?" "I'm crying," says the little boy, "because I can't do what the big boys do." And with that the old man sits down next to him on the kerb and starts crying, too.

By the time a man is old enough to read a woman like a book, he's too old to start a library.

Q: How is a 60-year-old man like an ageing television set?
A: Both are hard to warm up, losing their colour and have difficulty maintaining their horizontal hold.

As a man gets older he realizes there are basically only three styles for his hair: parted, un-parted and departed.

Two elderly ladies were discussing the upcoming dance at the country club. "We're supposed to wear something that matches our husband's hair, so I'm wearing black," said Mrs. Smith. "Oh my," said Mrs Jones, "I'd better not go."

Old men are dangerous. It doesn't matter to them what is going to happen to the world.

George Bernard Shaw

No man is ever old enough to know better.

Holbrook Jackson

An old man goes to a wizard to ask him if he can remove a curse he has been living with for the last 40 years. The wizard says, "OK, but you will have to tell me the exact words that were used to put the curse on you." The old man says without hesitation, "I now pronounce you man and wife."

The best way to get an ageing man to do anything is to suggest he's far too old to be capable of it.

Two old women are watching their husbands. "I can't believe your husband is still chasing after women," says one. "Doesn't worry me," says the other. "Even if he catches them he wouldn't be able to remember what he wanted them for."

I'm at the age now where just putting my cigar in its holder is a thrill.

George Burns

Two old men are walking down the street together when they see a pair of teenage girls walk by. "Oh," says the first, "I wish I was 20 years older." "You stupid old fool," says his friend. "You're 90 years old. You don't wish you were 20 years older. You wish you were 20 years younger." "No," says the first. "I mean 20 years older. That way I'd be past caring."

Q: How are old men similar to bumper stickers?
A: Once you get them on they're both very difficult to get off again.

There are three ages of men: under-age, over-age and average.

It is said that at the age of 55 each man becomes what he most despised at the age of 25. I live in constant fear lest I become a badly organized trip to Bournemouth.

Simon Munnery

Have A Heart, Wrinklies

Except for an occasional heart attack I feel as young as I ever did.

Robert Benchley

An old man goes to the doctor's for an examination. On his way out of the surgery he has a heart attack and drops dead on the spot. The doctor leaps into action and tells the receptionist, "Quick! Turn him round and make it look like he was just walking in."

A man is recovering after major heart surgery. The surgeon comes to see him and gives him strict instructions, places him on a very strict diet, tells him he mustn't drink or smoke and advises him to get at least eight hours of sleep a night. Finally, the patient asks, "What about my sex life though? Will it be all right for me to have intercourse?" "Yes," says the surgeon, "as long as it's just with your wife. Nothing too exciting you understand."

A very old man went to the doctor's and was given some medicine. "This is pretty strong stuff," said the doctor, "so take some the first day, then skip a day, take some again and then skip another day, and so on." A month later the doctor saw the old man's wife in the street and asked how he was getting on. The doctor was horrified to hear that the man had died. "I didn't think the medicine was that strong," said the doctor ruefully. "No, it wasn't the medicine," said the widow. "It was all that skipping."

An old man is in hospital waiting for a heart transplant when the doctor comes to see him. "Good news!" he says. "We've found a donor. In fact, we have three so you have a choice. There's a young sportsman who was very fit. Or you can have a middle-aged doctor who never drank alcohol or smoked. Or alternatively a 70-year-old lawyer." "I'll have the lawyer's heart if that's all right," says the old man. "Did you hear me right?" asks the doctor. "I said it's from a 70-year-old lawyer." "Yes. I know," says the patient. "So it's never been used, has it?"

The trouble with heart disease is that the first symptom is often hard to deal with: sudden death.

Michael Phelps

Archie and Agnes had been married for over 60 years, so when Archie suddenly died Agnes couldn't face life without him and decided to end it all. She found Archie's old army revolver in the drawer and, just to make sure it wouldn't go wrong, she phoned her local hospital to find out exactly where her heart was. She was told it was just below the left breast. So she poured herself a large gin and fired the fateful shot. Half an hour later she was admitted to casualty with a gunshot wound to her left knee.

When she hears that her elderly grandfather had passed away, a young woman rushes to her grandmother to offer comfort. When she asks how granddad died, her grandmother tells her he had a heart attack while they were making love on Sunday morning. The young woman is shocked and says that two people aged nearly 100 should have realized the dangers of carrying on in such a way. "Oh no!" says granny. "Despite our advanced age we've managed perfectly well for years. We always used to take care by making love in time to the slow chime of the bells in the village church." She pauses and wipes away a tear before continuing, "And if it hadn't been for that ice cream van going past, your granddad would still be alive today."

Toilet Problems

An old couple are in the middle of the congregation at church one Sunday. Halfway through the service, the old man leans over and tells his wife, "I think I just broke wind. Luckily it was a silent one. But do you think I should do anything?" "Yes," says his wife. "Put some new batteries in your hearing aid."

An old lady goes to her doctor and asks what can be done about her terrible constipation. "Oh, it's awful, doctor," she says. "Do you know, I haven't moved my bowels for more than a week now." "I see," says the doctor. "And have you done anything about it?" "Oh, yes," says the old lady, "I sit there in the bathroom waiting for half an hour every morning and half an hour every evening." "No, no," says the doctor. "I mean, do you take anything?" "Yes, of course I do," says the old lady. "I take a magazine!"

Three old men are comparing ailments. "I've got problems," says one. "Every morning at seven o'clock I get up and I try to urinate, but I can never manage it." The second old man says, "You think you have problems. Every morning at eight o'clock I get up and try to move my bowels, but it never works." The third old man speaks up, "Every morning at seven o'clock I urinate and every morning at eight o'clock I defecate." "You've got no problem then," says the first man. "Yes I have," says the third man. "I don't wake up till nine."

Problems Of Ageing For Wrinkly Women

Another of nature's cruel jokes – the menopause (menopause – you just knew men would have something to do with it, didn't you?). A lot of men don't even realize their wives are going through the change of life. Yes, they see the mood swings, the odd behaviour, etc, but how are they supposed to know it's not just the usual mood swings and roundabouts? Women, of course know all about it, with the hot flushes and everything, but at least it's the end of that dreadful monthly ritual – and no we're not talking about sex with their husbands.

Q: What does a 70-year-old woman have between her breasts that a 20-year-old doesn't?
A: Her navel.

I'd love to slit my mother-in-law's corsets and watch her spread to death.

Phyllis Diller

If you're a woman it's not any easier, you get to a certain age, you know, you've finished bearing children, all that part of your life is over, perhaps you're not quite so attractive as you once were... and then Mother Nature thinks, "What can I do to improve the quality of this woman's life? How can I help? What can I do for her? What is that magic thing...? I know, a beard!"

Dylan Moran

Have you heard about the new bra they've invented for women in later life? They call it the sheep dog. That's because it rounds them up and gets them pointing in the same direction.

If you're a woman and you get called in for a mammogram, look on the bright side. At least this is one kind of film they still want you to appear topless in.

Two old ladies are talking one day. One says to the other, "Even though I'm 75 men still look at my boobs." "Oh yes," says the second. "I bet they have to squat down a bit first though."

Old age is when a woman buys a sheer nightie and doesn't know anyone who can see through it!

Two ageing ladies are long-time rivals in their social circle. One year they bump into each other at a Christmas party at their country club. "Why, my dear," says the first, noticing the other's necklace. "Don't tell me those are real pearls?" "Yes they are," says the second. "You may say that," says the first woman with a thin smile, "but of course the only way I could tell for certain would be to bite them." "Well I'd be happy for you to do that," says the second woman. "The only trouble is you'd need real teeth."

A woman is as old as she looks before breakfast.

Edgar Watson Howe

The only time a woman wishes that she were a year older is when she is expecting a baby.

An old man tells his friend, "Despite her age, my wife really doesn't seem to be growing old gracefully. Last week she took part in a wet shawl contest."

Q: How does an ageing woman manage to keep her youth?
A: By giving him lots and lots of money.

Keith asks his girlfriend Karen to marry him and she says yes, but on one condition: that he buys her a solid gold boy scout knife. He asks around, he looks on the Internet, he tries everywhere, but he can't find a solid gold boy scout knife anywhere. But because he is really keen to marry Karen he goes to a jeweller's and asks them to make one specially. He is told it will be very expensive, but he tells them to go ahead anyway. When it's ready he presents it to Karen, who then agrees to marry him. "So why on earth did you want a solid gold boy scout knife?" asked Keith. "What are you going to do with it?" I'm going to put it away somewhere safe, then, when I'm old and grey, and wrinkled with half my teeth missing, and my boobs sagging and no man will look at me twice, I'll get it out. Because a boy scout would do almost anything for a solid gold pocket knife."

Q: How is a 50-year-old woman like a used tube of toothpaste?
A: They may be old and wrinkled, but if you squeeze hard enough, you'll find there's something left over.

A middle-aged woman goes to the doctor for a check-up and comes back delighted. "What are you so happy about?" asks her husband. "The doctor said I have the body of a 25-year-old," she replies. "OK," says her husband, "but what did he say about your 45-year-old arse?" "He didn't mention you at all," says the wife sweetly.

Signs That Your Brain Isn't What It Used To Be

You bend down to see if you can still touch your toes and you can't remember where they are.

When members of your family come to visit they have to introduce themselves.

When you tried one of those brain-training games your brain age was in three figures.

When you meet people you can never remember their names so constantly employ the greeting "Hello stranger!" – which is now almost literally true.

You spend ten minutes calling the cat in every night until you remember it died three years ago.

You've started counting on your fingers again.

You're the only member of the family who doesn't realize just how many of the TV programmes you watch are repeats.

You tie knots in a hanky to remember things, then you can't remember where you left the damn hanky.

You still have to convert all prices to pounds shillings and pence to understand their value and are constantly shocked to find that a packet of cigarettes is now the same price as a retirement bungalow.

You've downgraded from the "quick" crossword to the junior crossword and even then struggle a bit.

It's All In The Mind

In the town centre a slightly odd looking old man keeps wandering around yelling to no-one in particular. "Why does that man keep doing that?" asks a passer-by. "Oh, that's old Mr Jones," says a local. "He can't help it. He's just talking to himself in the street again." "Well, if he's talking to himself," says the passer-by, "why does he have to shout so much?" "He has to," says the local, "because he's deaf."

Three old men are at the doctor's to have their memories tested. The doctor says to the first old man, "What's three times three?" "Two hundred and seventy four," is his reply. The doctor worriedly says to the second old man, "It's your turn. What's three times three?" "Tuesday," replies the second old man. The doctor sadly says to the third old man, "OK, it's your turn. What's three times three?" "Nine," says the third old man. "Excellent!" exclaims the doctor. "How did you get that?" "Oh come on, doctor. That was simple," says the old man. "I just subtracted two hundred and seventy four from Tuesday."

An old man goes to see a psychiatrist. Afterwards the psychiatrist is concerned and has a word with the old man's wife. "I believe your husband may be psychotic," says the psychiatrist. "He says that when he goes to the toilet during the night God switches the light on for him when he opens the door and turns it off again when he's done." "Ah," says the old lady. "You recognize the problem do you?" says the psychiatrist. "I certainly do," says the old lady. "He's been getting up in the night and going to wee in the fridge again."

Two paramedics were dispatched to pick up a 92-year-old man who had become disoriented and take him to the hospital for evaluation. En route, with their siren going, they tried questioning the old man to determine his level of awareness. Leaning close, one asked, "Sir, do you know what we're doing right now?" The old man slowly looked up at him, then gazed out of the ambulance window. "Oh," he replied, "I'd say about 50, maybe 55 or so."

Three elderly women are talking about their grown-up sons. "My son is such a good boy," says one. "Last week he gave me an all-expenses paid trip to Europe for the summer. How nice is that?" "That's nothing," says the second woman. "Yesterday, my son bought me a new car that cost £30,000. Now there's a boy who loves his mother!" "You think so!" scoffs the third old lady. "My son goes to a top Harley Street psychiatrist, he pays him £500 an hour, he sits there all afternoon and you know the only thing he talks about? Me!"

The Wrinklies' Head To Toe Body Check (For Wrinkly Men)

If you're still not convinced that you truly are a wrinkly, take this simple body test.

Head: If you have a) a full head of skin and you are not a baby, b) "pink highlights" and you are not a baby whose hair is starting to grow, c) honest grey and you are not George Clooney, or d) jet black dyed hair and you are not a teenage goth, you are a wrinkly.

Chest: If you have a) wrinkles on your chest and are not somebody who is suffering from post-bodywax pucker, or b) grey hair on your chest and are not an after-bath child who has been over-liberal with the talcum powder, you are a wrinkly.

Stomach: If it is a) bloated and you are not a 25-year-old darts professional, or b) if it sags over your waistband and you are not an up and coming Sumo wrestler, you are a wrinkly.

Legs: If a) your knees crack when you sit down and you are not a professional sportsman who has punished his body daily to reach the top, or b) you have varicose veins and are not a toddler playing with a blue felt tip, you are a wrinkly.

Feet: If a) your toenails are a strange yellow colour and you are not a Goth with a disgusting taste in nail varnish, or b) your ankles swell up for no apparent reason and you are not pregnant, you are a wrinkly.

So, how did you do?

Wrinklies' Health Regimes

Eat well, stay fit, die anyway.

Plenty of exercise and a healthy diet can add years to your life. Unfortunately, they're always added on at the end when you're too old to enjoy them.

The only way to keep your health is to eat what you don't want, drink what you don't like, and do what you'd rather not.

Mark Twain

A man goes to his doctor and asks him if he thinks he will live to be 100. The doctor looks him over and asks, "Do you smoke or drink?" "No," replies the man. "I've never smoked and I never get drunk." "Do you gamble, drive fast cars and fool around with women?" inquired the doctor. "Of course not," says the man. "I've never done anything like that." "Well then," says the doctor. "What the hell do you want to live to be 100 for?"

Alf is celebrating his 105th birthday and a reporter from a national newspaper is sent to interview him. "That's amazing, 105, eh?" says the reporter. "What do you think is the secret of your longevity?" Alf answers, "Well, I never drank, I never smoked, I did a five-mile run every morning, followed by a cold

shower, and I always made sure I ate fresh fruit and vegetables."
"Well that's fantastic, but I heard that your twin brother Jim
followed exactly the same programme and he died at 55. Is that
true?" "That's true," says Alf. "But you see his problem was he
didn't keep at it long enough."

Two old men are talking outside the doctor's. "He's put me on
the cardiologist's diet," says one. "What's that?" asks the other.
"If it tastes good, spit it out," says the first.

The wrinkly's diet: forget the health food. I need all the
preservatives I can get.

A little boy is sitting on a bus eating a chocolate bar, and as soon
as he finishes it he produces another one from his pocket and eats
that. Then he has a third and a fourth, and a fifth. When he starts
eating the sixth an old man sitting nearby says, "I don't think
that's a very good idea young man." "Why?" asks the boy. "It's
bad for your teeth," says the old man, "it'll make you fat and
give you spots, and when you're older you might even have heart
problems." "Well," says the boy, unwrapping yet another bar of
chocolate, "my granddad lived to be 102." "And did he eat half a
dozen chocolate bars a day?" asks the old man. "No," snaps the
boy. "Most of the time he just minded his own flipping business."

Old Tom used to swear by a glass of liver salts. He used to drink
a glass after every meal, every single day of his life. Finally he
died at the grand old age of 95 and at the funeral the mourners
had to beat his liver to death with a stick.

An elderly lady sends her husband out to the local market to
buy some organic vegetables. The old man asks one stallholder,
"These vegetables are for my wife. Have they been sprayed
with any poisonous chemicals?" "No," says the market trader.
"You'll have to do that yourself."

Agnes is celebrating her hundredth birthday and the local paper
sends round a young reporter to interview her. "So, Mrs Ellis,"
he says, "what do you put your long life down to?" "Well,"

replies the old lady, "I think a bit of what you fancy does you good. I've always eaten in moderation, and I've drunk in moderation, and hardly ever smoked, and I've always done gentle exercise." "I see," says the reporter, "But your daughter tells me you've often been bedridden." "Of course I have," says Agnes, "but don't put that in your flipping newspaper, will you?"

The secret of longevity is deep breathing. Just try and keep doing it for 90 years or so.

At the age of 70 Tom starts going to a local senior citizens' exercise club and the instructor says to him one day, "You know, Tom, it's hard to believe you're 70. From the shape you're in I would have said you were 55 at the most. How do you do it?" "Lack of stress," says Tom. "You see early on in our marriage the wife and I decided that if we ever started to argue she would go to the bedroom and I'd go out into the garden." "I see," says the instructor, "and how do you think that has helped?" "Well for the past 50 years," says Tom, "I've been living almost permanently out in the fresh air."

You will always stay young if you live honestly, eat slowly, worship faithfully – and lie about your age.

A man asks his elderly father what his secret was for living such a long life. "I'll tell you, son," says the old man, "every morning I sprinkle a little bit of gun powder on my cereal." The man follows this advice to the letter. Amazingly it works and, when he finally dies at the age of 100, he leaves 14 children, 28 grandchildren, 35 great-grandchildren and a 15-foot diameter hole in the wall of his local crematorium.

A woman notices a little wizened old man rocking in a chair in his back garden. "I couldn't help noticing how happy you look," she calls across to him. "What's your secret for a long happy life?" "What? Me?" the little man croaks back. "I just enjoy life to the full. I smoke three packets of cigarettes a day. I also drink a case of whisky a week. I don't worry about what I eat at all and I never do any exercise." "That's amazing," says the woman. "So how old are you?" "Twenty-six," says the man.

The Wrinklies' Head To Toe Body Check (For Wrinkly Women)

Head: If your hair is a) a strange shade of blue and you are not a Chelsea football supporter, b) of a rigidity that would be immoveable in a tsunami and you have not had a no.1 razorcut, or c) white and you are not an albino, you are a wrinkly.

Chest: If it is a) heading south and you are not a frequent flyer to sunny climes, or b) it needs more support than the England football squad and you are not Jordan, you are a wrinkly.

Stomach: If you a) have the profile of Alfred Hitchcock in one of his famous cameos and you are not actually pregnant, or b) wear a figure-squashing girdle and are not some young pop star saucepot trying to attract attention, you are a wrinkly.

Legs: If a) your calves resemble sides of mutton and you are not an all-in wrestler, or b) you wear dark-coloured tights and you are not the principal boy in your local pantomime, you are a wrinkly.

Feet: If they: a) have to be put up and rested after walking and you are not Ian Botham raising money for charity, or b) you haven't actually seen them for some time and you are not extremely short-sighted, you are a wrinkly.

There, how did you do?

Exercise Your Wrinklies

Look after your body and your body will look after you. Rubbish! You've given your body everything it has wanted or craved over the years – chocolate, alcohol, big fat juicy burgers, chips, the finest cigarettes, supersize me doughnuts, a permanent holiday from any strenuous exertion; in short, you've spoiled it rotten and how does it repay you? By packing up when you need it most! Call that gratitude? And now, just when you feel old enough to really indulge yourself and shy away from any arduous work, you've got doctors, nurses, health "gurus", the government and the rest of the blinkin' nanny state telling you to get on your bike and cut down on all the things you enjoy most. Typical!

"You know I exercise every single day," says an old man to his friend. "So you know what that means." "Yes," says his friend. "When we die you'll be much healthier than I am."

"My husband's taken up jogging," says an old woman to her friend. "He says he thinks it's the only way he'll ever hear heavy breathing again."

An old lady decides her body has got out of shape, so she joins a fitness club to do some exercise. She signs on to do an aerobics class for senior citizens. On her first day she bends, twists, gyrates, jumps up and down, and perspires for an hour. But, by the time she manages to get her leotard on, the class has finished.

A little old lady tells her friend, "I've just bought myself one of those treadmills so I can do a bit of exercise." "What's it like?" asks her friend. "Oh, it's quite hard work," says the old lady. "So at the moment I'm just doing widths."

An old lady of 95 goes to a gym and asks if she can join the aerobics class. "Ooh, I don't know," says the instructor. "I'm not sure whether that's a very good idea." He looks her up and down and asks, "How flexible are you?" "Oh, very," replies the old lady. "But I can't do Wednesday mornings."

Old Ned says his doctor told him to take up jogging and it would add ten years to his life. He's only been doing it two weeks and it's worked. He already feels ten years older.

Two old women are chatting over coffee one morning and Mildred says, "How's your husband doing in the bedroom department these days?" Ethel replies, "Ooh, Mildred, I tell you what, he makes me feel like an exercise bike. Every day he climbs on and starts pumping away, but we never seem to get anywhere."

You can take up jogging and it will help you live longer. Unfortunately it will feel absolutely awful. So that way it will help your life seem to last even longer again.

You have to stay in shape. My grandmother started walking five miles a day when she was 60. She's 97 today and we don't know where the hell she is.

George Carlin

Old John decides to start doing some exercise to get his weight down so he joins his local health club and has a go on the running machine. He does very well on his first day and manages to lose one and a half stone. Unfortunately he manages this because the machine tears his leg off.

Gentle Exercise For Wrinklies

When you get to a certain age you get out of the habit of doing exercise. You don't run for the bus anymore and, quite frankly, just running for secretary of your local gardening club would puff you out. But you shouldn't give up! No, exercise doesn't have to involve pulling on running shorts, trainers, track suits, body warmers and all that stuff. You can get all the exercise you need at your age by simply adapting your daily routine slightly, as follows:

If you're too lazy or too old to change channels on the TV without the remote control at least press the buttons with your toes to give your feet a bit of exercise. Come on, tone up those toes!

Even combing your hair can give much-needed exercise to ageing arms. And if you're bald, there's absolutely no excuse, simply comb the hair under your arms or sprouting out of your ears.

Replace all your zips with buttons – that extra finger twiddling will help keep your digits young!

Have a cold bath now and then – the shivering will shake off those extra pounds in no time.

If you must eat sweets make sure they're nice and chewy – those really gluey toffees will give your face muscles a first class workout.

Read the paper without your glasses – the constant backwards and forwards motion when attempting to alternate between large and small typefaces will tone up those flabby arm muscles.

Buy a large, energetic and thoroughly disobedient dog, and the constant tug of war you have when taking him out for walks will have your biceps looking like Arnold Schwarzenegger's in a couple of weeks.

Keep those hands supple by varying which finger you use for punching in phone numbers, scratching head, pushing glasses up nose etc.

With advancing age the knees are one of the first things to go, so stop using them so much – cut down on stroking cats, crouching down to talk to small children or bothering to pick up any coin you've dropped that's under a pound. And the good news is it'll get you out of cleaning the toilet!

But Mother Nature has her own way of keeping you wrinklies moving about and this is why your memory goes. You get so much exercise hunting round the house looking for mislaid glasses, keys, teeth, etc that you hardly need to go to the gym.

Not Long For This World!

A 60-year-old woman is getting some test results at the hospital and the consultant says, "I'm sorry, Mrs Arbuthnot, but you haven't got long to live. I give you twenty-four hours at the most." Distraught, the woman goes home and says to her husband, "Come on, you! I've only got twenty-fours to live! I want you to take me upstairs and make wild passionate love to me all night!" Her husband looks at her tetchily and says, "It's all right for you, you haven't got to get up in the morning."

A woman accompanied her husband to the doctor's surgery. After his check-up, the doctor called the wife into his office alone. He said, "Your husband is suffering from a very severe disease, combined with horrible stress. If you don't do the following he will surely die. Each morning, make him a healthy breakfast. Try to be pleasant, and make sure he stays in a good mood. For lunch make him a nutritious meal. For dinner prepare something nice and healthy again. Don't burden him with chores, as he has probably had a hard day. Don't discuss your problems with him, it will only make his stress worse. And most importantly, make love with your husband several times a week and satisfy his every whim. If you can do this for the next one to two months, I think your husband will regain his health completely." On the way home, the husband asked his wife, "What did the doctor say?" "You're going to die," she replied.

An old dying man is lying in bed. One day he feels his senses begin to slightly revive as the smell of home baking comes wafting up the stairs and sets his mouth watering. With his last remaining strength he manages to pull himself out of bed and slowly clambers down the stairs to the kitchen. There he finds his wife has been busy baking a delicious looking chocolate cake. "Oh look," says the dying old man, "isn't that lovely? You've gone to the trouble of making me my very favourite cake." Just as he's about to cut himself a slice, his wife suddenly whacks his hand with a wooden spoon. "What's the matter with you?" asks the dying man. "Get your hands off that!" his wife tells him. "That's for the funeral!"

What The Doctor Says And What You Hear

When you get to a certain age you're naturally more concerned about your health and when you get to be a bit older than that you're more than likely getting slightly paranoid about your health. So when a doctor asks a simple question or makes a passing observation you might find that you're reading more into it than you should.

What the doctor says	What you hear
Can you pass urine into this tube?	Are you still capable of actually passing water at will at your age?
Do you suffer from any allergies?	You are covered from head to foot in giant purple spots
Breathe in	Just checking to see if you're still alive
Breathe out	Just checking in case that was a fluke or possibly a death rattle
What's your name?	Next I'll ask him/her who the Prime Minister is to see if he's doolally
Can you come back and see me in two weeks?	With a bit of luck he/she will be dead by then and I'll have a quiet life
Does this hurt?	Poor old soul probably hasn't got any feeling left at his/her age
Take your clothes off	I haven't had a good laugh all day
I'm going to refer you	I don't want you keeling over in my surgery and scaring the other patients
You're remarkably fit for a man of your age	You can't expect your luck to last for much longer can you?
Are you a bit hard of hearing?	I'm just about to mumble some very bad news

Your blood pressure's a bit on the high side	You are about to spontaneously combust
Well I don't think you need to come back and see me	You'll be dead by the end of the week
You're amazing for your age	It's amazing you're still alive
It's nothing to worry about	It's fatal, so worrying won't help
I can't seem to find anything wrong with you	Let's just say you're very very old and you're bound to feel terrible
Let's have a listen to your chest	I can hear this funny creaking sound and I'm not sure where it's coming from
Lie on the couch please	It'll be so much easier to get you to the mortuary later

You Know You're Getting Old When...

You find yourself on the stairs, and you can't remember if you were downstairs going up or upstairs going down.

You find yourself taking pleasure in comparative shopping for cemetery plots.

You find yourself telling people what a loaf of bread used to cost.

You get out of the shower and find you're glad the mirror is all fogged up.

You get the same sensation from a rocking chair that you used to get from a roller coaster.

You get tired just watching the fish swim around in the aquarium.

You get two invitations to go out on the same night... and you pick the one that will get you home the earliest.

You get up at night, go to the bathroom, then can't remember why you're there.

You get winded playing chess.

You get your full share of exercise acting as a pallbearer for healthy friends who spent all their spare time exercising.

You give up all your bad, unhealthy habits, and you still feel crappy.

You go into a record shop and wonder why you don't see any records.

You go to a garden party and you're mainly interested in the garden.

You go to a museum and find most of your favourite childhood toys are on display.

You go to a restaurant and complain that the butter is too tough for your teeth.

You go to your local barber's and your local barber asks why.

You have breakfast in bed as a necessity rather than as a luxury.

You have delightful dreams about mouth-watering prunes.

You have more patience, but it is actually that you just don't care anymore.

You have stopped counting freckles and started tabulating age spots.

Things To Avoid When You're Older

Botox on forehead – unless you can have your entire face and body Botoxed it's going to look a bit odd with a completely smooth bit shining out like a sandy island in a sea of wrinkles.

Don't have your face lifted more than twice – you'll end up with eyes in the back of your head.

Ditch those youthful nicknames like "Spider", "Babs", "Tiger" etc – you're going to feel a bit of a fool when you get that 100th birthday message from the Queen addressed to Bert "Kid" Smythe, aren't you?

You often read about those plucky grannies or granddads who suddenly decide at the age of 90 that they're going to do their first bungee jump, parachute jump or some other wildly adventurous exploit. But remember, you only tend to hear about the ones that survive...

Giving up drinking. It's hardly worth it now is it? And with your liver pickled in enough alcohol to launch the *Queen Mary* it would be too much of a shock to your system and might just finish you off anyway.

Getting drunk. Yes, you've spotted a possible contradiction here, but a little of what you fancy and all that is fine, though if you find yourself getting paralytic you will forget that you're actually knocking on a bit and the sight of you stripping off and dancing on the table will not be welcomed – even at the day centre.

Toy boys/girls. They'll only accentuate how old you actually are with their smooth skin, shining hair and well-toned bodies, and not only that, you just won't be able to keep up with them. Mind you, what a way to go!

Living in a bungalow. This is the ultimate indicator that you are officially old. Before people even knock on your door they'll know you're old. "Ah, bungalow!" the prospective charity collector/conman/burglar will say, "Here lives a soft touch/mug/ easy target." Mind you, the upside is that they may think you're too poor to be worth bothering with.

Other old people. Before you know where you are you'll all be sitting around having a moanathon about the "kids of today", "political correctness gone mad" and the price of walking sticks.

Wrinklyspeak

Elsewhere in this book you will find a section in which you can determine your wrinkly age through the language that you use, i.e. you can find out whether you're quite old or very old. But some phrases will be used by all wrinklies. If you find yourself using any of the following phrases regularly, congratulations, or possibly commiserations – you are now officially a wrinkly.

Question/statement	Wrinkly response
How are you?	Mustn't grumble
Did you have a good Christmas?	It was very pleasant
Did you have a nice holiday?	It was very pleasant
Would you like a cup of tea?	Only if you're making one
See you	Not if I see you first
Goodbye then	Don't do anything I wouldn't do

Other useful wrinkly phrases include:

(At bedtime) I'm off up the wooden hill to Bedfordshire

The country's going to the dogs

It's political correctness gone mad

It's health and safety gone mad

Let's agree to disagree shall we?

Ta muchly

Thanks ever so

A bit of what you fancy does you good

Not at my age

Giving me gyp

She's no spring chicken

Food doesn't seem to taste like it used to

I'm A Senior Citizen...

I wake up a few hours before my body allows me to get out of bed.

I'm a walking storeroom of facts... Unfortunately I seem to have lost the key to the storeroom.

I'm anti-everything now: anti-fat, anti-smoke, anti-noise, anti-inflammatory.

I'm having trouble remembering simple words like... er...

I'm not grouchy, I just don't like traffic, waiting, children, politicians...

I'm so cared for: long-term care, eye care, private care, dental care.

I'm sure everything I can't find is in a secure place somewhere.

I'm sure they are making adults much younger these days.

I'm the first one to find the toilet wherever I go.

I'm the life of the party... even when it lasts till 8pm.

I'm usually interested in going home before I get to where I'm going.

I'm very good at opening childproof caps with a hammer.

I'm walking more (to the toilet) and enjoying it less.

I'm wrinkled, saggy and lumpy, and that's just my left leg.

The real reason I have to smile all the time is because I can't actually hear a word you're saying.

I'm a Senior Citizen and I think I am having the time of my life... Aren't I?

Songs For Swinging Wrinklies

"Hit Me With Your Walking Stick" – Ian Dury and the Blockheads

"Bifocal Race" – Queen

"Pick Me Up Before You Go-go" – Wham

"It's a Beautiful Day Centre" – U2

"Cocoa" – The Sweet

"Bus Pass the Dutchie" – Musical Youth

"Old" – Spandau Ballet

"My Degeneration" – The Who

"Papa's Got a Brand-New Colostomy Bag" – James Brown

"Stairlift to Heaven" – Led Zeppelin

"I'm So Retired" – The Beatles

"Sunny Afternoon Nap" – The Kinks

"Ovaltine-age Kicks" – The Undertones

"Don't Make Me Over The Hill" – Dionne Warwick

"I Can't See Clearly Now" – Jimmy Cliff

Things You Spend More Time Doing As You Get Older And Wrinklier

Well, to be honest, pretty much everything you do takes longer as you get older, whether it's climbing the stairs or remembering what you went up there for in the first place. But that's OK, you wouldn't want to use up what little energy you have on racing around like some daft youngster, would you? Oh, you would? But isn't it nice to take your time, stop and smell the roses – even if it is at yet another funeral – and just relax a bit? Of course it is, though you don't want to relax so much that you sleep past your bus stop, drop off in mid-conversation or look so comatose that the rest of the family start making *your* funeral arrangements. But it's true, you will find as you get older that you spend more time:

Thinking about the good old days, and the good thing is that the older you get the more good old days there are to look back on.

Trying to remember where you left things – such as your husband or wife when out shopping.

Getting out of bed – one foot, then the other, ooh! Little rest. Up onto elbows. Another little rest. Swivel body slowly round... oh, sod it, I'll have another five minutes...

Getting your shopping. Parkinson's Law states that work expands to fill the time available for doing it and the same goes for shopping. If your weekend isn't a non-stop melee of partying and debauchery, then choosing just the right thing to have for your dinner can take the best part of a Saturday morning – leaving the afternoon free to choose what you have for pudding.

Moaning. Yes, it's an easy target and a bit of a cliché, but when you're old you need a hobby. The good news is that the older you get the more there is to moan about: everything's changing, you don't understand anything about the world anymore, young people are so damn... young, your body won't do a thing you tell it to, your mind's got a mind of its own, and it's bloody raining again.

Talking to yourself. For a start you're the only one who listens and, secondly, you're the only one talking any blooming sense so it stands to reason, doesn't it?

Trying to look younger. Even if you haven't actually booked a session with Dr Plastic, you'll find that you're now getting more than your money's worth out of the NHS, clocking up zillions of points on your Boots loyalty card and spending a large percentage of your day rubbing in creams, taking potions and vitamins, teasing your last few strands of hair into something approaching a style, and generally indulging in some extreme body maintenance. Though when you get to the further extremities of wrinklyhood you may well say, "Oh bugger it, they can take me as I am." You will then be regarded as a charming old eccentric – who whiffs a bit.

Wrinkly Pets

A vicar goes to visit a little old lady who lives in his parish. She shows him into her living room and there sitting on a perch is her pet parrot. "I can't help noticing," says the vicar, "that you seem to have tied a ribbon to each of your parrot's legs. What are they for?" "Well," says the old lady, "if I pull the left ribbon he sings 'Abide With Me'. And if I pull on the right ribbon he sings 'All Things Bright and Beautiful'." "Oh my goodness!" chuckles the vicar. "I wonder, though, what happens if you pull both ribbons at the same time?" "I fall off the flipping perch," says the parrot.

An old lady orders a new carpet for her living room and a man turns up to fit it for her. After he's put the carpet down, the man feels in his pocket for his packet of cigarettes and finds they're missing. He then notices a lump in the middle of the old lady's new carpet. "Oh no!" he says to himself. "I've dropped my fags and laid the carpet on top of them." In the end he decides the easiest thing is to get a hammer and gently tap the lump until it's completely flat. Just as he's got the bulge level, the old lady walks in with his pack of cigarettes in her hand. "Look!" she says. "You must have dropped these in the hall. Now I wonder if you could help me to find something. My pet budgie seems to have gone missing somewhere..."

A lady had a beautiful cat that she adored. One evening as she sat stroking it by the fireside, she dreamed of her cat turning into a handsome prince. Suddenly there was a flash of light and, lo and behold, there stood before her the most handsome prince anyone could possibly imagine. The prince took her hand in his and murmured, "Aren't you sorry now that you took me to the vet last week?"

An old man tells his wife he thinks their dog is getting a bit long in the tooth. "I think Rover is getting a bit old," he says, "he seems to be going deaf." "Absolute nonsense!" says his wife. "Just watch this! Rover sit!... Oh dear, maybe you're right. Fetch the shovel and clean that up!"

Wrinkly World: Pets

Do you possess any of the following:

A little dog with a tartan coat

A budgie

A cat with a very unoriginal name such as Tiddles

A dog with a name that sounds like one of the family –
e.g. Timothy

A cat wearing a collar with a bell on it

A cat that looks as though it weighs about four stone

A sad and solitary goldfish in a lonely bowl

Framed pictures of all your deceased pets

A chair that your cat or dog has all to itself

A tortoise

If you answered 'yes' to any of the above then welcome to Planet
Wrinkly

The Wrinklies' Morning Routine

Get up

Go to toilet

Go back to bed because it's only 2.30am

Get up

Go to toilet

Go back to bed because it's still only 4.45am

Get up

Go to toilet

Take handful of pills for various ailments

Have bath/shower, then rub on various creams, lotions, embrocations for various other ailments

Have breakfast

Read paper and have rant about "the world going mad", "political correctness gone mad" and people becoming celebrities despite being totally devoid of talent

Go to work, complain about the weather, the traffic, the useless bloody public transport system; swear at anyone who dares to invite you to "have a nice day"

Arrive at work and have audience-enhanced rant about the blooming weather, the blooming traffic and anything else you can blooming well think of

Christmas Test

If you're still not sure whether you qualify as a wrinkly then take this simple test:

Before Christmas you:

Moan about the fact that it's coming earlier every year

Complain about the fact that everything's too expensive

Say you'll be glad when it's all over

During Christmas you:

Moan about the house being full of relatives, with the older ones getting on your nerves, the little ones getting under your feet and the teenagers getting under the influence

Complain that all this rich food is giving you heartburn

Say you'll be glad when it's all over

After Christmas you:

Moan that it's gone on far too long (even though it was exactly the same length as last year)

Complain that the council still hasn't collected all the discarded Christmas trees and that the shops are already selling Easter eggs

Say you're glad it's all over

If you have found that you agree with at least three of the above statements you are officially a wrinkly. You may well be only 35, but your attitude screams 65 – you miserable old git!

A Wrinklies' Guide To The Modern World

iPod – a portable gramophone crossed with a hearing aid.

Rocket salad – lettuce that tastes funny.

Reality TV – home movies of people you've never met.

Celebrity – anyone who has appeared on the television more than once. This now comprises about half the population.

WAGs – the wives and girlfriends of footballers who achieve celebrity in their own right by... well, by being photographed a lot. Not to be confused with the "kiss and tell" girls who sell their "I slept with a footballer" stories to the Sunday papers and are known as "Sexual Liaisons And Gold-diggers" or SLAGS.

HDTV – a useful new type of TV that shows pin-sharp pictures that will enable you to read the letters on *Countdown* more easily.

MRSA – the proof that you will finally get something out of the NHS after paying in for all those years.

Jeremy Clarkson – one of the very few people under 70 whose views you agree with.

Email – a marvellous new way of sending messages, but when will they finally invent a stamp that will stick to the computer screen without falling off?

Blog – a bit like one of those round-robin letters people send at Christmas – without the interesting bits. May possibly stand for Boring, Long Or Godawful.

Texting – after a hundred years of telecommunications technology and all those "it's good to talk" BT ads we have finally reached the stage where you can communicate with one another by telephone without talking. And they call it progress.

The Wrinklies' Guide To Modern Technology

It's a sure sign of ageing when you can't cope with new technology. In the Stone Age there were probably old people struggling with the wheel. "How do you work this thing again? I just can't get my head round it. It's all right for you youngsters with your new-fangled ideas – what's wrong with the bison for goodness sake?" And when Alexander Graham Bell unveiled his new telephone there were probably oldsters galore refusing to have any truck with it. "If I wanted to talk to my sister in Wales I wouldn't have moved to East Anglia, now would I? What excuse have I got now?" And even when TV came along there were probably people who just couldn't get the hang of it. "That there announcer told me he'd be bringing me the news at six o'clock; I waited in especially and did the bugger turn up?"

A company has just brought out a new mobile phone specially adapted for older users – it has a bigger keypad, rotary dialling and, best of all, less memory.

An old lady receives a computer for her birthday. Her son tells her he is keen to teach her the advantages of the World Wide Web. He sets up the computer and sits his mother down in front of it. He demonstrates how to switch it on, how to access the internet and how to search for information. "I'm not sure about this," says the old lady. "It's easy, Mum," says her son. "Just pretend the search engine is a person you're talking to. Just ask it a question, press return and it'll answer anything you want." The old lady reaches for the keyboard and types into Google: "Hello. How are Auntie Ginnie's varicose veins?"

For the first time in many years, an old man leaves his house out in the countryside and travels into the nearest town to go to see a film at the cinema. After buying his ticket, he stops at a kiosk to buy some popcorn. He is astonished at the price he is charged and tells the popcorn seller, "Do you know what? Last time I came to the cinema, a bag of popcorn only cost sixpence!" "Well, you're certainly going to enjoy the film this evening," says the popcorn man. "They've got sound now and everything."

Ways To Tell If You Are A Wrinkly

OK, you've taken the wrinkly test, but you're still not convinced that you're a member of the grey army. You imagine somehow that you've been tricked or conned into outing yourself as a budgie-fancier. In short, you think those tests have been rigged, don't you? You scored highly, but you aren't having any of it. You are in denial. All right then, let's get specific. Do you recognize any of the following?

When you open your bathroom cabinet you realize that the cosmetics are outnumbered by the medicines.

You find it easier to sit down than to stand up.

When the binmen ask for a tip at Christmas you say, "Here's a tip – don't drop half the flaming rubbish in the road on your way to the dustcart, then you might get a Christmas box!"

You fondly reminisce about the days when there were "proper" programmes on the telly and not all this "How Clean Is Your Big Brother Supernanny Get Me Out Of Hell's Kitchen Love Island" so-called reality TV (it's all fixed anyway) and if that's reality I'm glad I'm not long for this world.

You have one or all of the following on your front door: "No junk mail", "Callers will be asked for ID", "Neighbourhood Watch", "Bugger off", a security chain, a picture of a ferocious looking dog with the quite transparent porky "I live here" emblazoned underneath.

The only downloads you are interested in are regular bowel movements.

You don't need to listen to the weather forecast, because you can predict the climate by the noise your joints make as you get out of bed in the mornings.

You can't understand why Radio 2 is playing so much rubbishy modern music and has young upstarts like Jonathan Ross presenting shows – disgraceful!

When it's time to go to bed you have the totally irrational wish that the bed could come down to you instead.

You are constantly shocked to find that policeman, politicians and other figures of authority appear to be fresh-faced youths who don't look like they've even started to shave yet.

You find it impossible to read a newspaper without your blood pressure rising to dangerously high levels.

Wrinkly World: Wrinkly Menswear

Do you possess any of the following:

An off-white or olive green windcheater

A green tartan or grey flat cap

A blue blazer with silver buttons

A collection of ties that your wife won't let you wear

A trouser press

A tie hanger

Hush Puppies

A hand-knitted scarf

A grey or olive green cardigan with brown buttons that look like footballs chopped in half

Spectacles on a string round your neck

A trilby with a little feather in the band

A boater that you wear semi-ironically in the summer

Grey flannels

Shoe trees

Cuff links that you haven't worn for 30 years, but haven't quite got round to throwing away

Striped pyjamas

A tartan dressing gown

Tartan or "comedy" slippers

An old leather belt

A proper hanky

Braces

A walking stick that is not a mobility aid, but a fashion statement (e.g. one with a carved animal head on the top)

If you have answered 'yes' to any of the above you are well on the way to being a wrinkly.

Films For Wrinklies

Gran Theft Auto

Butch Cassidy and the Tea Dance kid

The Big Snooze

The Pipe, The Slippers and the Rose

Granny Hill

Four Funerals and Another Funeral

Saving Private Pension

Stairlift Express

Grandchildren of the Damned

Saga Holiday

Senior Citizen Kane

Retirement Home Alone

Oldfinger

Grumble Fish

The Pruning of the Rose

Help! The Aged

A Gran Day Out

Loo Stop

Old Git Carter

Speak Up Pompeii

The Mild Bunch

Moaner Lisa

Being Nice To Older People

If you're one of the younger people reading this book who seems to be always putting their foot in it with the older generation, then here are a few tips on being more diplomatic.

Old people are not DEAF AS POSTS, they are A LITTLE HARD OF HEARING

Old people are not AS BLIND AS BATS, they are SLIGHTLY MYOPIC

Old people are not OLD GITS, they are IMBUED WITH THE WISDOM OF AGE

Old people are not SENILE, they have MEMORY RETENTION ISSUES

Old people are not STUCK IN THEIR WAYS, they GOT IT RIGHT FIRST TIME

Old people are not BIGOTS, they have FIRM VIEWS

Old people are not TECHNOPHOBES, they are DIFFERENTLY COMPETENT

Old people are not OVER THE HILL, they are OUTASITE!

Old people are not WRINKLY, they have CHARACTERFUL FACES

Old people are not SLOW, they just like to TAKE THEIR TIME

Old people are not JUDGEMENTAL, they TELL IT LIKE IT IS

Old people are not MOANERS, they like to EXPRESS THEIR INNER EMOTIONS

Old people are not DANGEROUS DRIVERS, they just like to MIX IT UP A BIT

Old people are not FORGETFUL, they are MENTALLY SELECTIVE

Old people are not DODDERY, they MOVE IN MYSTERIOUS WAYS

Old people are not LIVING IN THE PAST, they EXPERIENCE TEMPORAL SHIFT

Old people are not GRUMPY, they have A HAPPINESS DISCONNECT

Old people are not PENSIONERS, they have ALTERNATIVE WAGE ARRANGEMENTS

You Know You're Getting Old When...

All the cars behind you turn on their headlights.

All your midnight oil is all used up by 9.30pm.

Christmas starts to piss you off.

Complete strangers feel comfortable calling you "old-timer".

Conversations with people your own age usually turn into a bout of "ailment duelling".

Even dialling long distance makes you feel tired.

When you're just visiting a friend in hospital, a member of staff comes toward you with a wheelchair.

Every time you suck your belly in, your ankles balloon out.

Everything that works hurts and what doesn't hurt doesn't work.

Fortune tellers offer to read your face instead of your palm.

Funeral directors call and make idle conversation about how you're feeling.

Getting a little action means you don't need to eat any fibre today.

Getting lucky means you take less than ten minutes to find your car in the supermarket car park.

Half the stuff in your shopping trolley has the words "for fast relief" printed on the label.

Happy hour is a 30-minute nap.

You start having dry dreams and wet farts.

It gets harder and harder for them to make those sexual harassment charges stick.

It takes longer to rest than it did to get tired in the first place.

It takes you a couple of tries to get over a speed bump.

It takes you longer and longer to get over a good time.

Lawn care has become a highlight of your life.

Wrinkly Appearance

Age brings with it some difficult wardrobe choices. On the one hand you're not going to want to look old before your time with flat caps, headscarves and tweedy clothes; people will either think you're ancient or you've suddenly become a member of the Royal Family. On the other hand you don't want to look like old hen dressed as spring chicken. Think how embarrassing it must be for the children of certain rock stars to see their wizened old parents tottering around in high heels and make-up – and yes, we mean you female rock stars, too. You need to strike just the right balance between dignity and fashion. So if you must dye your hair, do it properly otherwise you'll end up looking like a patchwork Cruella De Ville; if you insist on having a tattoo make sure it's one that's out of sight and won't look too weird when it's stretched or shrunk dramatically over the years; and if you absolutely can't help yourself wearing a thong, a tiny swimsuit, tight jeans or way too much make-up, please take this simple and kindly meant tip – don't leave the house!

Time may be a great healer, but it's a lousy beautician.

Grey hair is God's graffiti.

Bill Cosby

Two ageing ladies are talking in the beauty parlour one day. "Of course I've always had a nice firm chin," says one. "Yes," says the other one, "in fact now I see the firm has taken on a couple of partners."

A man goes to a reunion of all his old classmates from school. The next day his friend asks him how it went. "It was OK," he says, "but unfortunately all my old friends had become so old and overweight, hardly any of them seemed to recognize me."

Two old men are talking. The first says, "Back in the 1960s my wife used to spend all her time and money trying to make herself look like Elizabeth Taylor." "What about now?" asks his friend. "Now," says the first old man, "she spends all her time and money trying NOT to look like Elizabeth Taylor."

She doesn't show her age, but if you look under her make-up it's there.

She's thinking of having her hair dyed back to its original colour. The only problem is now she's got to try and remember what that was.

An old man tells his friend, "You know, my wife is still as beautiful today as she was the first time I saw her." "That's nice," says his friend. "Yes," says the old man, "it takes her a couple of hours in the morning to get there mind."

As you get older you learn that beauty comes from within...
from within bottles, jars, phials, compacts...

A husband and wife are getting ready for bed. The wife is
standing in front of a full-length mirror, taking a long hard
look at herself. "You know dear," she says, "I look in the
mirror and I see an old woman. My face is all wrinkled, my
hair is grey, my shoulders are hunched over, I've got fat legs
and my arms are flabby." She turns to her husband and says,
"Tell me something positive, to make me feel better about
myself." He studies hard for a moment, thinking about it, and
says in a soft, thoughtful voice, "Well, there's nothing wrong
with your eyesight."

His face is so wrinkled it's capable of holding three whole days'
worth of rain.

I've only got one wrinkle and I'm sitting on it.

Jeanne Calment

Of course older people say they don't have wrinkles, they have
laughter lines. So we must all do a hell of a lot more laughing
once we pass 50.

Two old ladies are chatting at a day care centre. Alice says, "You
know I like that man who brings round the tea; he said I've got
the skin of a 20-year-old." "Hmm," replies Gertrude, "Well I
think you'd better give it back to her then – look how wrinkled
you've got it!"

Saffy: Mountaineers have died falling in to shallower ravines
than your wrinkles!

Absolutely Fabulous

A little boy watches as his grandmother applies a face mask and
asks, "What's that for?" "To help make me more beautiful,"
says the grandmother as she removes the mask. "Hmm," says
the boy. "Doesn't seem to have worked, does it?"

A middle-aged woman goes off to a health centre for a week and has a series of beauty treatments, including waxing, facials, a special diet, saunas and more. When she gets back home fully revitalized and glowing with health, she asks her husband, "So, if you'd never met me before, just on the way I look now, how old would you say I was?" Her husband looks her up and down and says, "I'd say from your skin, 26. From your hair about 20. And from your body..." The woman giggles girlishly and says, "You old flatterer, don't you think you're overdoing it a bit?" "Hold on," says the husband, "I haven't added them up yet."

A woman says to her husband, "I don't look 38 do I?" "No," he says, "but you did when you were."

An old couple are getting ready to go out one night. The old man admires his wife. "Wow," he says, "you look great." "Thank you," she says. "Yes," says the old man, "it must have taken you ages."

An old man tells his friend, "My wife tried putting on a mudpack to make herself attractive." "Did it work?" asks his friend. "It did for a bit," says the old man, "but then it fell off."

Old Albert is complaining to his mates in the pub: "Every night before she goes to bed my missus puts curlers in her hair, a mudpack on her face and bits of cucumber over her eyes. It's a waste of time if you ask me, I can still tell it's her."

I have flabby thighs, but fortunately my stomach covers them.

Is it really a coincidence that the Roman Numerals for 40 are "XL".

Sally: Remember: Every morning your face has slipped a little bit more. Since I turned 30 I've had to put a daily limit on facial expressions. I only ever smile at single men, so I can justify the loss of elasticity.

Coupling

Old Mavis has got lovely sleek black hair all the way down her back. It would be nice if she had some on her head as well but you can't have everything.

People who knew him 20 years ago say he looks the same now as he did then – old.

Artificial De-Wrinkling: Cosmetic Surgery

You know how when some people, as they get older, fail to recognize others – even members of their own family? Well now, due to the wonders of modern cosmetic surgery, you can even forget what you used to look like yourself! How fabulous is that? Despite being on the wrong side of middle-age you can wake up in the morning, go into the bathroom and be confronted by a gorgeous, fresh-faced thing with perfect teeth, beautiful hair and a youthful body. Yes, you forgetful old fool, you've forgotten that one of your grandchildren is over to stay!

I don't plan to grow old gracefully. I plan to have face-lifts until my ears meet.

Rita Rudner

A man tells his friend, "Now my wife's getting a bit older, she's getting into all this cosmetic surgery and beauty treatment business. Yesterday she was at the beauty clinic for over two hours. And that was just for the estimate."

An ageing woman is worrying about the cosmetic surgery she has booked. "Is it going to hurt?" she asks her doctor. "Yes," he says, "but not until you receive my bill."

Advice for wrinklies trying to get rid of the wrinkles: I don't know much about plastic surgery but a good rule of thumb is that you know it's time to stop when you look constantly frightened.

A definition of unhappiness: a woman who has her face lifted only to find an identical one lurking underneath.

A middle-aged man goes to his wife's plastic surgeon to complain. "You've given her a face lift, a bottom lift, a breast lift and a tummy lift," he says. "So what's the problem?" asks the surgeon. "What's the problem?" splutters the man. "She's 18 inches off the flipping ground now!"

A 60-year-old man decides to have a face-lift for his birthday. He spends £10,000 and is really happy with the results. On his way home, he stops at a newsagent and buys a paper. While he's there, he asks the sales assistant, "I hope you don't mind me asking, but how old do you think I am?" "About 40," says the sales assistant. "I'm actually 60," says the man feeling very pleased with himself. After that, he goes into a chip shop for some lunch and asks the assistant there the same question. The assistant says, "I'd say about 35." "Thanks very much," says the man, "I'm actually 60." Later, while he's waiting at a bus stop, he asks an old woman the same question. She replies, "I'm 85 years old, and my eyesight is going. But when I was young, there was a sure way of telling a man's age. If I have a feel in your pants for a minute, I will be able to tell you your exact age." As there is no-one around, the man lets her slip her hand down his pants. Ten minutes later, the old lady says, "Right. You're 60 years old." "That's incredible," says the man, "you're exactly right. How do you do that?" "I was behind you in the chip shop," says the old lady.

The best way to prevent sagging: just eat till the wrinkles fill out.

A woman with terrible bags under her eyes finally decides to do something about it, so she goes to a plastic surgeon and asks him to get rid of them. He performs the operation and tells the woman afterwards that to save her from having to keep coming back in years to come he has fixed a discreet handle to the back of her neck. "If those bags start coming back," he says, "just turn the handle a bit and it'll tighten up your skin and the bags will just disappear like magic." "Well thank you," says the woman, delighted. Every so often, when the bags under her eyes begin to show she turns the handle and they disappear, but after many years two bags appear which are just impossible to remove, however much she turns the handle so she goes back to the surgeon. He takes a look and says, "Madam, those aren't eye bags – they're your breasts. You've been turning that handle too hard." "Oh my goodness!" exclaims the woman. "I suppose that'll explain the goatee as well."

A famous old actor was bemoaning his lot on a chat show: "Some women get their good looks from their mothers. Mine gets hers from the plastic surgeon – and it's costing me a fortune!"

A man tells his friend, "My wife went in for a face lift operation last week." "Did it work?" asks the friend. "Not really," says the man. "When they saw what was under it, they dropped it again."

Two women are sitting in the old people's home bitching about the other inmates. One old lady says to the other, "Look at her, she's had her face lifted so often, when she raises her eyebrows her bedsocks shoot up her legs."

Edna is a 45 year-old woman. One day she has a heart attack and is taken to hospital. While on the operating table she has a near death experience. Seeing God she asks, "Is this it? Is my time up?" God replies, "No, Edna, my child. You have come here too soon. In fact you have another 43 years, two months and eight days to live." Upon recovery, Edna decides to stay in the hospital and have a face lift, liposuction, breast implants and a tummy tuck. She even has someone come in and change her hair colour and brighten her teeth! Well, she thinks to herself, since I have so much more time to live, I may as well make the most of it. After all her cosmetic surgery and treatment, she gets out of hospital, but, while crossing the street on her way home, she is run over by an ambulance and killed. She arrives up in Heaven in front of God and is completely furious. "What's going on?" she asks God. "I thought you said I had another 43 years? Why didn't you pull me from out of the path of the ambulance?" "Oh, sorry, Edna," replies God, "I didn't recognize you!"

Two men are sitting in a pub and opposite them is an attractive, young looking woman sitting on her own sipping a glass of wine. One of the men indicates the woman and says, "I reckon that woman has had a face lift you know." The other one says, "How can you tell?" And the first man replies, "Every time she crosses her legs her mouth suddenly closes."

Wrinkly World: Fashions For The Wrinkly Woman

Do you possess any of the following:

A tweed skirt

Toffee-brown stockings or tights

Stocking or tights that show extensive repairs

A collection of hats

Spectacles on a string round your neck

Sensible shoes

A light summer headscarf that holds several megawatts of static electricity

Various items of clothing in a variety of tartans

A bra that looks as though it could double as a comfy hammock for two

A selection of pastel-coloured "woollies"

An off-white or pale pink nightie

A brown dressing gown

Fluffy slippers

An ancient suspender belt the colour of a sticking plaster

A perfume that smells as though it may well kill 99% of all known household germs

A proper hanky

A ballgown that hasn't see active service since 1972

A selection of pale pastel blouses with mother-of-pearl buttons

A hairnet

Curlers

A large collection of cheap toiletries given to you by young members of family that you can't use but can't throw away either

A few old hatpins that even you don't use any more

An extensive collection of floral frocks

If you have answered 'yes' to any of the above you are well on the way to being a wrinkly.

You Know You're Getting Old When...

You remember the days when you could get tired legs from using a sewing machine.

You remember when service stations actually gave you service.

You start repeating all the stupid, irritating things your mother used to say to you as a child.

You sink your teeth into a juicy steak and they stay there.

You start to answer questions with the phrase, "Because I said so!"

You start to appreciate the attractions of accordion music.

You start to clean out your ear with a cotton bud, then realize you forgot to take out your hearing aid.

You step off a curb and look down one more time to make sure the street is still there.

You suddenly find you are proud of your lawn mower.

You take a metal detector to the beach.

You tap your feet and hum along to the music in lifts.

You think you know all the answers, but nobody will ask you the questions.

You throw a wild crazy party and none of your neighbours even notice.

You wake up looking like the photograph on your passport.

You walk around barefoot and get compliments about your new alligator shoes.

You wonder how you could be over the hill when you don't even remember getting on top of it.

You wonder why you waited so long to take up macramé.

Your back goes out more than you do.

Your birthday cake can no longer support the weight of the candles.

Your chemist offers to carry the bag of medicines to the car for you.

Out And About With The Wrinklies

An old man is trying to get his reluctant old friend to come out for a walk. "What happened to your get up and go," he asks. "It got up and went without me," says his friend.

An old couple arrive at the airport just in the nick of time to catch the plane for their summer holiday. "Do you know what?" says the old lady. "I wish I'd brought the piano with us." "What on earth are you talking about?" says her husband. "Why would you want to bring the piano with you." "Because," says the old lady, "I've left our tickets on top of it."

At the seaside there are two old men on their annual holidays standing in the sea with their trousers rolled up, smoking their pipes and watching the boats go by. One of them glances down at the other one's feet and says, "Blimey, mate, look at the state of your feet, they're absolutely filthy!" The other one looks down and agrees. "Yeah, I know," he says, "we couldn't come last year."

Cliff and his wife Esther go to their local county fair every year and every year Cliff tells his wife, "You know what I'd really like to do. I'd like to ride in that helicopter they've got over there." And every year Esther replies, "Cliff, you know very well that they charge £50 a ride. That's a lot of money to us pensioners." Finally Cliff tells Esther, "Esther, look, I'm 85 years old. If I don't get a ride in that helicopter this year, I might never get another chance." "Cliff," says his wife, "I've told you, £50 is a lot of money to pensioners like us." The helicopter pilot happens to hear the old couple's conversation and says to them, "OK, I'll make a deal with you. I'll take the both of you for a ride. If you can stay quiet for the entire trip and not say a word I won't charge you! But if you say one word, I'll have to charge you £50." Cliff and Esther agree and up they go in the helicopter. The pilot does all kinds of fancy manoeuvres, but doesn't hear a word from the couple. He does some daredevil tricks over and over again, but still not a word from the back. When they land, the pilot turns to Cliff and says, "Goodness me, I did everything

I could to get you to scream back there, but you didn't. I'm impressed!" Cliff replies, "Well, to tell you the truth, I almost said something when Esther fell out, but you know... £50 is a lot of money to pensioners like us."

Two old men are looking round a National Trust property when one says to the other, "You know, visiting these historical sites isn't so much fun when they all turn out to be younger than you are."

Albert and Henry are taking a stroll along the sea front one day when a seagull flies over and drops a blob of excrement right on the top of Albert's bald head. Henry is horrified at what has just happened and says in great concern, "Wait right there. I'll be back in a moment." Henry waddles off as fast as he can go to the nearest public convenience and returns a few minutes later with a length of toilet paper. "It's a bit too late for that," says Albert. "That seagull will be miles away by now."

One night, at the lodge of a hunting club, two new members were being introduced and shown around. The man guiding them said, "See that old man asleep in the chair by the fireplace, he's our oldest member and can tell you some hunting stories that you'll never forget." They woke the old man up and asked him to tell them a hunting story. "Well, I remember back in 1944," said the old man, "we went on a deer hunt in Canada. We were on foot and hunted for three days without seeing a thing. On the fourth day, I was so tired I had to rest my feet. I found a tree that had fallen, so I laid my gun down, propped my head on the tree and fell asleep. I don't remember how long I slept, but I remember the noise in the bushes that caused me to wake up. I was reaching for my gun when the biggest buck that I had ever seen jumped out of the bushes at me like this WHOOOOHHHHHH!!!!!!!!!!!... I tell you, I just filled my pants." The young men looked astonished and one of them said, "I don't blame you, I would have filled my pants too if a huge buck jumped out at me." The old man shook his head and said, "No, no, not then, just now when I said WHOOOOHHHHHH!!!!!!!!!!!"

Two old ladies were sitting in the park enjoying some music. "I think it's a minuet from Mignon," said one. "I thought it was a waltz from Faust," said the other. So the first old lady got up and shuffled over to a nearby notice board. "We were both wrong," she said. "It's a Refrain from Spitting."

A plane has a rough flight over the ocean. Suddenly a voice comes over the intercom: "Ladies and gentlemen, please fasten your seat belts and assume crash positions. We have lost our engines and we are trying to put this baby down as gently as possible on the water." "Oh stewardess! Are there any sharks in the ocean below?" asks a little old lady, terrified. "Yes, I'm afraid there are some. But not to worry, we have a special gel in the bottle next to your chair designed especially for emergencies like this. Just rub the gel onto your arms and legs." "And if I do this, the sharks won't eat me any more?" asks the lady. "Oh, they'll eat you all right, only they won't enjoy it so much," answers the stewardess.

Two old golfing partners are at the airport, booking a flight. One of them says, "Do you think we should take out any insurance?" "No," replies the other one. "I never bother any more. I used to, but it never seemed to make the slightest bit of difference."

Solly, an old Jewish man, gets on a train. The second class compartments are full, so he takes a peek into first class and sees an empty seat temptingly close to the door. The train is about to leave, so Solly reckons it's a safe bet the seat won't be taken. He slips inside the carriage, sits down and gets out his copy of the *Racing Post*. He happily spends the next half hour reading his paper while munching on a salt-beef sandwich and dipping into a jar of pickled herrings. Suddenly he's tapped on the shoulder by a steward. "Excuse me, sir," says the steward. "But this seat is reserved for the Archbishop of Canterbury." "So?" says Solly. "Who says I'm not the Archbishop of Canterbury?"

The Wrinklies' Holiday Test

All right, you're still not sure whether you're a wrinkly. You're borderline. OK, we believe you, but are you brave enough to take this test to find out whether you are winging your way to Planet Wrinkly? Go on, we dare you! Unless you're too old for such things of course...

Before going on holiday

You moan that there aren't any proper travel agents anymore and why should you have to book online when you know all computers hate you, but you suppose if you really must then you'll have to get your 12-year-old nephew to help you...

You complain that converting to the Euro has taken all the romance out of foreign travel and you hark back to the days when you could wander around the Dordogne with a pocket full of Francs and, yes, you would take a holiday in England but it's more expensive than Spain and the weather's so unpredictable...

You say it's costing you a fortune and in two weeks what will you have to show for it apart from sunburnt arms and a gyppy tummy?

During the holiday

You moan that it's too hot or too wet (if you did take that holiday in England) and you can't sleep at night because of British hooligans lowering the tone of the place and...

You complain that the food is too greasy/spicy/bland/foreign and they can't make a decent cup of tea, and oh for a good old British fry-up...

You say you're going to try and bloody well enjoy it because you're bloody well paying enough for it, but you won't be sorry to see a good old bit of British rain and have a decent cuppa...

After the holiday

You moan that, typical (!), the whole time you've been away the weather at home has been glorious, and the bank is ripping you off by charging you to change back your currency that you've got left over, and someone (not you, naturally) forgot to cancel the flipping papers.

You complain that you're exhausted and you've got to be back at work in two days and you really need another holiday to recover from your holiday and that's it for another year, 50 weeks of saving before you can afford to go again...

You say you had a great time, but you can't work out how to download your holiday pics from your digital camera, and you certainly didn't vote for getting rid of proper films, but then nobody asks your opinion about anything do they...?

All right, admit it. Be honest. Have you found yourself agreeing with at least three of those statements? We thought so. Welcome to Oldsville.

Wrinklies At The Wheel

With age comes experience – or is it the other way round? Anyway, this truism doesn't seem to apply to driving. Probably because they keep changing the rules. It's not your average senior citizen's fault is it? One decade you're driving down a perfectly normal road quite happily, then next decade it's become a one-way street! No-one told you did they? Old habits die hard. And motorways? Don't even start on motorways. Now, if I'm not meant to drive slowly, why do they call it the "slow lane"? Yes, all right, three miles an hour is pretty slow, but when your eyesight's as bad as mine and your reaction speeds make a tortoise look a bit nippy, it's the only safe way to drive. If only some of these hot-headed youngsters took a leaf out of my book...

Two old women, Millie and Dolly, are out driving in a large car. Both can barely see over the dashboard. As they cruise along they come to a junction and go through a red light. Millie, in the passenger seat, thinks to herself, "I must be losing my mind. I swear we just went through a red light." After a few minutes they come to another junction and go through another red light. Millie is almost sure that the light was red, but is concerned she might be mistaken. At the next junction they go through another red light. Millie turns to Dolly and says, "Millie! Did you know we just ran through three red lights in a row! You could have killed us!" Millie looks around and says, "Oh! Am I driving?"

Being 55 years old is like driving at 50 miles an hour. Everybody seems to pass you.

An old man is out driving on the motorway when his mobile rings. It's his wife calling. She says she's just heard a news report about a car that's driving the wrong way up the motorway. "I know," says the old man. "But it's not just one car. It's hundreds of them."

An old lady decides one day that she really should learn to drive. So after many attempts she passes her test and tells her husband that to celebrate she's going to drive him over to France for a holiday. But then a week before the trip she suddenly announces the holiday is off. "Why did you change your mind?" he asks. "Well," says the old lady, "it's this business of driving on the right. I've been practising round town for three weeks now and I just can't get used to it – in fact, I've nearly killed three people."

A police officer is driving along one day when he sees an old lady in her car, driving along while knitting at the same time. The police man attempts unsuccessfully to get her attention, but to no avail. Finally he drives right alongside her, winds down his window and calls out, "Pull over, madam!" At which points the old lady turns to him and says, "No. Socks actually."

A dilapidated and ancient Ford pulls into a petrol station. "Could you let me have two litres of petrol?" asks the old fellow at the wheel. "Why don't you fill her up, now that you're here?" asks the attendant. "Well," says the old man, "she might not run that far."

An elderly couple are driving around the M25 in their ancient Skoda with the wife at the wheel. A police car pulls them over onto the hard shoulder. "Do you realize you were speeding back there?" says the policeman. The woman being slightly deaf, turns to her husband and asks, "What did he say?" The old man shouts back, "He says you were speeding." The policeman says, "May I see your licence?" The old woman turns to her husband and asks, "What did he say?" The old man shouts, "He wants to see your licence." The woman hands over her licence. The officer says, "I see you're from Farnborough. I spent a bit of time there once. Do you know what? I had the worst sex I've ever had in my life with a woman in Farnborough. Oh she was a dreadful, unresponsive old bag!" The woman turns to her husband and asks, "What did he say?" The old man yells back, "He thinks he knows you!"

An old man is driving slowly round the supermarket car park, looking for a space, when finally he spots one in the corner. He carefully and gingerly tries to reverse into it, but as he does so a young man in a zippy hatchback swerves in front of him and pinches the space. The old man gets out to remonstrate with the youngster, but the young man says, "Tough luck, mate, that's what you can do when you're young and quick." So the old man climbs out of his car, lifts up his walking stick and starts bashing in the bonnet of the young man's car. "And that's what you can do when you're old and rich," says the old man, walking off.

The Wrinklies' Driving Test

Even if you've passed all the other wrinklies' tests, perhaps one of the surest ways of finally establishing whether you're one of life's elder statesmen/women is the way in which you drive.

Before going out in the car do you:

Moan about the fact that you have to go out on the roads with all those other lunatics

Complain that you're taking your life in your hands and it's going to cost you a fortune in car parking charges when you get wherever you're going

Say nobody under the age of 30 should be allowed on the roads anyway

During a car journey do you:

Moan that you're the only one observing the speed limit and not chatting on a mobile phone while you're driving

Complain about all the blooming road works, confusing one-way systems and the gaps between toilet stops on motorways

Say half these kids don't look old enough to drive anyway

After a car journey do you:

Moan about the state of the roads/the volume of traffic/the rudeness of other drivers

Complain you don't know why you bother taxing and insuring your car when no one else seems to bother

Say that if young women want to drive tanks why don't they join the army

So how did you do? If you found yourself agreeing with at least three of the above statements then congratulations, you have entered the magical realm of Wrinkliedom!

Wrinkly World: Furnishings And Household Accessories

Do you possess any of the following:

A shiny three-piece suite that is not meant to be shiny

A card table

A tallboy

A proper old-fashioned free-standing wooden wardrobe

A cake stand

Artexed ceilings

A set of occasional tables

A tablecloth "for best"

Curtains hanging on rings

A bureau

A set of doilies

Little cloths that go over the arms of the sofa

A set of fire accessories such as tongs, shovel and poker on a little stand

A draught excluder (possibly made to look like a snake or a dachshund)

A clothes horse

A Teasmade

A radio alarm permanently set to Radio 2

A fan heater

A two-bar electric fire

A Formica-topped kitchen table

A tin bath for soaking your "poor old feet"

A tin of toffees with a picture of one of the royal castles on it

A pouffe

Anything made from "leatherette"

An umbrella stand

A hatstand

Eating Out

A rich old man goes to a dating agency and ends up going to have dinner with an elderly dowager. The next day at his London club a friend asks him if he enjoyed himself. "Well, I would have done," says the man. "Would have done?" asks the friend. "What do you mean?" "Well," says the old man, "I would have done if the melon had been as cold as the soup, and the soup had been as warm as the wine, and the wine had been as old as the chicken, and if the chicken had been as young as the maid, and the maid had been as willing as the old dowager then, yes, I would have had a very good time indeed."

An elderly couple go to a trendy restaurant, but are turned away because it's full. They return the next night, but again it's full and they go home disappointed. The next night the same thing happens again. "Look," says the *maitre d'*, "to save you time, why don't you make a booking?" The old couple agree this would make sense, but discover that the restaurant is booked solid for the next three weeks. "Tell you what," says the *maitre d'*, "try phoning tomorrow. There might be a cancellation." The old man rings the next day and discovers that there haven't been any cancellations and now the restaurant is booked solid for the next five weeks! The old man complains bitterly. "You know," he says, "your restaurant would do a lot more business if you weren't so bloody full all the time!"

Wrinkly Birthday To You...

It's a sure sign of wrinkliehood when you stop looking forward to your birthdays. Remember how proud you were when you first become a teenager or turned 18 (or 21 for you older folk)? You may have even felt slightly proud of the fact that you reached the grand old age of 30 with all your own hair, teeth and fashion sense intact. But then what your friends joshingly referred to as the "big four O" loomed and as it got closer the feelings of dread, queasiness and slight panic began to take over. With all the enthusiasm of going to have your teeth pulled you celebrated your 40th with wry and rueful jokes, and self-deprecating remarks, and then relaxed a bit, because, frankly, 41 or 42 isn't a whole lot different from 40. But when the "big five O" starts looming wheezily and wizened on the horizon, that's when you start to use subterfuge, evasion and downright lying. Just one tip – people usually notice if they're asked to attend your second 40th birthday party.

Keith tells Harry, "We've recently had a terrible tragedy in our family. My grandmother died on her 99th birthday." "Oh no," says Harry. "That's sad." "I know," says Keith. "And we were only halfway through giving her the bumps at the time."

A man asks his wife what she'd like for her 40th birthday. She says she'd like to be six again. Next day the man buys his wife a party hat and a big sticky cake, and hires a clown to show her some magic tricks, and sings songs. The wife looks at her husband as if he's crazy. "But I thought you'd be happy," says the husband. "You said you wanted to be six again." "You idiot," she fumes. "I meant my dress size."

People ask me what I'd most appreciate getting for my 87th birthday. I tell them, a paternity suit.

George Burns

There is still no cure for the common birthday.

John Glenn

A newspaper reporter visits a very old man on his birthday. "Have you lived in this town your whole life?" asks the reporter. "Obviously not, you young fool," says the old man. "I haven't died yet, have I?"

It's a terrible thing having to grow old by yourself. My wife hasn't had a birthday for the past five years.

Old Bill is known as the most boring man in his neighbourhood. He spends his days constantly bragging to anyone who will listen about how fit he is, how active he is and how young he feels despite his advanced years. "Look at that!" he says to a group of other elderly people as he pats his well-honed stomach. "That's the result of 100 sit ups a day – and I can still do them," "How else do you keep so fit?" asks one of his audience. "I don't smoke," says Bill, "I don't drink, I never eat unhealthy processed foods or snacks, and I've never chased loose women! And tomorrow – guess what! I'm going to be celebrating my 95th birthday." "Really?" says another old man. "How?"

Wrinklies' Party Games

Sag – You're It!

Pass the Paracetamol

20 Questions followed by 20 "Eh?"s

Pin the Toupee on the Bald Wrinkly

Kick the Bucket

Simon Says Something Incoherent

Doc, Doc, Grouse

Hide and Sleep

Musical Wheelchairs

Cup of Char-ades

What Was That Simon Said Again?

Spin the Bottle of Sanatogen

Monotony

Short-sighted Man's Buff

Postman's Knock-knees

Shakes and Bladders

Blimey! Is That The Time Already Mr Wolf?

Ring a Ring an Ambulance

Here We Go Round the Flipping Mulberry Bush Again

Pass The Kidney Stone

It's Murder In the Dark When You're Trying To Find the Toilet at 3am

Chinese Whispers – What's Wrong With English Whispers Then?

Wrinkly Antiques And Artworks

A wealthy old dowager goes to the National Gallery one day and tries to impress one of the attendants with her knowledge of art history. "Oh, look!" she says. "Now correct me if I'm wrong, but isn't this a Goya?" "Er, no, madam, it's a Gainsborough actually," corrects the attendant. "Ah," says the old woman, "but that one over there… now that is definitely a Renoir isn't it?" "Sorry madam," says the attendant, "actually it's a Seurat." "Oh," says the woman, glancing around hastily to find one she definitely knows. "Now that horrible, ugly scary looking one; I know that for certain. It's *The Scream* by Edvard Munch." "No, madam," says the attendant. "That is in fact a mirror."

A man tells a friend, "You know, I am a keen collector of antiques." "I know," says his friend. "I've seen your wife."

Two old ladies are visiting an art gallery one day and walk through the sculpture section. A few minutes later they emerge looking rather shocked and shaken. "Blimey!" says the first one. "Did you see that statue of that feller?" "What the feller with the big doodah hanging out for everyone to see?" says her friend. "Yes I did see that. Absolutely enormous wasn't it?" "I know," says the first one, "and it was so cold in that art gallery as well."

I'm very proud of my gold pocket watch. My grandfather, on his deathbed… sold me this watch.

Woody Allen

106

They're Not Wrinkles, They're Smile Lines: Looking On The Bright Side

Psst! Do you want to know a secret? Getting older isn't as bad as you think. Oh people like to make jokes about false teeth, grey hair, hearing aids, corsets, impotence, forgetfulness, stairlifts, Zimmer frames, loss of brain cells and all the rest, but unless you're extremely unlucky it won't *all* happen to you. And, if the loss of brain cells comes first you won't realize that the rest of it is happening to you! Sorry, cheap shot. But the good news is that people are staying healthier longer, they're living active lives and showing the youngsters a thing or two. But enough about the Rolling Stones; with the oldies of this world due to outnumber youngsters any time soon it's going to be a wrinkly world – everyone else will just have to live in it.

Looking on the bright side, when you're in your 40s the glass is still half-full. On the down side, pretty soon your teeth will be floating in it.

Don't forget: being "over the hill" is a lot better than being underneath it!

If things get better with age, then I must be approaching "magnificent".

It feels great to be nearly 100. I mean, for those parts of me that still have feeling.

Bob Hope

Nice to be here? At my age it's nice to be anywhere.

George Burns

A reporter goes to interview a 104-year-old woman. "What do you think is the best thing about being 104?" asks the reporter. "Very little peer pressure," says the old woman.

God put me on earth to accomplish a certain number of things. Right now I'm so far behind I will never die.

There are some nice things about old age, like I can sit here and think how it's great that wrinkles don't hurt.

Whenever I begin to feel a little blue, I remember to start breathing again.

You know that inside every old person there's a young person trying to work out what the hell happened.

I intend to live forever. So far, so good.

I'm not confused, I'm just well-mixed.

Another good thing about being poor is that when you're 70 your children will not have declared you legally insane in order to gain control of your estate.

Woody Allen

Here's something you won't want to live to see. Do you realize that in about 40 years we'll have hundreds of thousands of elderly men and women running round covered with shrivelled old tattoos?

One of the nice things about being senile is you can hide your own Easter eggs.

The good thing about being over the hill is that you then start to pick up speed.

The older you get, the better you realize you were.

I used to dread getting older, because I thought I would not be able to do all the things I wanted to do, but now that I am older, I find that I don't want to do them.

Lady Nancy Astor

The Perks Of Getting Older And Wrinklier

All that money you've been investing in the NHS over the years will now finally start to pay off.

If you've never smoked, what the hell? Why not start? What's the worst that can happen?

In a hostage situation they're more likely to keep the young, pretty ones.

In general kidnappers will be less interested in you.

Nobody will expect you to run a marathon.

Nobody will expect you to run into a burning building.

You can buy things now and know they will never wear out.

You can eat your dinner at four in the afternoon and not feel ridiculous.

You can enjoy heated arguments about pension plans with your friends.

Men can stop trying to hold their stomachs in, even if a supermodel walks into the room.

You get to hear all about other peoples' operations.

You no longer have to think of a speed limit as a challenge.

Your doctor will no longer immediately dismiss you as a hypochondriac.

Your eyes won't get much worse.

You've finally got your number of brain cells down to a manageable size.

You've got nothing left to learn the hard way.

Nostalgia

It's hard to be nostalgic when you can't remember anything.

I can remember when the air was clean and sex was dirty.

George Burns

Old Tom tells Old Bert, "I was young once you know." "Cor!" says Bert. "You must have a good memory."

Nostalgia is a longing for a place you'd never think of moving back to.

After the age of 80, everything reminds you of something else.

Lowell Thomas

Two old men are talking over some sad memories. "You know it's 40 years today I lost my wife and children," says one. "Is it really?" says the other. "That's terrible." "Yes it is," says the first. "I'll never forget that poker game."

Nostalgia isn't what it used to be.

Then And Now

Then: "Whatever". Now: "Depends".

Then: dreaming of moving to California because it's cool. Now: dreaming of moving to California because it's warm.

Then: Getting out to a new, hip joint. Now: Getting a new hip joint.

Then: Growing pot. Now: Growing a pot belly.

Then: How high are you? Now: Hi! How are you?

Then: Long hair. Now: Longing for hair.

Then: Parents begging you to get your hair cut. Now: Children begging you to get their heads shaved.

Then: Passing the driving test. Now: Passing the vision test.

Then: Screw the system. Now: Upgrade the system.

Then: Seeds and stems. Now: Roughage.

Then: the Rolling Stones. Now: the kidney stones.

Wrinkly World: Outside The House

Does your property "boast" any of the following:

Stone cladding

Pebble-dashing

Crazy paving

A wooden letterbox on a pole

A house name such as "Dunlivin"

Overshoes in the porch

A "Please shut the gate" sign

A boot scraper

A hedge shaped like a bird

Any instruction sign headed "Polite notice"

Traffic cones for "reserving" your parking space when you're out

A coal bunker

A dustbin with your house number painted on it

A handrail to help you up and down the front step

A birdbath

A wishing well

If you answered "yes" to three of more of the above you are now officially a wrinkly.

Crafty Old Wrinklies

They say there's no fool like an old fool, but that's exactly what wrinklies want you to think. When you get to a certain age you suddenly have a whole armoury of tricks and ruses to keep you one step ahead of those grasping and demanding young whippersnappers, otherwise known as your family.

"Eh? What's that? You want to borrow how much? Sorry, you'll have to speak up..." "Ooh with my knees/heart/arthritis I can't carry the shopping on my own/clean the house/take the dog for a walk...", "All my money's tied up in investments, but as soon as I go it'll be left to the son or daughter who's done the most for me....", "What's that officer? Shoplifting/speeding/reckless use of mobility scooter? Oh, take pity, I'm only a poor old pensioner..."

An elderly man bought a large farm in Florida and fixed it up with walkways, orchards, tennis courts and a pond at the furthest edge of the property. One evening he decided to go down to the pond and took a bucket with him to bring back some fruit. As he got nearer, he heard voices shouting and laughing with glee. As he came closer he saw a bunch of young women skinny-dipping in his pond. He made the women aware of his presence and they all went into the deep end. One of the women shouted to him, "Hey, you old pervert! We're not coming out of here until you leave!" "That's OK," said the old man, "I didn't come down here to watch you ladies swim naked or make you get out of the pond naked." Then he held up his bucket and said, "I'm just here to feed my alligator!"

An old man calls his son on the other side of the country and tells him, "Your mother and I have something to tell you, but we don't really want to discuss it over the phone. We're just telling you because you're our oldest son and we thought you ought to know. We've decided to split up and get a divorce." "What do you mean?" asks the son, horrified at this news. "You've been married for over 50 years." "Sorry, but there it is," says the old man. "I don't understand," says the son. "Why would you want to get a divorce after all this time?" "We don't want to talk about it, because it's far too painful. We've made our minds up and that's it," says the old man. "We just want you to call your brothers and sisters, and pass on the news to spare us any further grief." The son insists on talking to his mother, but the old man tells him there's nothing he can do. "Just hold on, Dad," says the son, "don't do anything rash! Next week is Christmas and I'll be taking time off work anyway, so I'm going to come straight over to you and help you get this whole thing sorted out." Over the next hour all the other children call saying they too are going to come over to help sort things out as well. After all this the old man turns to his wife and says, "Well, there we are. It worked like a charm. But what are we going to do to get them to come over to us again next year?"

One night an old woman is horrified to see a police car pull up outside her house, even more so when she sees her husband brought out of the back and led up to the door. "What happened?" the old lady asks the policeman. "I'm sorry, madam," says the policeman, "we found this elderly gentleman at the local shopping centre. He was lost and couldn't remember how to get home." "Oh no!" says the old woman. After the police have gone she turns to her husband and says, "The shopping centre's only half a mile away. How could you have forgotten your way home? You're not losing your marbles are you?" "Of course not," says her old husband. "I wasn't lost. I was just too tired to walk."

An old man goes up to a young man at the Post Office and says, "Excuse me, would you address this postcard for me?" The young man gladly does so and then says, "Would you like me to write a short message on here for you as well?" "Yes, please," says the old man and dictates what he would like to say. Finally the young man, feeling very pleased with himself for his good deed, asks, "Now, is there anything else I can do for you?" The old man thinks a moment and says, "Yes, please. At the end could you just add, 'Please excuse the sloppy hand writing.'"

An elderly gentleman walks into a West End furriers with his young lady and says he wants to buy her a mink coat costing £15,000. "Will a cheque be OK?" asks the man. "Certainly, sir," says the sales assistant. "But we'll have to wait a few days for it to clear. Can you come back on Monday to take delivery?" "Certainly," replies the old man, and he and his girlfriend walk out arm in arm. Next Monday the man returns. The sales assistant is furious, "You've got a nerve coming back here. It turns out there's hardly a penny in your bank account and your cheque was worthless." "Yes, sorry about that," replies the man. "I just came in to apologize… and to thank you for the greatest weekend of my life."

Ancient Wisdom

A rambler in the country sees old farmer sitting on his porch, holding a small length of rope and studying it intently. "Good afternoon," says the rambler. "Tell me, what's that piece of rope for?" "I can use it to tell the weather," says the old farmer. "Really?" says the rambler, impressed. "How does it work?" "Well," says the farmer, "when the rope shifts slightly from side to side, that means it's windy. And when it feels wet, that means it's raining."

An old Cherokee chief sat in his reservation hut, smoking a ceremonial pipe, eyeing the two US government officials sent to interview him. "Chief Two Eagles," one official began, "you have observed the white man for many generations, you have seen his wars and his products, you have seen all his progress and all his problems." The chief nodded. The official continued, "Considering recent events, in your opinion, where has the white man gone wrong?" The chief stared at the government officials for over a minute and then calmly replied: "When white man found the land, Indians were running it. No taxes. No debt. Plenty buffalo. Plenty beaver. Women did the work. Medicine man free. Indian men hunted and fished all the time." The chief smiled and added quietly, "White man dumb enough to think he could improve system like that."

You Know You're Getting Old When...

The pharmacist has become your best friend.

The reason you walk around with your head held high is you're trying to get used to your trifocals.

The twinkle in your eye is the reflection of the sun on your bifocals.

The waiter asks how you'd like your steak... and you say, "pureed".

Those issues of *Reader's Digest* just can't come fast enough.

"Tying one on" means fastening your Medic Alert alarm.

When you do the "Hokey Cokey" you put your left hip out... And it stays out.

When you look in the mirror, one of your parents is looking back at you.

You and your teeth have given up sleeping together.

You answer to Bill, or George, or Mary... in fact, anyone's name but your own.

You are cautioned to slow down by the doctor instead of by the police.

You are on a first name terms with the chief nurse at your local hospital.

You have become obsessed with the price of petrol.

You begin every other sentence with the word "Nowadays..."

You begin to lose hope of ever finishing that Green Shield Stamp book you've had on the go since 1973.

You begin to outlive enthusiasm.

You bought your first car for the same price you paid for your kid's new trainers.

You buy a compass for the dashboard of your car.

You call the ambulance service and they're able to tell you your address.

You can clean your teeth in the dishwasher.

You can go out with someone who is a third of your age without breaking any laws.

Wrinkly Wisdom

In some cultures the elders are revered for their sagacity (No kids, sagacity is not a theme park for wrinklies!) and wisdom.

In our culture they are revered for how much money they might leave you when they die. The rest of the time wrinklies are marginalized, ignored and otherwise discarded by a culture obsessed with youth. But if you take the trouble to sit down and listen to what a wrinkly has to say you might learn something, such as the fact that the world's gone mad, a state pension is hardly worth walking down to the post office for and they don't write decent songs anymore. But no, that's just cynical and patronising stereotyping. George Burns was still cracking great gags in his 90s, and at a similar age George Bernard Shaw was still writing plays, Pablo Picasso was still painting and Bertrand Russell continued to be an active philosopher and campaigner. True, they may also have thought the world had gone mad, pensions were lousy and nobody was writing songs like they used to, but just consider this: they may have been right.

People say that age is just a state of mind. I say it's more about the state of your body.

Geoffrey Parfitt

Age is a very high price to pay for maturity.

Age is important, but only if you are a cheese or a fine wine.

Old age comes at a bad time.

By the time a man is wise enough to watch his step, he's too old to go anywhere.

By the time you're 80 years old you've learned everything. You only have to remember it.

George Burns

Now you're finally able to make ends meet, someone seems to have moved the ends.

Anyone who tells you that he can do the same things at 40 as he did when he was 20 probably didn't do much at 20.

Don't let old age get you down. It's too hard to get back up again afterwards.

One of the many things no-one tells you about ageing is... that it is such a nice change from being young.

Don't complain about getting old. A lot of people are denied the privilege.

Don't forget, age is largely a matter of mind over matter. If you don't mind it, it won't matter.

Life is like riding a bicycle; you won't fall off unless you stop pedalling.

Don't worry about avoiding temptation. As you grow older, it will avoid you.

What most persons consider as virtue, after the age of 40 is simply a loss of energy.

Voltaire

When you're old you love to go round sharing your wisdom and giving people the benefit of your advice. It compensates for your inability to set a bad example any more.

Growing old is mandatory. Growing up is optional.

Half our life is spent trying to find something to do with the time we have rushed through life trying to save.

Just when you've learned to make the most of your life, you realize most of your life has gone.

Everything that goes up must come down. But there comes a time when not everything that's down can come up.

George Burns

Opportunities always look bigger going than coming.

Remember: don't ever let anyone tell you you're getting old. If they do just run over their toes with your mobility scooter.

Remember: never ask old people how they are. At least, not if you have anything else to do that day.

There comes a time when you should stop expecting other people to make a big deal about your birthday. When you turn 11...

I'll never make the mistake of being 70 again.

Casey Stengel

The older we get, the fewer things seem worth waiting in line for.

People never seem to get too old to learn new ways of being stupid.

Maturity means being emotionally and mentally healthy. It is that time when you know when to say yes, when to say no, and when to say WHOOPEE!

By the time you're older you should have learnt that the real art of conversation is not only to say the right thing in the right place, but also to not say the wrong thing at the tempting moment.

If you live to the age of 100 you have it made because very few people die past the age of 100.

George Burns

Experience is a wonderful thing. It enables you to recognize a mistake when you make it again.

Experience is what causes a person to make new mistakes instead of the same old ones.

Experience is what you get when you didn't get what you wanted.

The secret of growing old is having lots of experience you can no longer use.

Wisdom is the comb that life gives you shortly after all your hair has fallen out.

Children are a great comfort in your old age. And they help you reach it faster, too.

Lionel Kauffman

Remember to be nice to your kids. They're they one who will choose your nursing home.

Remember that age and treachery will always triumph over youth and ability.

Blessed are the young, for they shall inherit the National Debt.

Herbert Hoover

The only truly consistent people are dead.

The secret of longevity is to keep breathing.

Sophie Tucker

You're only young once – but you can be immature forever.

Wrinkly World: In The Garden

Would an unsuspecting visitor find any of the following:

Gnomes

Cherubs

Men made out of flower pots

A little pond (possibly with another gnome fishing in it)

Grey stone ornaments with amusing messages emblazoned on them

A bird table

A little windmill

Stone birds, squirrels or rabbits

A vegetable patch

Fairy lights

Garden chairs with holes in the arms to put your drinks

A selection of footballs, tennis balls, frisbees and other paraphernalia that you refuse to throw back, because they'll only bloody well chuck them back again as soon as your back's turned

Wind chimes

A lawn mower that you don't have to plug in

His 'n' hers sun loungers

A swinging chair

A hammock (possibly constructed from one of the wife's bras)

If you answered "yes" to any of the above then welcome to Wrinkly World.

The Wrinklies' Guide For Putting The World To Rights

The trouble with the world today, according to wrinklies, is that it's run by young people. And young people, as most wrinklies will tell you, don't know anything. Not even the fact that they're born. If only they'd consult their wiser elders occasionally they'd soon start putting things right. So here, for the edification of youngsters and the gratification of wrinklies are a few tips on getting the world into shape – and boy, does it need it!

Crime

Bring back the birch/tawse/cat o' nine tails/rack/thumbscrew/ Dixon of Dock Green/Hanging, drawing and quartering/national service (it never did me any harm)

Put more bobbies on the beat – proper ones, ones with moustaches, not four-foot high women with "equality and gender awareness" training

Lock 'em up and throw away the key – yes, even for parking in the "disabled" bay at the supermarket

Education

Go back to the three Rs – reading, writing and arithmetic (yes, I know that's one R, a W and an A, but that's how we were taught so it must be right)

Bring back the cane – it'll instil a bit of discipline into the little blighters and teach them never to do it again, and I should know, I was caned every day when I was at school

Go back to chalk and talk – none of this new-fangled computer nonsense. Where did computers get anyone? Well, apart from the Moon obviously... all right, and Mars, and yes, OK, making Bill Gates the richest man in the world, and....

Global warming

If all this global warming stuff is true how come my flat's so cold? Eh? I could do with a bit of global warming round my chilblains of an evening, I can tell you....

OK, if London is under water in 50 years who cares? I won't be around to see it and Venice seems to manage all right, so what's the problem?

If the icebergs had melted 100 years ago the *Titanic* would never have sunk so think on...

Why they have to put those energy-producing windmills in the middle of the sea beats me – have the fish got TV down there or something?

The environment

We didn't have an environment in my day; we had indoors and outdoors – load of nonsense if you ask me

Cardboard in this bin, glass in that bin, tins in the other one – it's a load of rubbish isn't it? Ah! Aha! "Load of rubbish!" Get it? All right, suit yourselves. At least it was clean, not like half the so-called comedy on TV these days

They ruined the atmosphere when they started firing all those rockets into space if you ask me. Yuri Gagorbachov or whatever his name was. And as soon as the Cold War ended global warming started. Whichever way you look at it, it's obviously the Russians' fault isn't it?

Health

They should close down these mixed-sex wards straightaway. They shouldn't be having sex in hospital in the first place

Bring back matron!

Let's go back to the days when you had trust in the hospital and not the hospital in a trust

When I was a nipper the hospital staff were super and the bugs were nowhere to be seen. Now it's the other way round!

Give It Up For The Wrinklies!

As you get older you give up some things and some things give you up. You start getting a bit wheezy so you give up smoking, you find it difficult to concentrate so you cut down on your drinking. You begin to begin to get a spare tyre so you cut down on the Michelin star meals. You start to find pleasure in the simple things, like your spouse. You enjoy walking in the fresh air – especially since you had to give up driving due to being a menace to other road users (in the humble opinion of the local magistrates) and you don't even watch so much TV because of the terrible language – i.e. you swearing at the telly every time there's yet another reality show instead of a proper Wednesday play or something sensible.

And you find you're no longer a slave to fashion, because it's moved on so much that you don't know whether your clothes are retro, ironic or just simply a bit naff, so you give up and refuse to have anything to do with it. Similarly, your senses suddenly turn into nonsenses and your body goes on strike, refusing to do what you tell it. Suddenly you go from life in the fast lane to life in the "five items or fewer" lane – and that's just your brain cells.

You can live to be 100 if you give up all the things that make you want to live to be 100.

Woody Allen

An 80-year-old man is having a check up at the doctor's. As the doctor listens to the man's heart, he mutters, "Uh oh!" "What's the problem?" asks the old man. "Well," says the doctor, "you have a serious heart murmur. Do you smoke?" "No," says the old man. "Are you a heavy drinker?" asks the doctor. "No," says the man. "Do you have much of a sex life?" asks the doctor. "Yes," says the old man. "That's my sole remaining pleasure in life." "OK," says the doctor, "but now you've got this heart murmur, you're going to have to give up half your sex life." "OK," says the old man, "but which half do you want me to give up? The looking or the thinking?"

An old man sits reminiscing and says, "Do you know, I can remember the time I gave up both booze and sex at the same time. Dear me, that was the worst half hour of my life."

Your Wrinkly Age – Language

You might not think you're old, but one of the giveaways is the language you use, and no, we're not talking about the cursing under your breath as you try to extricate yourself from the armchair at bedtime. No, we mean those everyday words and phrases that mark you out as a wrinkly, even though you may still be dressing like a teenager. For example:

If you're young you refer to the radio, if you're quite old you might call it the wireless, and if you're very old you can't quite remember off the top of your head what it's called and refer to it as "the thingy".

If you're young and wish to convey to somebody that you find the winter weather inclement you might refer to it as "freezing", if you're quite old you may make reference to "brass monkeys", but if you're very old, and made of sterner stuff you will merely say "it's a bit parky".

If you're young you will probably download your musical entertainment from the internet, if you are quite old you may seek out what is quaintly known as a "record shop", if you are past the first few flushes of youth you will pick up your *Fifty Golden Oldies* or the *Best of Paul Anka* at the supermarket or possibly a petrol station.

And you may find as you get older that certain phrases spring to your lips, seemingly unbidden. For example, if a young child shyly refuses to speak to you, you may find the celebrated wrinkly phrase "What's the matter, cat got your tongue?" issuing forth from your ancient lips.

Similarly, on reading in the paper of some crazy bureaucratic decision you will start spouting off that the world has "gone mad" and that thank goodness, you won't be long for this Earth, etc etc.

You'll find you can't help yourself, and it is just another indicator that you have reached wrinkliehood, or what is sometimes known as World of Leather Features.

But sometimes this wrinklyspeak is tinged with an ironic wrinkly humour. So when you don't quite hear what somebody has said to you, you may respond with "You'll have to speak up a bit, I'm deaf in one eye!" And when the other person does indeed raise their voice you may find yourself shouting, "All right! I'm not deaf you know!"

And as the years advance and you find yourself at the mercy of unyielding joints, unsympathetic petty officials and other travails of senior life, you may find that you tend to swear a bit more than you used to. Following any such choice language you will wittily quip "Pardon my French!" *Tres amusant* of course, but it will mark you out as a wrinkly, because no one under the age of 45 has ever been heard to use this off-the-peg *bon mot*.

You Know You're Getting Old When...

You lose an argument with a phone answering device.

You nod off and other people in the room fear you may have died.

You realize you can't find your glasses without having your glasses on in the first place.

You realize that a postage stamp now costs more than a cinema ticket did when you were 14.

You recall when milk came in glass bottles and they were recycled automatically.

You regularly get into arguments with your friends about which denture adhesive is better.

You have to get up from a couch in stages.

You have to have an airbag fitted onto your walking frame.

You have too much room in the house and not enough room in the medicine cabinet.

You hear snap, crackle and pop at breakfast time as you sit down at the table – and it's not your cereal, it's your joints.

You know your way around, but you don't feel like going.

Everything either dries up or starts to leak.

You know you're getting old when the candles cost more than the cake.

Bob Hope

You know you're getting old when your wife decides to give up sex for Lent and you don't notice the difference until the August bank holiday.

You like sitting in a rocking chair, but you can't get the damned thing started.

You look at the celebrity birthdays and don't have a clue who they are.

You look both ways before crossing a room.

You look forward to a dull evening.

You light the candles on your birthday cake, and a group of campers form a circle round it and start singing "Kumbaya".

Lessons In Life That Wrinklies Should Have Learnt By Now

A penny saved is worthless.

A person who is nice to you, but rude to the waiter, is not a nice person.

Going to church doesn't make you a Christian anymore than standing in a garage makes you a car.

Friends may come and go, but enemies accumulate.

Artificial intelligence is no match for natural stupidity.

Don't worry about what people think – they don't do it very often.

If you look like your passport picture, you probably need the trip.

If you're too lazy to start anything, you may get a reputation for patience.

My father was a very wise old man. He once told me, "Son, don't worry about trying to understand women. If you ever do manage to eventually understand them, you won't believe it anyway."

Never, under any circumstances, take a sleeping pill and a laxative on the same night.

One-seventh of your life is spent on Monday.

There is always one more imbecile than you counted on.

If there really is a God who created the entire universe with all of its glories, and He decides to deliver a message to humanity, He will not use, as His messenger, a person on cable TV with a bad hairstyle.

If you had to identify, in one word, the reason why the human race has not achieved, and never will achieve, its full potential, that word would be: "meetings".

No matter what happens, somebody will find a way to take it too seriously.

Nobody cares if you can't dance well. Just get up and dance.

Nobody is normal.

People who feel the need to tell you that they have an excellent sense of humour are, in fact, telling you that they have no sense of humour whatsoever.

People who want to share their religious views with you almost never want you to share yours with them.

The badness of a movie is directly proportional to the number of helicopters in it.

The main accomplishment of almost all organized protests is to annoy people who are not involved.

The most powerful force in the universe is gossip.

The one thing that unites all human beings, regardless of age, gender, religion, economic status or ethnic background, is that, deep down inside, we all believe that we are above-average drivers.

There is a very fine line between "hobby" and "mental illness".

When trouble arises and things look bad, there is always one individual who perceives a solution and is willing to take command. Very often, that individual is crazy.

You should never say anything to a woman that even remotely suggests you think she's pregnant unless you can see an actual baby emerging from her at that moment.

You should not confuse your career with your life.

You will never find anybody who can give you a clear and compelling reason why we observe "Daylight Saving Time".

The Wrinklies' Visitor Test

If you've passed any of the other wrinklies' tests and still consider yourself just about on the right side of wrinkliehood, but there's still a little cloud of doubt in your mind, try this one:

Before visitors are due to come do you:

Moan that they always come at the most inconvenient time and you've got nothing in common with them and you're only inviting them because your other half wants them round

Complain that you've got to clean the house from top to bottom especially and cater to their faddy dietary requirements and put up with their blooming dog/flipping kids/irritating habits

Say that if you had your way you wouldn't bother keeping up with all these people and could enjoy a quiet life instead

During the visit do you:

Moan to your other half in the kitchen about the visitors and hope they can't hear you

Complain in general about blooming dogs/flipping kids/irritating habits in the hope that the visitors will take the hint

Say how lovely it is to see them again whilst stifling a yawn and glancing at your watch

After visitors have been do you:

Moan that they outstayed their welcome/bored the pants off you/ couldn't take the hint when you started putting on your pyjamas

Complain that they hardly touched the food you got in specially and never once complimented you on your new Jack Vettriano print/pine coat stand/novelty doorbell chimes

Say that you can't really see the point in having them over just for the sake of it and why don't we just keep it to Christmas cards and have done with it?

If you have found yourself agreeing with at least three of the above statements, then welcome to the one club where you won't be turned away by a bouncer with a youth-biased door policy!

Married For Ever Such A Long Time

When you take your wedding vows you are signing up for the long haul, the full Monty, the whole "till death us do part" thing. Though these days a lot of people seem to have slightly rewritten that last phrase to "till divorce us do part". But if you're one of those who has stuck at it through thick and thin, in sickness and in health, from a roll in the hay to a roll in the café, then congratulations! Of course you've had your ups and downs, well at least until you moved into that retirement bungalow, and the lust may have been lost, but these days you prefer companionship, loyalty and affection – which is precisely why... you bought a dog.

A wife asks her husband, "How do you think we should celebrate our 60th wedding anniversary?" "How about a two minute silence?" he suggests.

We've just marked our tenth wedding anniversary on the calendar and threw darts at it.

Phyllis Diller

The old farmer and his wife are getting ready for their 50th wedding anniversary dinner. The farmer's wife says, "Albert, should I go out in the yard and kill a chicken?" Albert says, "Oh come on Phyllis, why blame a chicken for something that happened 50 years ago?"

Bryan says to Dave, "It's your 20th wedding anniversary soon, isn't it, Dave? What are you going to buy the missus?" "A once-in-a-lifetime trip to Australia," says Dave. "Wow!" says Bryan. "I'm sure she'll be absolutely thrilled, but how on earth will you top that on your 25th anniversary?" "Well," says Dave, "I was thinking maybe then I could send her the money to pay for her ticket back."

Q: What's the definition of a cheapskate?
A: A man who buys his wife a pack of cards on their diamond wedding anniversary.

Henry's wife tells him, "Henry, for our 40th wedding anniversary I want you to take me somewhere I've never been before." "OK," says Henry under his breath, "how about the blooming kitchen?"

An old couple have gone back to their honeymoon hotel every year on their wedding anniversary. One year, when they're shown to their room, they find they've been given a whole suite rather than the usual double room. "Excuse me," says the old man to the hotel porter. "I think there's been a mistake. This is the bridal suite." "That's all right sir," says the porter. "There's no need to perform. If we'd put you in the kitchen we wouldn't be expecting you to knock up dinner."

Joe says to Pete, "On our silver wedding anniversary the wife and I went back to the same little country hotel where we spent our wedding night." "And was it all just the same?" asks Pete. "Almost," says Joe, "except this time I was the one crying my heart out in the bathroom."

On their 30th wedding anniversary a couple go back to the resort where they spent their honeymoon. On the way, they are driving through the countryside when the man says, "Look! Remember that field? Remember what we did on the way to our hotel 30 years ago?" The wife smiles and says, "Oh yes!" So they get out of the car and make love right up against the wire fence. When they get back in the car the husband says, "Wow! That was amazing! I think if anything you were even more animated this time round than you were 30 years ago!" "I know I was," says the wife, "because 30 years ago that bloomin' fence wasn't electrified!"

A married couple are celebrating their 60th wedding anniversary. At the party everybody wants to know how they've managed to stay together so long in this day and age. The husband tells them, "When we were first married we came to an agreement. I would make all the major decisions and my wife would make all the minor decisions. Well, can you believe it? I'm able to tell you today that in 60 long years of marriage, we've never needed to make a single major decision."

Every week, in church, the vicar notices one old couple who are always sitting in the same pew holding hands. Thinking that at their age this is rather charming he stops them one week on their way out to remark on it. "I can't help noticing," says the vicar, "how close you both seem even after all these years, holding hands and so on." "Close! Don't be so ridiculous!" says the old woman. "I'm just trying to stop the old bugger cracking his knuckles all the way through the service!"

A couple are celebrating their 40th wedding anniversary. A friend asks them, "What's your secret for such a long marriage?" "We take the time to go out to a restaurant twice a week," says the husband. "You know the sort of thing. A candlelight dinner, soft music and a slow walk home." "That's lovely," says the friend. "Yes it is," says the husband. "My wife goes on Tuesdays and I go on Fridays."

A 60-year-old couple are celebrating their 40th wedding anniversary. During the celebration a fairy appears and says that since they've been such a loving couple she'll give them each one wish. The wife wishes to travel around the world. The fairy waves her wand and poof! She has a handful of plane tickets. Next, it's the husband's turn. He pauses for a moment, then says, "I'd like to have a woman 30 years younger than me." So the fairy picks up her wand and poof! He's 90!

A married couple have been together for years. One night the husband is reading the newspaper when his wife tells him, "I wish I was your newspaper. Then you'd give me your full attention for hours every evening." "Oh that's nice, darling," says the man. "You know I wish I could have a wife like a newspaper as well." "Oh yes," says the woman. "Because then you'd be able to put your hands all over me every night?" "No," says the husband. "Because then I could throw the old one out each night and pick up a nice, fresh, new one every morning."

On their 40th wedding anniversary a man says to his wife, "Whatever you want, just name it and I'll buy it for you. It doesn't matter how much it costs. Just say what you'd like for our anniversary." She replies, "A divorce." "To be honest," he says. "I wasn't thinking of spending quite that much."

A 95-year-old man takes his 92-year-old wife to the solicitors and says they want a divorce. "But why?" asks the solicitor, "You've been married for over 70 years, why do you want a divorce now?" "We haven't been getting on for quite a few years," says the wife, "but we wanted to wait until the children had died before we split up."

Married Lots Of Times

My grandmother was a very tough woman. She buried three husbands and two of them were just napping.

Rita Rudner

He's been married so often, he signs the wedding certificate in pencil.

He's been married so often, his wedding certificate says "To whom it may concern..."

He's been married so often, they don't issue him with a new marriage licence now. They just punch the old one.

Marriage is the triumph of imagination over intelligence. A second marriage is the triumph of hope over experience.

She's been married so many times she has rice marks on her face.

Zsa Zsa Gabor was once asked, "How many husbands have you had?" She replied, "Do you mean apart from my own?"

Mixed Marriages Between Old Wrinklies And Young Non-Wrinklies

For some older people it's the ultimate achievement – to marry someone much younger than themselves. But what does the young person get out of it? If their sole aim was to go to bed with something wrinkly they could simply stop ironing their pyjamas. But by some strange coincidence the older half of these unlikely marriages is often rich or famous, or both. Of course, there are exceptions, such as... well, there must be some exceptions, but the older person also has to adjust when they marry someone much younger. No going to bed early with a cup of cocoa when the younger half wants to go out clubbing and then suffering the embarrassment of everyone laughing at them when they attempt to do the Twist to the latest hot dance floor track.

A 90-year-old man gets married to an 88-year-old woman. At the church door the guests don't throw rice, they throw vitamin tablets.

An 82-year-old man goes to his doctor for a check up. A few days later the doctor sees the old man walking along the road with a gorgeous young woman on his arm. The doctor calls the old man in again and says, "I saw you with your new girlfriend, but I'm not sure that's a good idea after what I told you last week." "What do you mean?" says the old man. "I'm doing exactly what you told me to do. You said I should get a hot mama and be cheerful." "No I didn't," says the doctor. "What I actually said was, 'You've got a heart murmur. Be careful.'"

Old Alf is 80 years old when he marries a 20-year-old woman and after a few months she is pregnant. "Are you sure this is a good idea?" Alf's doctor asks him. "It seems a bit late in life to be having another child." "I think it's the perfect time for me to have a baby," says old Alf. "After all I have to get up 12 times during the night now anyway!"

An ageing man marries a beautiful young bride many years his junior. On their honeymoon night they climb into bed and the old man asks his new bride, "Tell me, did your mother tell you what to do on your wedding night?" "Oh yes," she says. "She told me everything I needed to know." "That's handy," says the elderly gentleman as he turns out the light. "Because I seem to have forgotten."

An 80-year-old man marries a 20-year-old girl. After a few months of marriage the young woman goes into hospital to give birth. The nurse comes out to congratulate the ageing husband and says, "This is amazing. How do you do it at your time of life?" "Well," says the old man, "you've got to keep that old motor running." The following year the young bride gives birth again. The nurse comes out again to congratulate the old man and says, "You really are amazing. How do you do it?" "Well," he says again, "you've got to keep the old motor running." The third year of marriage, the same thing happens once again. Out comes the nurse to congratulate the old man saying, "Well, well, well! You certainly are quite a man!" "Yes, well," says the old fellow, "you've got to keep that old motor running." "Yeah," says the nurse, "actually if I were you I'd consider getting an oil change. This one's come out black!"

An old farmer gets married to an 18-year-old. A few weeks after the service, the vicar decides to call round at the farm to ask the old boy how things are going with his new young wife. "Oh," says the old man, "I can't keep my hands off her." The vicar mumbles his approval and goes on his way. A few weeks later he calls round again and asks the same question. "I still can't keep my hands off her," says the old man. "I suppose that's good," says the vicar. "Not really," says the old farmer. "She's gone and run off with one of them."

A 90-year-old man tells his doctor that he is planning to get married to a woman 65 years his junior. "Under the circumstances, do you have any suggestions for me?" asks the old man. "Yes," says the doctor thinking the old man's not going to be able to keep a young woman like that satisfied. "I think it might be an idea for you to take in a lodger." A year later the old man comes back for a check up. The doctor asks him how his marriage to the 25-year-old is going. "Oh fine," says the old man. "In fact, she's going to have a baby in a few weeks." "Oh yes," says the doctor knowingly. "So you took my advice and took in a lodger did you?" "Yes I did," says the old fellow. "The only problem is that she's pregnant now as well."

An ageing multi-millionaire gets married to a beautiful 19-year-old model. His friend tells him, "You're an old devil. How did you manage to marry a beautiful young girl like that when you're 60?" "It was partly the money," says the old man, "and partly the fact that I told her I was 95."

Ross: I would date her, but there is a big age difference.
Joey: Well think about when you're 90...
Ross: I know, she'll be 80 and it won't be such a big difference.
Joey: No. What I was gonna say is when you're 90 you'll still
have the memory of what it was like to be with a 20-year-old.

Friends

People's Manners Today!

An old couple are sitting at their dinner table when the old man
sneezes very loudly. "Well," says the old woman, "I notice that
you've finally learnt some manners and have started to put your
hand in front of your mouth when you sneeze." "I have to, don't
I?" says the old man. "It's the only way I can catch my teeth."

I was told to always respect my elders. Unfortunately it's getting
harder and harder for me to find any.

Old Alf says people spoke a lot more politely in the old days.
In fact when he was young he says he was a member of a gang
called Heck's Angels.

A feminist woman gets on a bus one day and all the seats are
taken, so an old man stands up and offers her his seat. "No
thank you!" says the woman, pushing him back in his seat. "I
think the world has moved on a bit." At the next stop a woman
gets on and again the old man stands up and offers his seat. Now
angry, the feminist pushes him back down. "We sisters don't need
your patronising gestures!" she fumes. At the next stop a third
woman gets on and again the old man stands up. "You just don't
get it, do you, granddad?" screams the woman. Now it's the old
man's turn to be angry, "Look, you old boiler, just let me off the
bloody bus will you! I've missed three stops already!"

Things older people don't want to hear from cheeky young
whippersnappers: Hey! Want some onions to go with those liver
spots?

Things older people don't want to hear from cheeky young whippersnappers: Hey, I know! Let's all play getting older! OK! You go first!

A Wrinkly And His Money

Remember when you wished for the income you can't live on now?

Sign outside a Scottish cinema: "Free admission for old age pensioners, but only if accompanied by both parents."

Sophia: I'm settling my estate.
Dorothy: What estate? Your bus pass and loofah sponge?

The Golden Girls

A reporter asks a rich old American man how he made his money. The old man replies, "Well, son, it was 1932. The depth of the Great Depression. I was down to my last nickel and I invested that nickel in an apple. I spent the entire day polishing the apple and, at the end of the day, I sold that apple for ten cents. The next morning, I invested those ten cents in two apples. I spent the entire day polishing them and sold them for 20 cents. I continued this system for a month, by the end of which I'd accumulated a fortune of $1.37. Then my wife's father died and left us two million dollars..."

A pretty young girl walks up to the fabric counter in a large department store and says, "I want to buy some material for a new dress. How much does it cost?" "To a pretty little thing like you, miss," says the unctuous male counter assistant, "it's one kiss per yard." "OK," says the girl. "I'll take ten yards." With expectation and anticipation written all over his face, the clerk hurriedly measures out and wraps the cloth, then holds it out teasingly. The girl snatches the package. "Thanks," she says and points to a little old man standing beside her. "My granddad says he'll pay the bill."

Harry gets to the age of 65 and decides to go and get his bus pass. When he gets to the council office he is asked to produce his pension book and other documents. He then realizes he's left them at home, but the woman on the desk feels sorry for him and says, "Don't worry about your documents; just let me have a look at your chest." "My chest?" asks Harry. "Why?" "Do you want a bus pass or not?" says the woman. So Harry opens his shirt to reveal grey chest hair. "OK," says the woman, "that's fine. I'm sure you're old enough to qualify." And with that she gives him his bus pass. When he gets home Harry tells his wife what happened. "You idiot!" she exclaims. "What's the matter?" asks Harry. "Well," says his wife, "if you'd dropped your trousers as well, she'd have probably said you were also entitled to disability allowance!"

Wrinklies In Retirement

With more and more people taking early retirement these days there's no reason that "retirement" should conjure up images of bus passes, rose pruning and church hall bingo, but it does. And even if your retirement is filled with exotic cruises, luxury hotels and playing *Chemin de fer* in Monte Carlo, it's difficult to escape the image that the word brings to mind. Perhaps it needs rebranding? Now there's a challenge for those young advertising execs – make retirement seem cool and youthful. Retirement – it's the new work!

Retirement must be wonderful. I mean, you can suck in your stomach for only so long.

Burt Reynolds

An ageing human cannonball goes to tell the circus ringmaster that, after 50 years in the job, he feels he's had enough and he wants to retire after tonight's performance. "Oh no," says the ringmaster, begging him to reconsider. "Where else will I find a man of your calibre?"

Retirement at 65 is ridiculous. When I was 65 I still had pimples.

George Burns

Now I'm retired I can do whatever I want. As long as it's not too far from a public convenience.

Why do they give you a watch when you retire? Don't they realize it's the first time in your life you don't care what time it is?

The bad thing about retirement is that it means you get twice as much of your spouse on half as much money.

The best time to start thinking about your retirement is before the boss does.

At his retirement presentation old Tom was told by his boss, "We don't know how we'll manage without you. Mainly because we're not sure exactly what it was you did here."

It is time I stepped aside for a less experienced and less able man.

Scott Elledge

Albert's boss is making a speech on the occasion of Albert's retirement. "Today we would like to thank Albert for his service to our company," says the boss. "Albert has always been someone who does not know the meaning of 'impossible task', who does not know the meaning of 'lunch break' and who does not understand the meaning of the word 'no'. So we have all clubbed together and bought Albert... a dictionary."

There's one thing I always wanted to do before I quit... retire!

Groucho Marx

You can always tell the guest of honour at a retirement dinner. He's the one who keeps yawning after the boss's jokes.

When you're retired you wake up in the morning with nothing to do and go to bed at night with it still not done.

When old Bill retired from his job, his boss made a little speech to all his colleagues and told them they weren't so much losing a worker as gaining an extra car park space.

What The Comments In The Retirement Speech Really Mean

Active socially: drinks heavily.

Character above reproach: still one step ahead of the law.

Excels in the effective application of skills: makes a good cup of coffee.

Shows tremendous flair and imagination: some of those expenses claims could qualify for the Booker prize.

Has the energy of a man half his age: he's worn out 14 young secretaries so far – and that's just this year.

Has the respect of all his staff: he scares the living daylights out of them.

His honesty is beyond reproach: covers his tracks extremely well, and he even bunged me a few quid to say that.

Has enjoyed a long career: that's "career" as in "going down hill extremely fast".

Fitted in well with the rest of the team: he doesn't understand what's going on either.

Has helped turn this company round: from one of the most profitable firms in the sector to the basket case it is today.

Popular with colleagues: shows them all the ways to fiddle their expenses too.

His departure will be a great loss: to all the local pubs, wine bars and betting shops.

Great communication skills: can yabber away on the phone at the company's expense for hours.

A born leader: a little Hitler.

Has made great personal sacrifices for the company: often keeps his lunch break down to two and a half hours.

Has a good relationship with his superiors: a right little creep.

Shows initiative: has set up a private business fully equipped with office machinery and stationery nicked from the company.

Possesses people skills: is a person.

Never misses an opportunity: to get out of working.

Will never be forgotten: we will pursue him through the courts until every last penny he embezzled has been repaid.

Visionary thinker: spends most of the day looking out of the window.

Irreplaceable: thank God!

Internationally known: likes to go to conferences and trade shows in Las Vegas.

Is well informed: knows all the office gossip and where all the skeletons are kept.

Tactful in dealing with superiors: knows when to keep his mouth shut.

Willing to take calculated risks: doesn't mind spending someone else's money.

A Wrinkly Looks Back At His Career

My first job was working in an orange juice factory, but I got canned .. couldn't concentrate.

Then I worked in the woods as a lumberjack, but I just couldn't hack it, so they gave me the chop.

After that I tried to be a tailor, but I just wasn't suited for it... mainly because it was a so-so job.

Next I tried working in a car spares factory, but that was too exhausting.

Then I tried to be a chef – figured it would add a little spice to my life but I just didn't have the thyme.

I attempted to be a deli worker, but any way I sliced it, I couldn't cut the mustard.

My best job was being a musician, but eventually I found I wasn't noteworthy.

I studied a long time to become a doctor, but I didn't have any patience.

Next was a job in a shoe factory... I tried but I just didn't fit in.

I became a professional fisherman, but discovered that I couldn't live on my net income.

I managed to get a good job working for a pool maintenance company, but the work was just too draining.

So then I got a job in a workout centre, but they said I wasn't fit for the job.

After many years of trying to find steady work, I finally got a job as a historian, until I realized there was no future in it.

My last job was working at a coffee shop, but I had to quit because it was always the same old grind.

So I retired and I found I am perfect for the job!

Homes For Retired Wrinklies

An old people's home gets a celebrity visit from Cliff Richard. Cliff arrives and before he leads them all in a sing-along, he goes round saying hello to all the elderly residents. Unfortunately no-one seems to recognize him, so Cliff says to one old lady, "What about you? Do you have any idea who I am?" "No, sorry, dear," says the old lady. "But let's call one of the nurses over. I'm sure they'll be able to tell you."

The old people's home next gets a special visit from Bruce Forsyth. Bruce tells the residents a series of funny jokes and they all seem to find his act extremely amusing. Afterwards Bruce says to the matron, "That seemed to go well, dear. A couple of the audience laughed so much they wet themselves." "Don't kid yourself, Bruce," says the matron, "they'd have done that whether you were here or not."

A man finds a place for his elderly mother at a care home. All the residents are given a wristband on which can be written details of any food allergies they have. Unfortunately the man is not told about this and, when he comes to visit his mother the next day, he is furious when he finds the staff have stuck a wrist band on her on which is written the single word, "Bananas".

A man goes to visit his elderly mother who is in a retirement home. When he gets there he is told his mother is asleep at the moment, but if he wishes he can sit by her bed and wait until she wakes up. As he sits there he looks through her newspaper and magazines, and eats his way through a packet of peanuts on her bedside cabinet. When she wakes up, he apologizes, "I'm terribly sorry, Mum. I think I've just eaten your entire packet of peanuts." "That's OK, dear," says his mum. "I'm not very keen on nuts. That's why I always just nibble the chocolate off and put them back in the packet."

Two very old men are sitting outside the Sunnyglades rest home watching the world go by when one asks the other how he's feeling today. "Oh," he says, "do you know what, I feel just like a little baby." "What happy and healthy and full of energy?" "No," says the other one, "bald and toothless, and I think I've just filled my nappy."

A charity organized a special Christmas lunch for elderly people in the area and a couple of weeks after the event they were charmed to receive a thank you letter from one of the guests. She wrote: "I am just writing to thank you for your kindness in inviting me to the Christmas lunch, where I was lucky enough to win a lovely portable radio in the raffle. In my retirement home I share a room with another elderly lady who would occasionally allow me to listen to her radio when she was feeling generous, until it broke recently. Now I have my own radio and when she asks if she can listen to it I can say, 'No, you can't you old cow!'"

The manager of an old people's home decides to hire an animal act to entertain everyone at the home's annual tea-party. He calls a theatrical agent and asks what sort of acts he has to offer. "I've got a tiger," says the agent. "It does a high wire act and juggles plates." "Too dangerous!" replies the manager. "It might fall on someone or bite them." "How about a performing seal?" says the agent. "It can play a variety of musical instruments." "Too noisy," replies the manager. "The old folk won't like it. What we need is something unusual, but nice and sedate, so it won't upset them." "I know," says the agent. "How about Morris the gibbon? He's very quiet. All he does is card tricks." "Perfect," replies the manager. "So... Let's try a mellow gibbon round the old folk's tea..."

The Wrinklies' Guide To Understanding The Modern World

The modern world can be a confusing and bewildering place for people who grew up with fewer than 200 TV channels. Some of these new-fangled terms, such as "user friendly" or "balsamic vinegar" are simply lost on folk who can still remember when all mail was first class. So here, for the help of you third-agers, are a few translations you might find handy:

Gender issues – when women think that they get a raw deal, but quite like being women when blokes buy them a drink, pay for them to get married, etc.

Internet chat room – where you can talk to complete strangers without ever meeting them – a bit like being cold-called by a telephone banking salesman.

Gay marriage – you've heard of the gay divorce? Well this is what immediately precedes it.

Pensions time bomb – something you hope will go off after you've gone off.

Biodegradable carrier bags – ones that will fall apart after a few years, unlike the unbiodegradable ones that fall apart as soon as you start lugging your shopping home from the supermarket.

Call centre – a place where British people can still indulge in their favourite hobby of queuing, even when they're housebound.

Supermodel – a model who can tell people to get stuffed.

Celebrity chef – just like a normal chef, but with swearing.

Farmers' market – where you can buy fresh produce without going to the supermarket, though for some reason they usually hold them just outside the supermarket, so you have to go there anyway.

Skinny latte – a glass of hot milk for two quid.

Rogue trader – just like an ordinary trader, but one who gets caught.

Virtual reality – like ordinary reality just after you've taken a couple of those little green pills the doctor gave you.

Second life – an alternative life in cyberspace where you can take on a new persona and live in a world divorced from reality – very similar to going gaga in old age.

Hoodie – item of clothing that hides the wearer's face – or, in other words, a cheap alternative to plastic surgery.

Love In Old Age

I don't date women my own age – there are no women my own age.

George Burns

An 85-year-old widow goes out on a blind date with a 90-year-old man. When she gets home later that night, she seems to be rather upset. "What happened?" asks her daughter. "Oh it was terrible," says the old widow. "I had to slap that man's face three times." "Oh no," says the daughter. "You don't mean he got fresh with you?" "I wish he had," says the old widow. "No, I kept thinking he was dead."

An old man and an old lady are sitting in their garden one evening. "I remember," says the old lady, "when we were first courting you used to kiss me every time we were alone." And so the old man stretches over and kisses her. Then she says, "And I remember when we were first courting you used to hold my hand whenever you could." And so the old man reaches over and takes her hand. Then old lady says, "And I remember when we were first courting you used to love to nibble my ears all the time." With this the old man groans, gets up and starts hobbling towards the house. "Where are you going?" asks the old lady. "I'll be back in a minute," says the old man. "I've just got to get my teeth."

An old man and an old woman have been dating for a little while and decide to get married. As part of the preparations for the wedding they visit their local chemist's shop. Inside the old man asks the chemist, "Tell me, do you supply a range of heart medicines here?" "Oh yes," says the chemist. "What about vitamin supplements?" asks the old man. "Of course," says the chemist. "Lumbago ointment?" "Yes." "Pills for arthritis." "Yes." "Viagra." "Yes." "Incontinence pants." "Yes." "Excellent," says the old man and then calls over to his bride to be, "Darling, I think we've found just the place to do our wedding list."

Old Bert falls in love with old Ethel and decides to propose. As a stickler for tradition, Bert takes Ethel's hand, gets down on one knee and tells her there are two things he would like to ask her. "What's the first?" asks Ethel. "Will you marry me?" says old Bert. "Oh yes," says Ethel. "What's the second?" "Can you help me back up?" says Bert.

Senior Citizens' Personal Ads

BEATLES OR STONES? I still like to rock, still like to cruise in my Camaro on Saturday nights and still like to play air guitar. If you were a groovy chick, or are now a groovy hen, let's get together and listen to my boss collection of eight-track tapes.

FOXY LADY: Sexy, fashion-conscious blue-haired beauty, 80s, slim, 5'-4" (used to be 5'-6"), searching for sharp-looking, sharp-dressing companion. Matching white shoes and belt a plus.

LONG-TERM COMMITMENT: Recent widow who has just buried fourth husband looking for someone to round out a six-unit plot. Dizziness, fainting, shortness of breath not a problem.

MEMORIES: I can usually remember Monday to Thursday. If you can remember Friday, Saturday and Sunday, let's put our two heads together.

MINT CONDITION: Male, 1932, high mileage, good condition, some hair, many new parts, including hip, knee, cornea, valves. Isn't in running condition, but walks well.

SERENITY NOW: I am into solitude, long walks, sunrises, the ocean, yoga and meditation. If you are the silent type, let's get together, take our hearing aids out and enjoy quiet times.

WINNING SMILE: Active grandmother with original teeth seeking a dedicated flosser to share rare steaks, corn on the cob and caramel toffee.

Wrinkly Sex

Wrinkly sex. Hmm, doesn't sound very attractive does it, but that's what light switches are for. Anyway, the older people get the less they are interested in sex, or possibly, the less sex is interested in them. When was the last time you saw anyone with grey hair in the Playboy centrefold? No, people find that they are more interested in things like gardening as they get older. Gardening is the new sex. And why not? It lasts longer, gives you more exercise and you don't have to expose your ageing body to the ridicule of your partner. And if you think about it maybe older people aren't supposed to be having sex. Nature generally only allows women to have babies up to the age of about 40-ish, anything after that is for the purposes of recreation rather than procreation. Mother Nature is basically saying, "All right, if you will insist on having sex even when you are not trying to have babies then I'm going to do my utmost to stop anyone wanting to go to bed with you" – and this is where the wrinkles come in.

An old couple are sitting on their sofa watching television one night. During one of the commercial breaks, the old woman asks, "Whatever happened to our sexual relations?" After a long thoughtful silence, her slightly deaf husband replies, "I don't know. We didn't even get a Christmas card from them last year did we?"

An old couple are sitting in the local park on a beautiful spring day. "Spring days like this really take me back," says the husband. "Do they?" says his wife. "Tell me, do you remember the first time we ever made love?" The old man sits and thinks for a moment and then says, "No. In fact to be honest with you, I can't remember the last time."

Two old soldiers are watching young girls walk by in the park one day when one says to the other, "You remember how when we were young servicemen, they used to put Bromide in our tea to stop us thinking about girls." "Yes," says his friend. "Well," says the first, "I think mine's finally begun to work."

An old man was passing a group of giggling teenagers in the park. "What's the joke, lads?" asked the old man. "Oh nothing," said one boy, "we were just seeing who could tell the biggest lie about their sex life." "You young boys just disgust me!" exclaimed the old man. "Do you know, when I was your age, I never even thought about sex." After a pause the boys all cried in unison, "OK, granddad! You win!"

One afternoon, an elderly couple are relaxing in front of the television. Suddenly, the woman is overcome with lust and says to her husband, "Let's go upstairs and make love." "Which would you prefer?" asks her elderly husband. "I'm not sure I can do both."

An old man shuffles very slowly into the doctor's surgery and says, "Doctor, I need you to give me something to lower my sex drive." "How old are you?" asks the doctor. "Ninety-six," says the man. "Ninety-six and you want to lower your sex drive!" says the doctor. "I would have thought at your age, it's all in your head." "It is," says the old man. "That's why I want you to lower it."

Two ageing married men are talking. "So, how's your sex life?" says the first. "I'm having old age pension sex," says the other. "Old age pension sex? What's that?" asks the first. "Oh, you know," says the second, "I get a little each month, but it's not really enough to live on!"

Sex for an old guy is a bit like shooting pool with a rope.

George Burns

Old Bernard gets talking to a young man at his local pub. When the conversation turns to the young man's sexual conquests, Bernard tries to impress him by telling him how he has managed to keep sexually active himself, despite his advancing years. "So how often do you sleep with a woman?" asks old Bernard. "A few times a week," says the young buck. "Huh!" says Bernard. "My wife and I make love nearly every day." "Nearly every day!" says the young man. "But you must be nearly 80 years old." "It's true. We make love nearly every day," says Bernard. "We nearly made love on Monday. We nearly made love on Tuesday…"

Three middle-aged women are talking about their love lives. Daphne says, "My husband is like a Rolls-Royce convertible; smooth, sleek and sophisticated." Beryl says, "Mine is like a Ferrari. Fast, furious and incredibly powerful." Blanche, the oldest one of the group, says, "Mine's like an old Morris Minor: needs a hand start and you have to jump on quick once you've got it going."

An 87-year-old woman comes home from bingo one night and finds her 92-year-old husband in bed with their home help. The old woman becomes violent. She attacks her husband and pushes him off the balcony of their 20th floor flat. At her trial she pleads not guilty. "What do you mean 'not guilty'?" asks the judge. "You were seen doing it." "I know," says the old woman, "but I thought it was a reasonable assumption that if he was able to get up to that kind of thing at his age, he'd be able to fly as well."

A famous sex expert worked out that people usually lied about how often they had sex. So he devised a test to tell for certain how often a person made love. To prove his theory, he filled a lecture theatre with volunteers and went round them all, asking each of them to smile. By looking at the size of the person's smile, the expert was able to accurately assess the truth about the frequency of their sexual relations. When he came to the last volunteer, an elderly gentleman, who was grinning from ear to ear, the expert guesses he must have sex twice a day. "Oh no," said the old man. The expert was surprised at this so he tried again and suggested, "Once a day then." "No, no," said the old man. "Twice a week?" "No." "Twice a month?" "No." "Once a month?" "No." Eventually the expert got as far as once a year and the old man said, "Yes!" "I can't believe it," said the sex expert. "This completely disproves my theory. So if you only have sex once a year what are you looking so damn happy about?" "Tonight's the night," said the old man.

A man decides to surprise his elderly grandfather by hiring the services of a call girl to visit him on his 90th birthday. The girl turns up on his doorstep and tells him, "Hi, I'm here to offer you super sex." "Oh really?" says the old man. "OK. I think I'll have the soup then please."

A senior citizen shuffles painfully into a house of ill repute and asks how much it will cost him for a night of pleasure. "Two hundred pounds," replies the madam. "Two hundred pounds!" splutters the old man. "Are you putting me on?" "We can if you want," says the madam, "but that will be an extra ten quid."

Albert Grimshaw was about to reach the grand old age of 100 and he decided to celebrate the event by making love for the first time in many years. When the happy day came the Queen sent him a telegram and the Duke of Edinburgh sent him a diagram.

An elderly man hobbles into a brothel and tells the madam he would like a young girl for the night. Surprised, she looks at the ancient wizened creature and asks how old he is. "I'm 90 years old," gasps the old fellow. "Ninety years old!" replies the madam.

"Sorry, pop. I think you've had it." "Oh, have I?" says the old man, fumbling for his wallet. "So how much do I owe you?"

An old lady goes to a specialist and tells him that she's obsessed with sex and believes she might even be a nymphomaniac. "I might be able to help you," says the psychiatrist. "But I better tell you, I charge £200 per hour." "I see," says the old lady. "How much would it be for the whole night?"

An old man and wife go to see their doctor and ask if they can have an AIDS test. The doctor is shocked and surprised. "But why?" he asks, "You've been together for 45 years, you've not had other partners." The old man replied, "No, but they said on the radio this morning that you should go for a test after having annual sex."

One evening in the retirement home 90-year-old Elsie came downstairs in a see-through negligee and approached three old men sitting on the sofa. "Now then, boys," she announced, holding up a clenched fist, "whoever can guess what I'm holding in my hand gets to spend the night with me making wild passionate love!" "An elephant?" suggested one appalled old man. "That's close enough, dearie!" she said, grabbing him by the hand and leading him away.

Q: How does an ageing car mechanic make love?
A: He attaches jump leads to his nipples and gets a start from a younger man.

Two old widows in their 80s are sitting in their chairs in their retirement home. "Tell me," says one to the other, "when you were married, did you and your husband have mutual orgasms?" The second old widow thinks for a few moments and then says, "No, I think we were with the Prudential."

Two old soldiers, Bert and Tom, are sharing a glass of malt in the corner of their club one evening. "Tell me," says Bert to Tom, "when was the last time you made love to a woman?" Tom considers this for a minute and says, "1947." "Good Lord!"

says Bert. "That's an awfully long time ago." "No it's not," says Tom. "It's only a couple of minutes past eight o'clock now."

Tips On Lovemaking For Wrinklies

Create that special mood by adjusting the lighting. Switch them ALL OFF!

Don't worry about making all the noise you want. Your neighbours are probably deaf too.

Keep extra Polygrip close by to avoid the embarrassment of losing your teeth under the bed.

Make sure you put 999 on your speed dial before you begin.

Put on your glasses and have a quick double check that your partner is actually in bed with you.

Set your bedside alarm for three minutes' time in case you happen to doze off halfway through the proceedings.

Write your partner's name on a pad at the side of the bed in case it slips your memory.

If it works, call everybody you know and tell them the good news.

And remember, whatever else you do, don't think about trying to do it a second time.

Signs You May Be Going Through The Menopause

The Phenobarbital dose that wiped out the Heaven's Gate Cult is the only thing that gives you four hours of decent rest.

You change your underwear after every sneeze.

You have to write post-it notes with your kids' names on them.

Your husband jokes that instead of buying a wood stove, he is using you to heat the family room this winter. Rather than simply saying you are not amused, you shoot him.

You're on so much oestrogen that you take your Brownie troop on a field trip to see the Chippendales.

Oooh, Young Man!

Three little old ladies are sitting on a park bench when a man in a raincoat jumps out from a bush and flashes at them. Two of the women have a stroke, but the other one can't quite reach.

A little old lady walks into a police station. "I want to report something, officer," she tells the desk sergeant. "I was walking through the park when a great big beast of a man leapt out of the bushes and molested me all over my body." "Oh yes," says the policeman, "and did this happen this morning?" "No," says the old lady. "It was in 1957." "That's quite a long time ago," says the policeman, "why are you telling me about it now?" "Oh, you know," says the old lady, "it's nice just to reminisce occasionally."

An old lady calls the police round to her house. She tells them she is shocked and appalled because the man who lives in the house opposite keeps wandering around his bedroom completely naked. The policeman looks out of her window to check and says, "But you can't see into his bedroom from this window." "No," says the old lady, "but you can if you climb on top of the wardrobe and look out of the skylight."

An old maid gets held up in a dark alley. She says she has no money on her, but the robber insists that she's lying and that she's got her cash hidden somewhere about her person. He then starts feeling all over her trying to find the money. After a few minutes of squeezing and fiddling with every bit of her body, the old lady says, "I told you, young man, I haven't got any money. But... ooo-er... if you keep doing that I could always write you a cheque!"

Two old dears go to the zoo and visit the elephants' enclosure. One male elephant seems to be in a bad mood and is rampaging around with a large erection. "Oh my goodness!" says Ethel. "Do you think he'll charge?" Her friend replies, "By the look of him, love, I think he'd be entitled to, don't you?"

An old lady calls the emergency services in a desperate state. "Send someone over quickly!" screams the old woman into the phone. "Two naked men are climbing towards my bedroom window!" "This is the Fire Department, lady," says the voice at the other end of the phone. "I'll have to transfer you to the Police Department." "No, no," says the old lady. "It's YOU I want! They need a longer ladder!"

Wrinkly Nudity

An old lady goes to the Chelsea Flower Show, where she whips off all her clothes and streaks through the judges' enclosure. In the end they decide to award her first prize for Best Dried Arrangement.

Two ageing university lecturers are sunbathing on the veranda of their apartment at a nudist resort. "So tell me," says one, "have you read Marx?" "Yes I have," says the other, "I think it must be this wicker chair I'm sitting on."

Two old men are sitting in the garden of a home for retired gentle folk. Suddenly one of the elderly female residents runs past them, streaking. "My goodness!" says the first. "Wasn't that Elsie Clitheroe?" "I think it was," says his friend. "She's 98, you know," says the first. "Yes," says the other. "What was that she was wearing?" "I don't know," says his companion. "But it looked like it could do with a good iron."

A little old lady goes out shopping on a windy day and as she's walking along the high street her hat blows off. She tries to grab it and her skirt is blown up over her head, revealing that she's not wearing any underwear. A passing policeman then books her for indecent exposure. When she gets to court the magistrate asks why she didn't use her hands to hold her skirt in place rather than trying to grab her hat. "Well," she says, "Everything under my skirt is 87 years old, but my hat was brand new!"

Viagra

If you're depressed and think you might need Viagra, see a professional. If that doesn't work, see a doctor.

Two old men are talking. "My doctor's refused to give me Viagra," says one. "Why?" asks the other. "Because," says the first, "he said it would be like sticking a new flagpole on a condemned building.

The marketers of Viagra have a new slogan, "Let the Dance Begin". This is better than the original, "Brace Yourself, Grandma!"

Jay Leno

An old couple are sitting at home one day when the old lady asks her husband, "So, granddad are you going to take any of those Viagra tablets I got for you?" The old man looks at her and says, "No, I'm not." "Why not?" asks the old lady. "Because," says the old man, "there's no point putting lead in your pencil if you haven't got anyone worth writing to."

I started my new diet this morning. It consists of Viagra and prune juice. Now I can't tell if I'm coming or going!

An ageing couple are in bed one morning in an amorous embrace when the wife says: "Darling, our love life is wonderful again now that you've started taking Viagra, but I think I'd better go and make us a full English breakfast." "Oh no," says her husband. "I'm not hungry at all. The Viagra takes away my appetite." Later in the day, the wife says: "Darling, I want to make you a nice wholesome lunch." "No, no," says the husband. "I'm just not hungry after using that Viagra." At dinner time, the wife tries again, "Are you hungry yet? I can make us a steak and kidney pie." "No," says the husband, "I'm telling you for the last time, Viagra seems to kill my appetite." "OK," says the wife, "but I need to get myself something to eat, so for the last time, will you just get off me so I can get out of bed!"

An old man is telling his friend about his Viagra tablets. "It's the greatest thing I've ever known," he says. "It's the Fountain of Youth! It makes you feel like you're young again." "Can you get it over the counter in the chemist's?" asks his friend. "You can if you take six," replies the first.

An old man walks into a chemist's and asks for a bottle of Viagra. The pharmacist says, "Do you have a prescription?" "No," says the old man, "but here's a picture of my wife."

An old man goes to his doctor and gets his prescription for Viagra. The doctor tells him to take the tablet now and then in an hour's time he'll be able to give his wife a nice surprise. When the old man gets home from the doctor's surgery he discovers that his wife has gone out shopping and won't be back for some time. He phones the doctor and tells him, "I've already taken the tablet and now it's going to be wasted." "That's a bit of a shame," says the doctor. "Do you have a housekeeper? If you do you could occupy yourself with her instead." "That's no good," says the old man. "Why not?" says the doctor. "Well," says the old man, "I don't need Viagra with the housekeeper."

Did you hear about the old man who made an appointment with an impotence clinic? He had to cancel because something came up.

An old man goes to the chemist to get himself some Viagra, but is horrified by the price. "I can't believe it, £40 for two tablets," says the old man. "That's a disgrace!" "It's not too bad," says his wife. "After all, it works out at only £20 a year."

An old man goes on holiday, but falls asleep on the beach and ends up with terrible sunburn. Wincing in pain, the old man hobbles off to the local doctor for help. The doctor takes one look at him and says, "There's not much I can do about sunburn this bad, but here's some Viagra for you." "What?" says the old man. "How is Viagra going to help my sunburn?" "It's not," says the doctor. "But it will help keep the sheets off you in bed tonight."

An elderly man goes to his chemist and asks for a prescription of Viagra. "OK," says the pharmacist. "How many do you want?" "I want 12 tablets," says the old man, "and I want you to cut each of them into quarters for me." "Why do you want me to do that?" asks the pharmacist. "A quarter of a tablet won't do much for you." "Look, son," says the old man, "I'm over 90 years old. I don't need the tablets for sex. I just need them to make sure that when I go to the toilet it's sticking out far enough so it doesn't go all over my shoes."

An old man is at his dentist's. The dentist examines him and says, "I'm going to have to take one of your teeth out. I'm going to give you a shot of Novocain and I'll be back in a few minutes." The old man grabs the dentist's arm. "No! Please," he says, "I hate needles!" "OK," says the dentist. "Then I'll have to give you gas." "That's no good either," says the old man. "The gas always makes me sick for days." "In that case," says the dentist, "you'd better take this Viagra tablet." "Viagra?" says the old man. "Will that kill the pain?" "No," says the dentist, "but it will give you something to hang on to while I'm pulling your tooth."

Some nursing homes are giving their elderly male patients Viagra in their night time mug of cocoa. Apparently the cocoa helps them sleep, while the Viagra helps stop them from rolling out of bed in the night.

Viagra claimed its first victim last week after an old man took an overdose. It wasn't the old man who passed away, however. It was his wife who died of exhaustion.

Did you hear about the boatload of Viagra that went down on Loch Ness? A few minutes later the monster came up.

Q: What do you get if you mix Viagra and Prozac?
A: An old man who is ready to go, but doesn't really care where.

A truck carrying a load of Viagra slid off the road and fell into the Ohio River. Now none of the lift bridges will go down.

Q: What happens to men who take Viagra at the same time as being on a course of iron supplements?
A: Every time they get an erection, it points north.

Q: What's the difference between Niagara and Viagra?
A: Niagara Falls.

An old man tries Viagra for the first time, but when he swallows the tablet it gets stuck in his throat. The next morning he wakes up with a stiff neck!

Q: What's the similarity between Viagra and Alton Towers?
A: They both involve an hour's wait before a two-minute ride.

Q: What do you get when you smoke pot and take Viagra?
A: Stiff joints!

Old men don't need Viagra, because they're impotent. Old men need Viagra because old women are very, very ugly.

Jimmy Carr

161

They May Be Wrinkly But They've Still Got It

An old man says to his friend, "You know, even though I'm old, I've definitely still got it." "Oh yes," says his friend. "Yes," says the old man. "The problem is nobody wants it any more."

A 90-year-old man has been married four times, but appears at his doctor's to announce that he is getting married again, to a highly sexed 18-year-old girl. "Are you mad?" says the doctor. "You realize that if you start having frequent sex again it could prove fatal." "Ah well," says the old man, "if she dies, she dies."

An old man goes to his doctor's and says he is worried about his failing sex drive and that his wife might stray if he is no longer able to satisfy her. "Hang on!" says the doctor to the old man. "How old are the pair of you?" "I'm 82," says the old man. "And my wife is 79." "OK," says the doctor. "And when did you notice this problem with your sex drive?" "Twice last night," says the old man, "and once again this morning."

An ageing spinster is sitting on a park bench one day all on her own. A rough looking man walks over and sits at the other end of the bench. After a few moments, the woman asks, "Are you a stranger here?" "I used to live here years ago," says the man. "Oh," says the woman. "So, where were you all these years?" "In prison," he says. "Oh," says the woman. "What did they put you in prison for?" And the rough man looks at her and very quietly says, "I got into a wild drunken rage one night and I killed my wife in the most violent terrible way imaginable." "Oh," says the woman. "So you're single then..."

An old man is celebrating his 100th birthday. The local newspaper sends a reporter to cover the story. "Well," says the reporter, "you seem in remarkably good shape. What's the secret of living so long?" "There's no secret," says the old man. "It's probably just because I've never messed around with women and I've never touched a drop of alcohol." Just then there's a crash and a scream from a room upstairs. "Oh my goodness," says the reporter, "what was that?" "Don't worry about that," says the old man, "it's just my dad. He's pissed again and chasing the home help round the bedroom."

Taking Precautions

An old lady goes to her doctor and asks for contraceptive tablets, claiming they help her sleep at night. "Why would contraceptive pills make you sleep any better than normal?" asks the doctor. The old lady replies, "Because I put them in my granddaughter's coffee."

Eighty-year-old spinster Miss Jones was the organist in her local church and was admired for her sweetness and kindness to all. One afternoon the vicar visited her at home and she showed him into her old fashioned living room. She invited him to take a seat while she made them some tea. As he sat facing her old Hammond organ, the vicar noticed a glass bowl sitting on top of it. The bowl was filled with water and in the water floated a condom! When Miss Jones returned with their tea and biscuits, the vicar couldn't help but ask about the condom floating in the glass bowl. "Oh, yes," Miss Jones replied, "isn't it wonderful? I was walking through the park a few weeks ago and I found this little package on the ground. The directions said to place it on the organ, keep it wet and that it would prevent the spread of disease. And do you know I haven't had a cold all winter?"

Two old ladies are standing outside their nursing home so they can have a smoke. The sky darkens and it begins to rain. Feeling the patter of raindrops, one of the old ladies reaches into her handbag and pulls out a condom. She cuts off the end, slides the rubber tube over her cigarette and continues smoking. "What are you doing?" says the old lady standing with her. "These things are really handy," says the other old lady, showing her packet of condoms. "If it starts to rain, you put them over your cigarette and it doesn't get all wet and spoilt." "What a good idea," says her friend. "Where can I get a packet of these miniature cigarette Pac-a-macs?" "You can get them at any chemist," says her companion. So the old lady hobbles off to the local chemist and announces loudly to the young man behind the counter that she wants to purchase a box of condoms. The pharmacist is rather taken aback by this, but asks her if there is any particular brand that she prefers. "No, that doesn't matter, young man," says the old lady, checking the pack of cigarettes in her bag, "just as long as they're big enough to fit a Camel."

Things That Make You Feel Old (Even When You're Not)

We all get old eventually – if we're lucky. But what about when you're not actually that advanced in years, but certain things make you feel old very suddenly and bring you up with a shuddering jolt? For example:

Bald punks

It doesn't seem five minutes ago that the nation was being shocked and horrified, largely via some lurid tabloid reportage, by those spitting, swearing, snarling punks. Maybe you were even a punk yourself, but now, thanks to all those TV documentaries about the 1970s or rock music, we suddenly find ourselves confronted by fat, bald, middle-aged men who apparently once used to be punk rockers. Suddenly they seem as threatening as suet puddings, but even worse they make you feel ancient.

Documentaries about the 80s

If punk seems five minutes ago, then the 80s are a mere nanosecond back in time. It's probably a sign that TV executives are getting younger and they want to trawl over the ashes of their recent youth, but for goodness sake, some of us are still wearing ripped jeans and playing with Rubik cubes. Nostalgia it ain't.

Rock star children

Just when you thought you'd heard the last of certain rock stars from the 60s and 70s, who should start popping up in the gossip columns but their flipping children! Spoilt brats with silly names falling out of nightclubs or launching their own doomed careers in a haze of cocaine and their own celebrity scent. And when *their* children hit the front pages you know it's time to apply for your bus pass – and hope that it will take you away from all this.

Fashion revivals

If you're past 50 then your flared trousers alone have probably necessitated you fitting a revolving door to your wardrobe. Those loons have been in and out more often than the cuckoo in your granny's favourite clock. And each time one of the fashions from your youth is revived you realize another decade has slipped by. Why can't these overpaid fashion designers think of something new instead of making you feel old?

Culture shift

Remember when you used to listen to Radio 1 because it had all your favourite music on it? Then you woke up one morning to find that they were playing modern stuff and all your faves had been relegated to Radio 2? Then you found all your favourite DJs had gone there too, or to oldies stations. Then there was the first time you heard one of your all-time favourite records being used as background music at your bank, or worse still in a lift, or on a TV advert for toilet rolls or something. It's almost as if they're trying to tell you something.

Troublesome Wrinklies

An old man comes out of the newsagents and crosses over to the car parked opposite where a traffic warden is writing a ticket. "Oh come on!" says the old man. "I'm a pensioner. I can't afford to pay that, can I?" The traffic warden ignores him and continues writing the ticket. The old man becomes more abusive. "You fascist!" he says. "You slimy piece of I don't know what. You've got no heart. You pathetic, jumped up stupid little man!" The traffic warden proceeds to write another ticket and then another as the old man keeps ranting at him about his lack of consideration. The car ends up with five tickets on the windscreen. "You should have spoken to him a bit more nicely," says a passer by to the old man, "and then he might have let you off." "I don't care," says the old man. "This isn't my car."

An old man is making a long distance call in the USA when all of a sudden he gets cut off. He hollers, "Operator, giff me beck da party!" She says, "I'm sorry, sir, you'll have to make the call all over again." He says, "What do you want from my life? Giff me beck da party." "I'm sorry sir," says the operator, "you'll have to place the call again." "Operator, ya know vat?" says the old man. "You can take da telephone and shove it in you-know-vere!" And with that he hangs up. Two days later he opens the door and there are two big, strapping men standing in his way telling him, "We've come to take your telephone away." "Vy?" asks the old man. "Because," they say, "two days ago you insulted operator number 28. But if you'd like to call up and apologize, we'll leave the telephone here." "Vait a minute," says the old man, "vat's da rush? Vat's da hurry?" He goes to the telephone and dials. "Hello? Get me operator 28. Hello, operator 28? Remember me? Two days ago I insulted you? I told you to take da telephone and shove it in you-know-vere?" "Yes?" says the operator. "Vell," he says, "get ready... they're bringin' it to ya now!"

An old lady from a remote village in Cornwall goes to stay with her niece in Surrey. Nearby is a very well known golf course. On the second afternoon of her visit, the elderly lady goes for a walk. Upon her return, the niece asks, "Well, Auntie, did you enjoy yourself?" "Oh, yes, indeed," says the old lady. "Before I had walked very far, I came to some beautiful rolling fields. There seemed to be a number of people wandering around them, mostly men. Some of them kept shouting at me in a very eccentric manner, but I took no notice. There were four men who followed me for some time, uttering curious excited barking sounds. Naturally, I ignored them, too. Oh, by the way," she says holding out her hands, "I found a number of these curious little round white balls, so I picked them all up and brought them home hoping you could explain what they're all about."

Two guys left the bar after a long night of drinking, jumped in the car and started it up. After a couple of minutes, an old man appeared in the passenger window and tapped lightly. The passenger screamed, "Look at the window. There's an old ghost's face there!" The driver sped up, but the old man's face stayed in the window. The passenger rolled his window down part way and, scared out of his wits, said, "What do you want?" The old man softly replied, "You got any tobacco?" The passenger handed the old man a cigarette and yelled, "Step on it!" to the driver, while rolling up the window in terror. A few minutes later they calmed down and started laughing again. The driver said, "I don't know what happened, but don't worry; the speedometer says we're doing 80 now." All of a sudden there was a light tapping on the window and the old man reappeared. "There he is again," the passenger yelled. He rolled down the window and shakily said, "Yes?" "Do you have a light?" the old man quietly asked. The passenger threw a lighter out of the window, saying, "Step on it!" They were driving about 100 miles an hour, trying to forget what they had just seen and heard, when all of a sudden there came some more tapping. "Oh my God! He's back!" The passenger rolled down the window and screamed in stark terror, "WHAT DO YOU WANT WITH US?" The old man gently replied, "I just wondered if you wanted any help getting out of the mud?"

An avid young golfer finds himself with a few hours to spare after work one day. He works out that if he hurries and plays as fast as he can, he could get in nine holes before he has to go home. Just as he is about to tee off an old gentleman shuffles onto the tee and asks if he could accompany the young man as he is golfing alone. The young golfer doesn't like to refuse and lets the old gent to join him. To his surprise the old man plays fairly quickly. He doesn't hit the ball far, but nevertheless plods along consistently without wasting much time. Eventually they reach the ninth fairway, and the young man finds himself with a tough shot. A large pine tree stands right in the direct line of his shot, between him and the green. After several minutes of debating how to hit the shot the old man finally tells him, "When I was your age I was able to hit the ball right over the top of that tree." With this gauntlet thrown down, the youngster swings as hard as he can and hits the ball right smack into the top of the tree trunk, where it thuds back on the ground less than a foot from where it started. "Damn it!" says the young golfer. "How on earth did you manage to hit the ball over that tree?" "Well," says the old man, "of course in those days the tree was only three feet tall."

A granddad is talking to his grandson. "How many miles do you walk to school?" asks granddad. "About half a mile," says the boy. "Huh!" snorts granddad. "When I was your age I walked eight miles to school every day. What grades did you get in your last report?" "Mostly Bs," says the boy. "Huh!" says granddad in disgust. "When I was your age I was getting all As. Have you ever been in a fight?" "Twice," says the boy, "and got beaten up both times." "Huh!" says granddad. "When I was your age I was in a fight every day. How old are you anyway? "Nine years old," says the boy. "Huh!" snorts granddad. "When I was your age I was 11."

An old man is telling his grandson about how he used to work in a blacksmith's when he was a boy. "Oh yes," says the old man, "I had to really toughen myself up to work in that place. Do you know I would stand at the back of my house, get a five-pound potato sack in my right hand and a five-pound potato sack in my left hand, and then raise my arms up and extend them straight out from my sides. I'd then stand there holding them out like that for as long as I could. After a while I moved onto ten-pound potato sacks, then 20-pound potato sacks. Finally I was able to do it with a pair of fifty pound potato sacks." "Wow, granddad," says the little boy. "That must have been hard." "Oh yes," says the old man, "it was. And it was even worse when I started putting potatoes in the sacks."

Three old men are chatting about their ancestors and boasting about what they had done in the forces. The first one says, "My great grandfather was in the First World War trenches and survived." The second one says, "Well my great grandfather was in the Boer War and he survived." Not to be outdone the third one says, "Well, if my great grandfather was alive today he'd be internationally famous." "Really?" say the other two, leaning forward. "Why's that?" "Because he'd be 153 years old," says the third old man.

An old man is finding it increasingly difficult to get around so he asks his similarly aged neighbour if he would mind popping into town to the post office to see if a package he is expecting has turned up yet. His old neighbour says he was going into town anyway to get his groceries. So off he totters, all the way down the street and into the town. The old man sits watching for several hours until eventually his elderly neighbour re-appears, slowly plodding all the way back down the street again. "So?" says the old man to his neighbour. "Was my package there?" "Oh yes," says the neighbour. "It's there all right."

Wrinklies And The Law

A little old lady is in court for stealing a tin of peaches after absent-mindedly popping them into her bag rather than her trolley. Under the circumstances the judge decides to be lenient and asks her how many peaches there were in the tin. "There were three peaches," she replies. "Very well then," says the judge, "in that case I sentence you to three days in prison." Just then her husband pipes up and says, "She stole a tin of peas as well!"

An elderly lady calls 999 on her mobile phone. In a panic she calls for the police to come quickly, because her car has been broken into and a number of items have been stolen. "What exactly has been taken, madam?" asks the operator at the other end of the line. "Oh it's terrible, officer," says the old lady.

"They've taken my car stereo. They've taken the steering wheel, the gear stick, the brake pedal and even the accelerator!" "My goodness," says the operator, "I've never heard of anything like this before. I'm sending someone out straightaway." A few minutes later the operator gets a call from the policeman attending the scene. "Case solved!" says the policeman. "The stupid old woman climbed into the back seat by mistake."

Old Tom and Old Ned used to meet in the park every day. One day Tom didn't turn up, but Ned presumed his friend must have caught a cold or something. A week passed by and Tom still didn't appear, so Ned began to worry. However, since the only time they ever met was at the park, Ned didn't know where Tom lived, so he couldn't check whether his friend was all right. A month passed by and Ned presumed he must have seen Tom for the last time, but then suddenly one day he reappeared. "Where have you been?" asked Ned. "I've been in prison," said Tom. "Prison!" said Ned. "How on earth did that happen?" "Well," said Tom, "you know the pretty waitress in the café I go to sometimes? One day she filed charges against me saying that I tried to molest her. I was taken to court and because I'm 89 years old, I was so proud that when I got in the dock I pleaded guilty and the judge gave me 30 days for lying under oath."

An elderly gentleman came home one night to find a homeless girl of about 18 ransacking his house. He grabbed her by the arm and was just about to call the police when the girl dropped down on her knees and begged him, "Please don't call the police! I'm in too much trouble already. In fact, if you don't call the police, I'll let you make love to me and do all the things you've ever wanted to do!" The old man thinks about this for a minute and finally yields to temptation. Soon the pair are in bed together, but despite the old man's very best efforts he finds he no longer has what it takes. Finally he gives up. He rolls over exhausted and reaches for the phone. "I'm sorry, young lady... but it's no use," he gasps. "It looks like I'm going to have to call the police after all."

Are You A Gaga Lout?

People complain about the young and their lack of manners, appalling language and general decorum, but what about some of the wrinklies? Oh, they may blame their boorishness on everything from the pills they're on to mild dementia, but the real reason they do it is because they know they can get away with it – and it's fun! So come on, own up – are you a gaga lout?

Do you use your walking stick not just as a mobility aid, but also as an offensive weapon? It's not for nothing that the humble and seemingly innocuous walking stick is known in some police circles as the "pensioners' baseball bat".

Do you elbow your way to the front of the bus queue in the full knowledge that if anyone younger (and most people are) tries to stop you that you will then become a frail old pensioner again and they're the ones who'll be in trouble?

Do you sit on city centre benches and swear at passers-by, knowing that the loopier you seem the less likely people are to come and sit next to you, and deprive you of somewhere to put your flask, sandwiches, newspaper and tartan blanket?

Do you make lewd remarks to younger people knowing that they'll simply regard you as a loveable old eccentric rather than the crusty old pervert you actually are?

Do you shoplift small items of groceries and then when caught say, "But I'm Napoleon, I own all ze shops in ze land and if you don't unhand me I will send you to the guillotine!"

Do you pretend to be a bit deaf when people come to the door trying to sell cleaning materials, double-glazing or religion?

Or do you simply go into scary old person mode and frighten them off with such phrases as, "Ah, another victim! Would you like to come in and try some of my especially prepared sooooup?"

When children come trick or treating do you remove your false teeth, contort your features into a hideous gurn and open the front door holding a torch beneath your face?

When cold calling telephone salesmen ring do you turn up the ga-ga-ometer to 11 and engage them in a long and rambling conversation, at their expense of course, about your medical history, views on immigration and other sundry matters, before breaking into bouts of hysterical laughter?

Have you ever (now be absolutely honest here) feigned a fall in the street to get a ride home in an ambulance because you simply couldn't be bothered to walk?

Have you ever charged in mob-handed with a bunch of other coffin-dodgers to a Help The Aged shop and demanded all the money out of the till on the grounds that you want to cut out the middle man?

He / She Is So Old That...

He's so old that when he orders a three-minute egg, they ask for the money up front.

Milton Berle

Even his kids are drawing their pensions.

He remembers when Barbara Cartland didn't need make-up.

He can remember when Glenn Miller was considered a teenage fad.

If you ask him if he remembers the war, he asks which one.

He has to convert decimal prices to pounds, shillings and groats.

He compares the millennium celebrations with the previous lot.

The first time he celebrated Guy Fawkes Night it was the original one.

His first telephone book was just one foolscap sheet.

He can remember when the Queen Mum was a bit of all right.

When he took his driving test he had to pay a man to walk in front waving a red flag.

He can recall when a Czar was a Russian leader and not somebody who advised the government on drugs.

His earliest memories are all in black and white.

He can remember when the world heavyweight boxing champion was a white man.

He can remember when trains used to run on time.

He can remember when fast food meant Lent.

His first job was as a lamplighter.

He was a suspect in the Jack the Ripper murders.

He thought a pair of trainers was two sports coaches.

His bald head is coming up to its golden jubilee.

He still refers to the pictures as "the talkies".

They have to get the fire brigade to attend every time they light the candles on his birthday cake.

He can remember when Heinz only had one variety.

He could have been a waiter at the last supper.

He was the hot dog salesman at Custer's last stand.

He owes Moses three pounds.

When God said let there be light, he was the one who hit the switch.

In my lifetime I saw the Berlin Wall come and I saw it go. George Burns can say the same thing about the Ice Age.

Bob Hope

When he went to the *Antiques Roadshow*, someone appraised him.

When he walks past a graveyard, guys come running after him with shovels.

When he was a boy rainbows were in black and white.

He has an original autographed edition of the bible.

His birthday expired.

I told him to act his age and he dropped dead.

I'm so old they've cancelled my blood type.

Bob Hope

Old Bert says he's so old that when he was in school they didn't have history. Then it was called current affairs.

Her birth certificate is in Roman numerals.

Her social security number is one!

In his school photo he was standing just in front of Moses.

He knew Burger King while he was still a prince.

She needs an archaeologist to do her make-up.

He's two years older than dirt.

When I was a boy the Dead Sea was only sick.

George Burns

You Know You're Getting Old When...

Your children start saying, "Hey! That looks like a nice place, doesn't it?" when driving past nursing homes.

Your doctor doesn't bother giving you X-rays any more, he just holds you up against a sunny window.

Your ears are hairier than your head.

Your friends phone you up at nine o'clock at night and ask, "Did I get you out of bed?"

Your idea of a "night out" is spending an evening on the patio rocking chair.

Your insurance company has started sending you their free calendar... a month at a time.

Your knees buckle but your belt won't.

Your last visit to a specialist cost you more than you earned in your first four years at work.

Your memory is shorter and your complaining lasts longer.

Your mind starts to make contracts your body can't meet.

Your new reclining chair has more optional extras than your car.

Your photographic memory finally seems to have run out of film.

Your underwear starts creeping up on you... and you enjoy it.

Your wild oats turn to prunes and bran.

You're driving in your car, but can't remember where you're going – but it doesn't matter, you're not in a hurry.

You're 18 around the neck, 44 around the waist, and 105 around the golf course.

You're on a high-stakes TV game show and you decide to risk it all to go for the rocker.

You're on holiday and your energy runs out before your money does.

You're sitting on a park bench and have to ask a passing Boy Scout for help crossing your legs.

You're trying to straighten out the wrinkles in your socks, then discover you aren't wearing any.

Are You Trying Too Hard To Stay Young?

We all try to fight old age in our own way, don't we? We take up exercise, we try not to wear fuddy duddy clothes, we try as hard as possible not to use phrases like, "well, in my day...", we take up new hobbies and interests, do a bit of silver-surfing on the internet, absolutely refuse to buy *Saga* magazine and 101 other things, but sometimes we go too far. Extreme youthism is a dangerous game for an oldster, so have a look at the following list and see whether you are overdoing it a bit.

Do you find your walking stick a help or a hindrance when skateboarding?

Ladies – last time you put on make-up were you mistaken for Barbara Cartland?

When the teenagers next door have their music on a bit loud do you bang on the wall and shout "turn down the volume!" or bang on your drum kit and shout "pump up the volume!"

Men – are you torn between not wearing a trilby because it reminds you of what you wore in your youth or wearing one because Pete Doherty does?

Women – do you wear skimpy swimsuits that leave young men gasping – and running in the opposite direction?

Do you find that wearing a baseball cap back to front actually confuses you about what direction you should be going in when you walk away from the hall mirror?

When you had a tattoo done did you find people asking if it was done while you were in a concentration camp?

When you attend raves in your hoodie do you find young people thinking they're hallucinating that you're a ghostly old monk and rush to the chill-out area?

Do you consider roller skates a fun mode of transport or an alternative mobility aid?

When you dance wildly at parties does a stranger attempt to pick you up – or just leave you lying on the floor?

Did you spend 45 minutes annoying the other people at your local internet cafe before you found out that you'd completely misunderstood what was meant by "internet chat room"?

When the local deli asks you if you want a "wrap" do you find yourself going into an impromptu impersonation of MC Hammer before being asked to leave by the management?

Do you need a specially adapted vacuum cleaner to administer your Botox injections?

Last Wishes

A very old man is lying on his deathbed. He summons his lawyer and tells him to make some last-minute changes to his will. "I wish to leave everything I own, all stocks, bonds, property, art and money to my nagging, spiteful, ungrateful, mean-spirited wife. However, there is one stipulation." "And that is?" asks the lawyer. "In order to inherit," says the old man, "she must marry within six months of my death." "That's a bit of an odd request," says the lawyer. "Why do you want to do that?" "Because," says the old man, "I want someone to be sorry I died."

Winston, an old Scotsman is dying and he calls for his best friend Rory to come to his bedside and listen to his dying wish. "Rory," whispers old Winston, his breath almost spent, "under my bed you'll find a bottle of the world's finest single malt. I've been saving it for this moment. When you come to my funeral would ye do me the great service of pouring the whiskey over my grave?" "Aye, of course I will, my friend," replies Rory and then adds, "But would you mind terribly if I pass it through my bladder first?"

A woman goes to the undertakers to see her late husband's body just before his burial. When she gets there she is shocked to find him dressed in a grey suit. "Oh no," she says. "I can't have him buried in a grey suit. He couldn't stand grey. He always said he wanted to be buried in a black suit." "I'm sorry, I can't do anything about it now, madam," says the undertaker. "It's too late. The funeral is going to begin in a few minutes." "But I insist!" shouts the woman, breaking into tears. "All right, madam," says the undertaker. "Calm down. I'll see what I can do." The undertaker pushes the trolley with the man's body out into the back room. A few moments later an assistant pushes the trolley back in with the woman's husband now dressed in a black suit. "My goodness that was quick!" says the undertaker under his breath. "How did you do it?" "Oh it wasn't too hard," says the assistant. "Luckily we had a bloke out there already dressed in a black suit so we just swapped the heads over."

An old lady in London decides to draw up her will and make her last requests. She tells her solicitor she is leaving her fortune to her daughters, but with two important conditions. Firstly, she says she wants to be cremated, and secondly, she wants her ashes scattered over the first floor of Harrod's department store. "Harrods!" says the solicitor. "Why Harrods?" "Well," says the old lady, "at least that way I'll be sure my daughters will visit my final resting place each week."

An old man lying on his deathbed summons his doctor, his lawyer and his priest. He hands out three separate envelopes to them. Each of the envelopes contains £30,000. "Gentlemen," he tells them solemnly, "they say you can't take it with you, but I am going to try. When they lower my coffin into my grave I want each of you to throw in these envelopes I have just given you." After the funeral the doctor confesses to the other two, "I've got to be straight with you. My health practice desperately needed some money to build a new clinic, so I kept £20,000 and just threw in £10,000." The priest also confesses, "The church is in desperate need of renovation. So I'm afraid I kept £10,000 and just threw in £20,000." The lawyer stands shaking his head in disgust. "I can't believe you two," he says. "Am I the only one of us who was decent enough to carry out the old man's dying wishes?" "So you threw in the entire £30,000!" say the doctor and the priest in astonishment. "Yes," says the lawyer. "Well... I threw in a cheque for the full amount."

Doris is dying and is already planning exactly how the funeral should be arranged, and calls in her husband. "Arthur," she says, "When you go to the church for my funeral I want you to promise that you'll sit next to my mother and keep her company." "Oh no," says Arthur, "Do I have to? You know I can't stand the woman, and she makes no secret of the fact that she can't stand me." "But Arthur," protested the woman, "it's my dying wish. Can't you make an effort just for me?" "Oh all right" says Arthur, "but I want you to know this is going to completely ruin the whole day for me."

The family of a rich old man gathers to hear his will being read. The solicitor solemnly opens the document and reads, "The last will and testament of John Smith. Being of sound mind, I therefore spent all my money."

You Know You're Getting Old When...

Licking the stamps to go on your letters to the hospital is a hard day's work.

Most of your co-workers were born the same year you got your last promotion.

Most of your day is spent making appointments with different doctors.

People tell you you're young-looking rather than telling you you're young.

Rocking all night means dozing off in your rocking chair.

Someone compliments you on your layered look – and you're wearing a bikini.

Taking out a year's subscription to a magazine is an act of positive thinking and real optimism.

The local "peeping tom" leaves a note saying: "Please pull the blinds down!"

The best part of your day is over when your alarm clock goes off.

The best way to make the wrinkles you see in the mirror disappear is simply to take off your glasses.

The car you bought brand new becomes a vintage model.

The clothes you put away until they come back in style... come back in style... for the second time.

The end of your tie doesn't come anywhere near the top of your trousers.

The girls at the office start confiding in you.

The little old lady you help across the street is your wife.

The names in your little black book are mostly doctors.

The only four-letter word you can think of to describe something you and your partner do in bed together is "read".

The only thing you find you ever exercise is caution.

The only thing you really want for your birthday is not to be reminded of your age.

The only time you kick-up your heels is when you fall down (and can't get up).

Wrinklies' End

Next time you hear anyone complaining about old age just ask them if they'd prefer the alternative. They'll probably say no – especially, of course, if the alternative is being bored to death with platitudes about old age. Death, they say is the last taboo. Well, it's the last everything really, isn't it? The good news is you only have to do it once – unless you're a stand-up comedian with a rather poor act, when you can die every night or possibly die a thousand deaths in one solitary open mike spot. In fact, the real thing might actually be preferable to the sound of a couple of hundred unhappy punters screaming for your blood and chucking Belgian beer bottles. It's not for nothing that one of the most fearsome weapons in the world is known as a Heckler.

Two old men are talking. "I reckon death must be the best part of life," says one. "Why's that?" asks the other. "Because," says the first, "it always gets saved till last."

Dying is not popular; it has never caught on. That's understandable; it's bad for the complexion.

George Burns

Either he's dead or my watch has stopped.

Groucho Marx

It's not that I'm afraid to die, I just don't want to be there when it happens.

Woody Allen

Two recently bereaved women are chatting at a support group and one says, "Don't talk to me about solicitors, I've had so much trouble sorting out my late husband's will that I sometimes wish he hadn't died."

An old lady tells her friend, "My husband died the other day." "Oh dear," says her friend. "What of?" "The doctors aren't sure," says the old lady, "but they don't think it was anything serious."

Two old ladies bump into each other at the supermarket. "Hello, dear. How are you?" asks the first. "Oh I'm fine," says the second. "And what about your husband?" asks the first. "Oh, didn't you hear?" says the second. "He died two weeks ago. He went out in the garden to dig up a cabbage for dinner, had a massive heart attack and fell over in the compost heap, stone dead." "Oh my goodness!" says the first old lady. "How absolutely terrible for you. What did you do?" "Well," says the second, "luckily I managed to find a tin of sweetcorn in the cupboard, so I had that instead."

True story:

A doctor had to inform an elderly lady that her husband had died as a result of a massive myocardial infarct. A short while later the doctor heard her reporting to the rest of her family that her husband had died of a "massive internal fart."

Two old men bump into each other in the park. One says to the other, "You've got to forgive me because my memory is getting terrible. Just remind me again will you, who was it died last week? Was it your wife or you?"

An old couple wake up one morning and the old man leans over to kiss his wife on the cheek. "No!" squeals his wife. "Don't touch me! I think I've died!" "What are you talking about, woman?" says the old man. "How can you have died when you're sitting up in bed with me." "I don't know," says the old woman, "but I think I've definitely died in my sleep." "Well, what makes you think that?" says the man. "Because," says the old woman, "I've just woken up and nothing's hurting."

I can't afford to die; I'd lose too much money.

George Burns

I don't mind dying, the trouble is you feel so bloody stiff the next day.

George Axlerod

I want to die peacefully, in my sleep, like my granddad. Not screaming and terrified, like his bus passengers.

Joe tells his friend Pete, "My granddad died last night." "Oh no," says Pete. "Yes," says Joe, "he was working late in the whisky distillery, he had to climb up to check in one of the vats, but being a bit doddery on his legs now he lost his balance and fell in." "Oh my goodness!" says Pete. "So what happened? Did he drown?" "Yes. After eight hours," says Joe. "Eight hours!" says Pete. "Why so long?" "Well it would have been quicker," says Joe, "but he had to get out three times to go to the toilet."

An old man asks his wife, "Darling, if I died, would you ever consider getting married again?" "I've no idea!" says his wife. "But maybe after a considerable period of grieving, I might consider it. After all, we all need companionship." "OK," says the old man, "but if I died and you got married again would your new husband live in this house?" "I've no idea!" says his wife. "But then again we've spent a lot of money getting this house the way we want it. I'm not going to get rid of it easily, so perhaps he would." "OK," says the old man, "and if I died and you got married again and your new husband came to live in this house, would he sleep in our bed?" "I've no idea!" says his wife. "But then again I suppose this bed is brand new and it cost us £2,000. It's going to last a long time, so maybe." "OK," says the old man, "and if I died and you got married again and he came to live in this house and slept in our bed, would you let him use my golf clubs?" "Oh no," says his wife. "He's left-handed!"

Roger and Catherine are talking one day and the subject turns to death. "What would you do if I died before you?" asks Roger. "Oh, I don't know really," says Catherine. "I suppose thinking about it, I'd have to sell this place, because it would be far too big for me, and then I'd get in touch with my best friend Julie and move in with her now her husband's gone. What about you?" "Hmm," says Roger, "probably exactly the same as you."

How young can you die of old age?

Steven Wright

There are worse things in life than death. Have you ever spent an evening with an insurance salesman?

Woody Allen

Fred tells Ethel, "Do you know, my granddad knew the exact date and the exact time that he would die." "That's uncanny," says Ethel. "Was he psychic then?" "No," says Fred. "The judge told him."

I know when I'm going to die... my birth certificate has an expiration date.

Steven Wright

Gertrude and Hilda are sitting in the bingo hall between games and looking out of the window. As they do so a funeral procession goes by and the name of the deceased, "Albert", is spelt out in flowers in the back of the hearse. Gertrude sniffs loudly and gets a hanky out of her handbag. Hilda says, "Oh you old softie!" "I can't help it," says Gertrude. "After all, he was a good husband to me."

Granddad was in hospital and one of his teenage grandchildren was looking after the cat while grandma was at work. One day the teenager went to visit her granddad in hospital and announced that the cat had died. "My poor old Polly?" said granddad, "You could have broken it to me gently. "How?" asked the teenager. "You could have said, Polly was playing on the roof, then she slipped and hurt herself, and you took her to the vet and he couldn't save her." "I see," said the teenager, "Sorry, Granddad." A week later the teenager went to visit granddad in hospital. "Hello," said Granddad, "How's Grandma?" "Well," said the teenager, "She was playing on the roof..."

Death is not the end. There remains the litigation over the estate.

Ambrose Bierce

If your time hasn't come, not even a doctor can kill you.

M A Perlstein

Funeral For A Wrinkly

Who was it who said, "Always go to other people's funerals or they won't come to yours" and was he speaking from experience? Still, it's the last chance you'll ever have of hearing lots of people saying nice things about you. Perhaps the only chance. And you in turn will have your last chance to inflict on them some dreadfully maudlin tune that may well have half of the congregation slitting their wrists and jumping in the coffin with you. Why should you be the only one who's suffering?

They say such nice things about people at their funerals that it makes me sad that I'm going to miss mine by just a few days.

Garrison Keillor

A funeral service is being held for a woman who has just passed away. At the end of the service, the pall bearers are carrying the coffin out when they accidentally bump into a wall, jarring the casket. They hear a faint moan! They open the lid of the coffin and are amazed to discover that the woman is still alive after all. She lives for another ten years before passing on. Once again, a funeral service is held and, at the end of it, the pall bearers pick up the coffin, and start carrying it out of the church. As they carry the coffin towards the door, the husband cries out: "This time will you watch out for that bloody wall!"

An elderly couple are discussing their funeral arrangements one day and the wife says to the husband, "So, Bert, when you die would you like to be buried or cremated?" "I don't know," replies her husband. "Surprise me!"

At an old man's funeral, the vicar talks at some length about the good life of the dearly departed, what a pillar of the community he has been, what a loving husband and kind father, and how he will be sadly missed by all his poor family. Listening to this, the old man's widow looks increasingly concerned. "Are you all right, Mum?" asks her son, fearing she is about to break down with emotion. "I'm fine," says the old lady, "but could you just go and have a quick look to make sure we've got the right person in the coffin. I'm not sure he can be talking about your father."

In the churchyard the undertaker is standing next to the grieving widow. The old woman is crying uncontrollably and so the undertaker tries to cheer her up by starting a conversation.

"How old was your husband then?" he asks. "My Bert was 97," replies the widow. "Only a few months older than I am." "Oh dear. Is that so?" says the undertaker. "So really when you think about it, it's hardly worth you going home is it?"

A man is walking down a steep hill while at the top a funeral car has stopped at the church. As the back of the car is opened the coffin falls out and starts to slide down the hill, gathering speed as it does so. The man hears the noise and turns round to see the coffin hurtling towards him, so he starts to run down the hill. By now the man and the coffin are rushing at breakneck speed, and the pharmacist comes out of the chemist's shop down the hill to see what the commotion is. As the man rushes past he shouts to the chemist, "Hey, can you give me something to stop this coffin!"

If you get fed up with elderly relatives coming up to you at weddings and saying, "You'll be next", try doing the same to them at funerals.

Jim's wife dies and he takes it very badly, breaking down during the funeral service and then being unable to face the guests at the wake. His best friend Tony goes up to his bedroom where he is lying on the bed weeping. "OK, mate, I know it's tough right now," says Tony, "but believe me, it'll get easier. You never know, in a year or two you may even meet someone else and have another relationship." "A year or two?" splutters Jim. "What about tonight?"

Did you hear about the local greengrocer's funeral the other week? Apparently there was a large turnip.

Wrinklies From Beyond The Grave

An old Jewish woman goes to a travel agent and asks for a holiday in Calcutta, because she wants to consult with the Indian mystics. "Oh, it won't be very suitable for a woman of your age," says the travel agent, "How about a nice cruise?" But the woman insists and takes the trip to Calcutta. When she gets there it's very hot, and there are flies buzzing round her as she comes out of the airport and boards a ramshackle old bus. She is on the bus for several uncomfortable hours and finally reaches a remote spot where there is a temple. There is a queue of people waiting to see the guru, so she waits and waits and waits until finally she is allowed in. "Now remember," says one of the men at the door of the temple, "You are only permitted to utter five words to the guru." The woman nods and goes in to where the guru sits in a dark corner. She approaches him and says, "Albie, come back home now!"

A widower who never paid any attention to his wife while she was alive now found himself missing her desperately. He went to a psychic to see if he could contact her. The psychic went into a trance. A strange breeze wafted through the darkened room and suddenly the man heard the unmistakable voice of his dearly departed wife. "Dearest!" he cried. "Is that you?" "Yes, my husband," she replied. "Are you happy?" "Yes, my husband." "Happier than you were with me?" "Oh yes, my husband, I am." "Wow," he said. "So Heaven must be an amazing place!" "I'm not in Heaven, dear," said his wife.

Everybody wants to go to Heaven, but nobody wants to die.

I want to die before my wife and the reason is this: if it's true that when you die your soul goes up to judgment, I don't want my wife up there ahead of me to tell them things.

Bill Cosby

A little old lady goes to a medium to help her contact her dead husband. "He's with me now, dear," says the medium, "Is there anything you want to ask him?" "Well," says the old lady, "just ask him if there's anything he needs." "He says he'd like a packet of cigarettes," says the medium. "OK," says the little old lady. "Did he say where I should send them to?" "No," replies the medium. "But he did say that where he is he won't be needing a lighter."

An old married couple have an accident in their car and go straight up to Heaven. When they get there they look round in amazement at the wonder and tranquillity of the place, and the overwhelming feeling of peace and contentment they feel. "Oh my!" says the wife. "It's so beautiful and peaceful, it's even better than I imagined." The husband hasn't said a word since they got there, so she turns to him and says, "What's the matter, Henry, don't you like it?" "Like it?" replies the husband. "It's fantastic! And if it hadn't been for you and your flipping health foods I could've been up here years ago!"

A lawyer and the Pope died at the same time and both went to Heaven. They were met at the Pearly Gates by St Peter who conducted them to their rooms. The Pope's room was spartan, with a bare floor, an army bunk for a bed and a single bulb for light. They came to the lawyer's room. It was huge, with wall-to-wall carpeting, king-sized water bed, indirect lighting, colour TV, stereo, jacuzzi and fully stocked bar. The lawyer said, "There must be a mistake. This must be the Pope's room!" St Peter said, "There's no mistake. This is your room. We have lots of Popes, but you're our very first lawyer!"

A lawyer dies and goes up to Heaven and waits in front of the Pearly Gates. A few minutes later St Peter appears and says, "Ah! Mr Smith, it's such an honour to have you here at last. At 1028 you're the first person to have lived longer than Methuselah himself." "What are you talking about?" says the lawyer. "I died aged 65." "But you are John Smith, aren't you?" asks St Peter. "John Smith the lawyer of 32 Sebastopol Terrace, Hackney." "That's right," says the lawyer. "Oh I see where we've gone wrong," says St Peter. "We've worked it out from your billing hours."

A woman goes on holiday to South Africa. Her husband is on a business trip and is planning to meet her there the following day. When the woman reaches her hotel in Cape Town, she sends her husband an e-mail, but sends it to the wrong address. The next day the grieving widower of a recently deceased Sunday school teacher checks his e-mail, shouts out in horror and drops dead from a heart attack. Afterwards his cleaner finds a disturbing message on his computer screen: "Darling, Just got checked in. Everything ready for your arrival tomorrow. Your loving wife. P.S. Wow it's really hot down here."

After losing her husband a woman decides to go to a medium to try and contact him. After a while the medium says she thinks the husband is with them. "How are you?" the widow asks. "I'm fine," says the husband. "In fact, I'm great. I'm in a lovely green field surrounded by cows." "Oh," says the widow, rather surprised. "And some of them are very attractive," says the husband. "Really?" says the widow. "And are there angels there?" "No, just cows," says the husband. "I think I'm going to enjoy myself." "Well, that's good I suppose," says the widow. "But why do you keep going on about cows?" "Didn't I tell you?" says the husband. "I'm on a farm at Ilkley Moor – I've come back as a bull!"

St Peter is guarding the Pearly Gates when he hears a knock at the door. He goes to answer it, but there's nobody there. A few minutes later there's another knock. Again he goes to answer it, but once more there's nobody there. After another few minutes there's yet another knock at the door and this time there's an old man standing there. "What's your game?" asks St Peter. "Have you been playing 'knock down ginger' on my door?" "No," says the man. "The doctors were trying to resuscitate me."

They Shall Never Die...

Old academics never die, they just lose their faculties.

Old accountants never die, they just lose their balance.

Old actors never die, they just drop a part.

Old anthropologists never die, they just become history.

Old archers never die, they just bow and quiver.

Old architects never die, they just lose their structures.

Old astronauts never die, they just go to another world.

Old bankers never die, they just lose interest.

Old bankers never die, they just want to be a loan.

Old football players never die, they just go on dribbling.

Old beekeepers never die, they just buzz off.

Old bikers never die, but they're hard on tires.

Old biologists never die, they just ferment away.

Old blondes never fade, they just dye away.

Old book-keepers never die, they just lose their figures.

Old bookshop owners never die, they just go out of print.

Old bowlers never die, they just end up in the gutter.

Old bridge players never die, they just lose their finesse.

Old bridge players never die, they just sit around on their fat aces.

Old bureaucrats never die, they just waste away.

Old burglars never die, they just steal away.

Old businessmen never die, they just get consolidated.

Old canners never die, they are just preserved.

Old cars never die, they just get run into the ground.

Old cashiers never die, they just check out.

Old chauffeurs never die, they just lose their drive.

Old chemists never die, they just fail to react.

Old chemists never die, they just reach equilibrium.

Old cleaners never die, they just kick the bucket.

Old composers never die, they just decompose.

Old computer operators never die, they just lose their memory.

Old computer programmers never die, they just byte the dust.

Old cooks never die, they just get deranged.

Old couriers never die, they just keep on expressing it!

Old doctors never die, they just lose their patience.

Old drug addicts never die, they just get wasted.

Old electricians never die, they just lose contact.

Old farmers never die, they just go to seed.

Old mechanics never die, they just retire.

Old hippies never die, they just smell that way.

Old horticulturists never die, they just go to pot.

Old investors never die, they just roll over.

Old journalists never die, they just get de-pressed.

Old lawyers never die, they just lose their appeal.

Old limbo dancers never die, they just go under.

Old mathematicians never die, they just disintegrate.

Old milkmaids never die, they just lose their whey.

Old musicians never die, they just get played out.

Old number theorists never die, they just get past their prime.

Old numerical analysts never die, they just get disarrayed.

Old owls never die, they just don't give a hoot.

Old pacifists never die, they just go to peaces.

Old photographers never die, they just stop developing.

Old pilots never die, they just go to a higher plane.

Old policemen never die, they just cop out.

Old preachers never die, they just ramble on, and on, and on.

Old printers never die, they're just not the type.

Old programmers never die, they just branch to a new address.

Old sailors never die, they just get a little dingy.

Old schools never die, they just lose their principals.

Old sculptors never die, they just lose their marbles.

Old seers never die, they just lose their vision.

Old sewage workers never die, they just waste away.

Old skateboarders never die, they just lose their bearings.

Old soldiers never die. Young ones do.

Old steel-makers never die, they just lose their temper.

Old students never die, they just get degraded.

Old tanners never die, they just go into hiding.

Old teachers never die, they just gradually lose their class.

Old typists never die, they just lose their justification.

Old white-water rafters never die, they just get disgorged.

Old wrestlers never die, they just lose their grip.

There is no conclusive evidence about what happens to old sceptics, but their future looks doubtful.

The Wrinklies Will Not Be Forgotten

At my age I do what Mark Twain did. I get my daily paper, look at the obituaries page and if I'm not there I carry on as usual.

Patrick Moore

A man dies and his wife phones the local paper to arrange for his obituary to be printed. She is put through to the correct department and tells them she doesn't have much money, so she just wants the obituary to say, "Alf is dead." "That's quite short," says the man at the newspaper office, "but if you're worrying about the cost, don't forget you're entitled to have up to six words for the same price." "In that case," says the woman, "make it, 'Alf is dead: Toyota for sale.'"

A woman is at the solicitor's listening to the reading of her late husband's will. She is shocked and outraged to find that he has left all his money to another woman, so she stomps off to the graveyard, where the man from the undertaker's has just laid his headstone reading "Rest in Peace". Despite her protests the undertaker says it's too late to change the inscription. "All right then," she says. "After 'Rest in peace' just add 'For the time being'."

A young man is building a brick wall outside his house one day when a man stops to congratulate him. "What a magnificent wall you've built, young man, I doubt whether even Cornelius Bagshot III could have built a wall as good as that." "Who?" says the young man. "Cornelius Bagshot III," says the passer-by. "He was an incredible man. He could do anything he set his mind to. An outstanding athlete, leading light of Mensa, a chess grandmaster, and a brilliant footballer, cricketer and mountain climber. And he was an incredible lover as well by all accounts. He knew exactly what women wanted in the bedroom department, if you know what I mean. He was certainly an incredible, brilliant man, the like of whom we will not see again." "So was he a friend of yours then, this Cornelius Bagshot III?" asks the young man. "No. I never met him," says the passer-by. "I just married his widow."

An old spinster dies a virgin and has asked that the following inscription be put on her headstone, "Born a virgin, lived a virgin, died a virgin." Being a bit short of time the undertaker shortens this to: "Returned, unopened."

The inscription on the hypochondriac's tomb stone: "I told you I was ill."

A rich old lady commissions an artist to paint her portrait. When he arrives she starts putting on some very expensive looking jewellery: a diamond necklace, diamond earrings and a diamond tiara. "Wow!" says the artist. "That's fantastic jewellery. It must be worth an absolute fortune, if you don't mind me saying." "Well, it is," replies the old lady, "but I've only rented it. I don't usually go in for this sort of thing." "Oh, I see," says the artist, "you just want it to look good for the portrait?" "No," says the old lady, "but when I die my husband will probably remarry and I want the little gold-digger to go mad looking for the jewellery."

Three old men are talking about what their grandchildren might be saying about them in 50 years' time. "I would like my grandchildren to say, 'He was successful in business,'" says the first old man. "Fifty years from now," says the second, "I want them to say, 'He was a loyal family man.'" Turning to the third old man, the first gent asks, "So what do you want them to say about you in 50 years?" "Me?" says the third old man. "I want them all to say, 'My! He looks good for his age!'"

Part Two: Your Bedside Companion

Now why would a wrinkly need another bedside companion? You already have your hot water bottle, your bedside drink, the book that you read a page and a half of before nodding off, and all your other bedtime bits and bobs. Not to mention your long-suffering wrinkly other half.

Ah, but this is something else. This is something to tickle your fancy, tickle your ribs and let you luxuriate in the joys of being a wrinkly.

On the pages from here on you will find everything you need to know to help you sleep like a baby. A rather wrinkled baby, naturally, but where else would you find the meaning of wrinkly dreams, the definitive list of wrinkly bedtime essentials or even wrinkly prayers?

With the aid of this part of the book you can delve into the history of sleep with Rip Van Wrinkly, run through the town in your nightgown with Wee Willie Wrinkly, or sing yourself to sleep with 'Wrinkly The Best'.

Or perhaps you could rearrange your bedroom for the ultimate sleep experience with your very own version of Feng Shui, plan your superannuated bedtime snacks with your very own menu du wrinkly or compose letters of complaint to all those companies, organisations, and thoughtless individuals who have upset you today.

You could marvel at the achievements of other people well into wrinkliehood, find out surefire cures for wrinkly insomnia, and look out for the tell-tale signs of things that might go wrinkly in the night.

Your bed is your final sanctuary after another day out there in the frankly confusing modern world. The world of blogs and tweets, bogofs, Asbos, and reality TV; the world of speed dialling, speed dating, laptops, Blackberries, iPhones, iPods, YouTube, Facebook, self-service tills, online banking, downloading, upspeaking, and celebrities you've never heard of; the world of sub-prime, super-sizing and global warming, and all those other mind-boggling things that have been put on this Earth to bewilder and befuddle your grizzled grey matter in the Autumn of your years.

But help is at hand!

From this point in this book you will find positive thoughts for grumpy wrinklies (yes, there are some, believe it or not), tips on getting a good night's sleep (without the aid of half the contents of your medical cabinet), and even a few sartorial pointers as to what the fashion-conscious wrinkly should be considering for his or her bedtime attire (anything described in your favourite mail-order catalogue as 'skimpy' will not be appropriate).

There are a thousand and one books out there about the meaning of dreams, but how many are there which interpret the nocturnal nightmares and three o'clock fantasies of the not-so-young-at-heart?

None, until now.

The dreams of the everyday wrinkly cannot be compared to those of the thrusting young things of the Twitterati. No, wrinkly dreams are something else altogether and need to be considered and analysed as a separate phenomenon in their own right.

Bedtime for wrinkies should not merely be considered a time to sleep, perchance to dream. It should be an experience, a joy, something to be looked forward to. This means making sure you have all your bedtime essentials close to hand when you retire for the night.

This enlightening book will provide a handy list of bedside can't-do-withouts to help you to ease your way through the night. And when you wake up at 4 o'clock in a cold sweat worrying about this, that or the other, then reach for your handy bedside companion to comfort, console and cosset you through the wee small hours.

It'll be just like having a hot water bottle that never goes cold, a nightcap that never needs topping up, or a partner who stays mercifully quiet while you have a good old grumble.

This part of the book is there for every circumstance, whether you imagine you hear something going bump in the night, fancy that you can see a ghostly spectre hovering at the end of the bed or worry that you're warming your feet on the cat and have actually put the hot water bottle out the back door for the night by mistake.

In the long hours of sleeplessness you will find lists of inventions that wrinkies like your good self are waiting for, stories that you look forward to reading in the news when your morning paper plops onto the doormat, plus of course, the wrinkies' guide to insomnia.

This bit of the book is not called a companion for nothing. It's there for you when no one else is and even your partner is snoring like a baby. It's handy at bedtime with its wrinkly bedtime check list, and it's handy in the morning when you get up, look in the mirror and need to read the section on How to Look Good Wrinkly. It's also there in between with lists of ideas on how to while away the hours when you just can't quite manage to drop off.

In short, it's the answer to your wrinkly bedtime prayers. It also contains a bit of blue sky wrinkly thinking such as: what if the entire world were peopled exclusively by wrinklies? You may think that it is already the case if you live in a retirement home, a gated community or certain parts of the south coast, but, in the words of the song, what a wonderful world this would be…

Yes, whatever the eventuality, you will find the answer here in these pages. It will even answer questions you never thought, or never dared, to ask.

An oracle, a treasure trove, an almanac and a bedtime snack tray all rolled into one. How did you ever manage without one?

So, stop worrying, lie back and forget all about it.

Say it loud, you're Wrinkly and you're proud!

So You've Survived Another Day Then!

There's a certain point in your wrinkly life when you see each day not just as a new challenge, but also as a personal achievement in actually getting through it and living to tell the tale.

And frankly, when you look at all the things a wrinkly has to contend with it's up there with Sir Edmund Hillary climbing Everest, Buzz Aldrin going on his zero-gravity walkabout on the moon, or Eddie 'the Eagle' Edwards being taken even slightly seriously as a contender in the Winter Olympics.

Up to around middle age your body performs well enough for you not to even have to think about it most of the time.

You take it for granted that you can get from A to B without the aid of an oxygen mask, that you can eat a bag of nuts without worrying what it's going to do to your teeth, or to be able to read a road map without holding it at arm's length outside the car.

Eventually you reach what's known in medical circles as 'the Dalek years' when you can no longer get up the stairs.

Bit by wobbly bit the wheels start falling off your bus.

Little bits of sight, little bits of hearing, mobility and grey matter fall by the wayside until you're like one of those mechanical monkeys that didn't have the long-life batteries installed, and you come to a shuddering halt.

So, to actually survive another day with these handicaps is quite an achievement in itself.

Of course, all these things aren't irritants to wrinklies exclusively, but it is the wrinkly who suffers most because the wrinkly grew up in a different world. A world of good manners, customer service and politeness.

Youngsters don't know any better. They expect people to be walking around wired up like robots to phones, iPods, laptops, pedometers, and all the rest of it.

They expect to have to bleep their own groceries, and remember their chip and pin numbers. They expect to have their picture taken by CCTV every 20 seconds and to have their bags checked when they visit a museum, or to have to put their rubbish in 15 different coloured bins no more than a foot from their front gate.

They have never known roads without humps that almost jolt your teeth into your lap every time you go over them. In short, they don't know how much nicer it all used to be.

But the wrinkly does; and it is for this reason that every day survived in the mad, bad and dangerous modern world is a personal triumph, a great achievement, an accolade-worthy, spine-tingling, air-punching success in the teeth of the mightiest foes the modern world can throw at them.

Probably just how Sir Edmund Hillary felt in fact.

Well done, wrinklies everywhere!

Ten Things A Wrinkly Needs To Survive The Day

1. A sense of humour

If you can't take a joke you shouldn't have joined the wrinkly army. So it's probably best to join in with everyone else and start enjoying a good old chuckle at yourself. After all from now on you are going to have practical jokes played on you every single day by your own body.

2. A sense of the ridiculous

Come on! Surely you can't still believe that life is ever going to make much sense. That's as bad as presuming that the people around you are going to behave sensibly or that it will ever be possible to elect a government that looks like it knows what it's doing. Surely you're not clinging onto these naïve delusions! Not after you've lived this long! Besides doesn't the daily hunt for reading glasses that are dangling from a string round your neck require a certain attitude de l'absurd?

3. Someone else who can remember 'the good old days'

Charming as some young people can be, there's not much point in discussing the past with them. There's nothing quite like a stroll down memory lane with someone of your own vintage to the times when shop assistants called you 'sir' or 'madam', when policemen were reassuringly middle-aged, and when you could phone any company in the UK and complain in person to a real, live human being – ah, bliss!

4. Those little home comforts

Imagine your worst nightmares: a traffic jam with tattooed lorry drivers swearing and gesticulating at you just because you are blocking 'their' lane, or a clothes shop where all the assistants seem to be about 15 years old and the clothes seem to be made for Twiggy's thinner young sister. Now imagine your comfy armchair, TV remote at your fingertips, the kettle boiling gently in the background, a nice piece of cake, and your battered old slippers. No contest really is it?

5. A good strong drink

The good news is that it's far too late to do you much harm now. And besides, you're so shaky on your pins people probably think you're half cut most of the time anyway.

6. At least two pairs of glasses

There's your main pair, of course; then there are your reading glasses, your 'spare' pair, your 'old' sellotaped pair for emergencies, possibly a tinted pair that you bought in a moment of madness or got in a 'buy one, get one free' offer, your driving glasses...

7. Some proper food

We all like a curry now and again, but for goodness sake, is it necessary for every pub and restaurant the length and breadth of Britain to be serving foreign food all the time? What exactly is a fajita anyway?

8. A bit of peace and quiet

Why people can't get through the day without that 'boom boom boom' racket going on – or why TV shows can't go two seconds without background music, or radio traffic reports can't be delivered without some ghastly 'rock' music playing in the background – is anybody's guess. And don't even get me started on road drills, personal stereos, shop muzak, ice cream vans...

9. A nice cup of tea

It's what the British Empire was built on.

10. A good old moan

Forget all your yoga, feng shui, Pilates, Indian head massages, body waxing, colonic irrigation, tanning salons, hot tubs and all that other old nonsense. There's nothing like a good moan to cleanse the system and put life back in the old wrinkly.

Positive Thoughts For Grumpy Wrinklies At The End Of A Long Hard Day

- If nobody complained nothing would ever get any better
- I'm not as miserable as that old bloke/old biddy next door
- I'm past the stage where I need to worry about what I eat
- I don't understand modern art, and frankly I'm quite glad
- My life insurance seems to be getting so much cheaper these days
- I'm beyond fashion
- The best tunes are played on the oldest violins
- If experience comes with age I should probably be running the country by now
- I drink, therefore I am
- The older you get, the more memories you have – well, at least, if you can remember them
- Fewer and fewer people can remember all the things I did wrong when I was younger
- OK, I go to more funerals these days, but at least they're not my own

The Obstacles You've Overcome Today

The average wrinkly has seen a great many changes in his or her lifetime. When you're young you take these in your stride. As the advancing years take their toll however you begin to find these continual changes unnecessary, excessive and, not to put to fine a point on it, a bit of a pain in the wrinkled old posterior.

Anyone would think that there is someone out there whose entire existence is spent in dreaming up annoying little changes to hamper your smooth progress through the day.

Let's call him Mr Scroggins!

Shopping

Shopping used to be so simple: you went to a shop, told the shop assistant what you wanted, handed over the cash (and it usually was cash), and they handed you your purchase and your change.

Then Mr Scroggins decreed that, oh no, that's far too simple! From this day forth you will be issued with a trolley at the supermarket and have to collect all your groceries yourself!

Then, because supermarket trolleys were being commandeered by local yobbos and being used as impromptu art installations in local ponds and rivers, Mr Scroggins decided that from now on you would have to pay a deposit of £1 before you could get your trolley. So, on arrival at the supermarket you probably have to make sure you've got some small change (or, more likely, some quite large change) for the car park, and a pound coin for the trolley.

For a few years all went smoothly (apart from the odd dodgy trolley wheel) until Mr Scroggins decided that what we all needed was loyalty cards.

So, not only do you have to remember your car park money, and your pound coin for the trolley, you also have to remember your loyalty card.

This is bad enough for people with quite good memories, but no so brilliant for people whose memories are not 100% reliable. Oh, and nowadays of course, you have to remember your chip and pin as well.

Then, with his green hat on, Mr Scroggins announced that you should start remembering to bring your own shopping bags to the supermarket. Hot on the heels of this little gem was turning the customer into his or her own cashier! That's right, bleeping your own bleeping groceries through the bleeper if you please! And then afterwards faffing around with the payment machine instead of having the cashier do it for you!

And has anyone ever managed to use one of these self service machines without it eventually getting confused and summoning the assistant to sort out the 'unexpected item' it has detected in the bagging area?

If this self-service lark goes any further they may as well just issue you with your own set of keys to the supermarket so you can go and help yourself whenever you want to. You'll probably be expected to mop the floor once in a while as well and chase shoplifters.

Happy shopping!

Driving

Another of life's little pleasures made a misery by jobsworths of all descriptions.

Do you realize that at one time you didn't even have to pass a test to be able to drive a car?

They soon put a stop to that!

Then came traffic lights, breath tests, yellow lines, traffic wardens, bollards, width restrictors, chicanes, speed limits, sleeping policemen, photo ID, penalty points, motorway hazard warnings – or sometimes just little bits of useful advice such as 'tiredness kills', or 'don't forget to breathe' – controlled parking zones, wheel clamps, bus lanes, and a thousand and one other petty annoyances that should make you want to never set foot in a car again, but actually increase your resolve to beat the system.

If you tried to read all the signs they put at the side of the road, you'd have no time left to watch the cars around you. And of course to read the signs at your age you have to constantly swap between your distance and reading glasses. All this just to drive round the corner to the shops!

Apart from the official interference, you also have to put up with other road users who are rude, inconsiderate or just plain daft.

Whether it's Lycra louts weaving their bikes in and out of the traffic, lorry drivers changing lanes without signalling, taxis stopping abruptly, or buses forming an unpassable convoy it's enough to leave you blubbing like a baby.

And who was the genius who invented the traffic lights that stay on green for five minutes as you're driving towards them only to then change at the very last moment? Why not just have done with it and have the message 'Ha ha! Got you again, sucker!' flash up over the red light?

Then there are the squeegee merchants who give your windscreen the once over while you're stuck at the lights. For one scary moment, as you see a massive white splodge suddenly appear on your windscreen, you imagine you have been targeted by a passing albatross.

Then you have charity collectors dressed as giant rabbits or something rattling buckets of money at you while you sit fuming in an interminable line of traffic, or people who stuff leaflets under your windscreen wipers the moment you've parked.

We should look on the bright side however. Our roads should all be in perfect condition by now. After all they seem to keep digging them up every time you leave the house.

The simple act of climbing into your car is like walking through a wardrobe into a Narnia of nonsense, annoyance, irritation and hassle.

What on earth would Henry Ford have made of it all? He probably thought the car would mean freedom for all. He said a man would 'enjoy with his family the blessing of hours of pleasure in God's great open spaces.' He obviously hadn't envisaged the M25 on a bank holiday weekend.

Walking

You would have thought walking would have been one of those things that came as naturally as night following day.

Try walking down a busy town high street though and it's a different matter altogether. If you can manage to go more than about 20 yards (oh, all right, metres if you must) without being accosted by a market researcher, a charity collector or a *Big Issue* seller then you're lucky indeed.

How did companies manage before they hit upon the idea of market 'ree-search' as its proponents insist on pronouncing it?

When Mr Coca and Mr Cola started their famous brand, they probably just had a hunch people might like it.

Same for Mr Heinz. He probably didn't mess around with market ree-search, he just jumped in feet first and launched 57 varieties. Good on him.

Then there are the charity collectors. Once upon a time you'd just pop your threepenny bit into the tin, collect your little flag and wear it with pride for the rest of the day. Whatever happened to those little flags by the way? Apart from anything else it protected you from being accosted by another charity collector five yards up the road.

These days, they don't want your threepenny bits or the modern equivalents anymore. They want you to sign up to have considerable sums removed from your bank account by direct debit every month. It's not for nothing these people are called 'chuggers', or charity muggers.

And then you have to contend with your fellow pedestrians constantly getting in your way. They seem oblivious to everything and everyone around them. Clearly the reason they're on foot is because if they were ever allowed behind the wheel of a car, a mass pile up would result as soon as they pulled out from their driveway.

Apart from these hazards in human form, we wrinklies also have to contend with loose paving stones, little green men at crossings that turn red before you can get halfway across the road, dropped chewing gum, banana skins, cars driving by with some dreadful rap music blaring out of the open windows, scary-looking people with shaven heads, tattoos, hoodies, and bits of metal sticking out of their faces, and people constantly yabbering away on mobile phones.

Add to this those geriatrics speeding down the pavement in their motorised scooters re-enacting the chariot scenes in Ben Hur, and a myriad other nuisances and it's a wonder any of us wrinklies are still around to tell the tale.

Around the house

Did you know that most accidents occur in the home? Apparently, eleven people every year die putting their trousers on. We can probably assume that a similar number die in the process of taking them off.

Not only do we feel terrified whenever we leave the house, clearly we should be terrified when we get home again as well!

Yes, never mind the mean streets, just getting down to the breakfast table can be fraught with danger for wrinklies.

You know what it's like, the alarm clock blasting down your ear almost gives you a heart attack. You lie there for a few moments until the terrible realisation hits you: you're still alive so you have to get up after all.

You drag yourself out of bed but haven't yet put your glasses on so you step on the cat at the top of the stairs. If the physical obstruction itself isn't enough to send you flying down the apples and pears at breakneck speed then the sound of your moggie making an ear-splitting yowl will be enough to bring on a cardiac arrest.

When you get to the breakfast table sans specs you need to be doubly vigilant that you are pouring cereal into your breakfast bowl and not the cat's crunchy treats.

Also, without your bifocals it may be difficult to read the small print warning that your breakfast may contain nuts, or that it has more E numbers than a 1967 vintage car rally.

Then you have to check the salt content and the sugar content, and make sure you're not putting that wicked full cream milk on it – heavens no, you might actually enjoy it!

Yes, whatever you do, don't forget that anything that makes life worth living will probably kill you. So in order to keep healthy, avoid anything enjoyable. Then not only will you live longer, it will seem longer as well!

OK, so you survived breakfast, now you've got to deal with all those flipping nuisances who knock on the door uninvited. Double glazing salesmen, Jehovah's Witnesses (what happens when a double glazing salesman calls at a Jehovah's Witness's house or vice versa?), charity collectors, jumble collectors, postmen with parcels for next door, people selling fresh fish or manure or some such thing, meter readers, people who can't tell Acacia Avenue from Acacia Close, children playing 'knock down ginger', people who want to prune your trees or fix your roof or pave your drive.

You begin to see why the rich employ butlers.

If they're not ringing your doorbell, they're ringing your phone. Cold-calling salesmen, wrong numbers, people doing surveys, people who hang up as soon as you pick up the phone, and those really irritating people who demand 'who's that?' when they've phoned you!

Yet, despite what life in your own home throws at you, you've survived another day. OK, you've been driven to distraction at times, but as you lay down your head to sleep you can feel quietly proud of yourself.

Things Your Body Is Trying To Tell You

Aching joints

You're trying to do too much. Lifting a cup of tea and working the remote control with the same hand all the time is going to lead to all sorts of problems, so alternate hands or get someone else to change channels.

Feeling tired all the time

You've not been having your afternoon nap have you?

Why do you think they made daytime TV so boring?

Yes, precisely – so you will nod off and catch up on your beauty sleep.

You don't think you're actually supposed to watch Weakest Antique Celebrity Bargain Deal House Cash Garden Makeover Roadshow Revisited do you?

Ringing in your ears

You've gone to sleep with the phone under the pillow again.

Forgetfulness

You're now at the age where you don't much fancy remembering exactly how old you are so your memory is starting to block out these unwelcome bits of information.

Listlessness

Your blood sugar levels are low. You should be eating more biccies, drinking more hot sweet tea and having regular slabs of cake.

The weight gain may even help to smooth out some of those wrinkles!

Blurred vision

Having a bottle or two of what you fancy around the house, or maybe even your very own fully-functioning bar with optics, beer mats, ice buckets et al constantly on hand is, to say the least, a bit of a temptation.

If the blurred vision isn't a sign of deteriorating eyesight then it may just be the constant gush of alcohol in your front room. It is probably no coincidence that 'cataract' is also another word for 'waterfall'.

Loss of balance

See above.

Back pain

Starting your TV viewing at 9am and ending when you drop off in front of the late night film could be a contributory factor. Either that, or it's the constant offers of 'buy one, get one free' that entice you to lug home twice as much you actually want from the supermarket.

Wrinklies Vs The Awkward Squad

Who are the Awkward Squad? The rest of the non-wrinkly world basically.

You're probably old enough to remember going to the shops and being served by a shop assistant. Then the supermarkets took over and you had to go round getting your own groceries and packing them yourself.

How long will it be before they expect you to dig your own potatoes out of the ground and climb up a tree in the supermarket car park to get your own apples too? Progress? Schmogress!

Even when you park your car you need the brain of Stephen Hawking to remember where you left it in some vast multi-storey car park.

This is all very well for people in the prime of life with grey cells to spare, but we wrinklies need our little grey cells for more important things such as remembering when Corrie starts (unless it's been moved again because of the flipping football) or how to work the microwave.

Yes, the big wide world out there is anti-wrinkly. We have laws against ageism, so that yes, seventy-five year-olds can apply to be nightclub bouncers if they really want to, but it's the little things that make life difficult. For example, why do they print instructions so small? You get your medicine home from the chemist's and inside is a leaflet folded up half a dozen times and which opens out into something the size of a judo mat.

At the top, in large letters, it says 'read carefully before starting treatment.' The rest is printed in type that could fit the entire contents of the Bible onto the back of a postage stamp.

This is not helpful for the average wrinkly, especially if the medicine in question is the eye drops without which you can see virtually nothing anyway.

You used to have a phone in the hall and that was that. Now you have to be available '24/7' on your mobile. Some people are so attached to their mobiles that they have a thing permanently clipped to their ear, making them look like a tagged dairy cow.

Even if you don't want a mobile you're virtually forced to have one because everyone else expects you to have one. Then there's the inter-bloody-net.

Want to go somewhere? The cinema maybe, a tourist attraction? You have to book online. No more of that simply turning up and buying a ticket. You have to go through more menus than Egon Ronay before you can do anything these days. And people are always telling you to 'check out our website.' Why?

It's as though all organisations want to keep you at arm's length while they continue with the important business of relieving you of your hard-earned cash.

Even if you phone the police to complain about the little yobbos graffitiing your fence you get put through to a call centre miles away. Typical!

The Awkward Squad – watch out, they're everywhere!

More Positive Thoughts For Grumpy Wrinklies At The End Of A Long Hard Day

- I'll probably get an MBE for moaning
- When my children have children it will be a rather delicious sort of poetic justice
- It don't mean a thing if it ain't got that whinge
- If God had meant me to climb stairs he wouldn't have invented the stairlift would he now?
- I'll never have to join a social networking site on the internet
- I don't care what my ring-tone sounds like or whether it's cool
- In some cultures I would be venerated as an elder statesperson
- I enjoy telling people the same old stories over and over again because my memory's so bad that I'm always quite surprised to hear the ending even though it's me that's saying it
- For the first time in my life I am a bit of a character thanks to the combination of senility, out of date opinions and 15 different tablets my doctor has prescribed for me each day
- People are still making all the same stupid mistakes I've seen my entire life. Now I can just sit back and enjoy watching them do it
- Doddering is better than actually falling over
- I'm old enough to know better but forgetful enough not to care
- If I were a wine, I'd be called vintage

- If I were an outfit of clothes or a car I'd be called a classic
- If I were a building, I'd be listed and have a preservation order slapped on me
- If I were some kind of mechanical object the same age as myself, a group of enthusiasts would be giving up their time to restore me to perfect working order
- I have to be given free access to public transport now because of the danger I'd pose if I tried to drive myself anywhere
- If every wrinkle is a laughter line then I must have brought joy and happiness to the world!
- If life is a bowl of cherries who gets the pits?
- Age before beauty? Does that mean I've still got the beauty to come?
- I should soon be of an age when I'll be preserved for posterity by the National Trust
- I'm still 21 on the inside!

The W Factor

In our youth-obsessed culture it's easy to forget that wrinklies rule the world. OK, we've got a few fresh-faced British politicians strutting their stuff on the world stage, but look at the woman who has the power to tell them when they can form a government.

Not that we'd dream of branding the Queen a wrinkly, but she is in her 80s remember and has seen off a dozen or so of these thrusting young Prime Ministers over the years.

Have you ever seen a young Pope? Exactly.

And who's that bloke who always puts the fear of God into stock markets the world over? Alan Greenspan. He was still Chairman of the Federal Reserve when he was 80. And the other one, what's his name? Warren Buffett, aka the Sage of Omaha (1930 vintage). Even relative whippersnapper Bill Gates is the wrong side of 50.

Sexiest man in the world? Sean Connery (born 1930). Sexiest woman? Dame Helen Mirren (born 1945). Greatest artist who ever lived? Pablo Picasso – still dipping his brush well into his eighties.

You're getting the picture now? Yes, young people can do all that supermodel/footballer stuff, and good luck to them, but all the important stuff is in the hands of wrinklies.

Ever heard of the Illuminati? It's a shadowy secret society of people who really run the world. Forget all your presidents and prime ministers and all that; these are the people who are really pulling the strings.

And you know what? They're all wrinklies.

Yes, the hands of power have liver spots on them. The Wrinkleati, as we should probably be calling them, have the entire future of mankind in their rheumatic grip. And so it should be.

Modern societies have got it all frack to bunt. They've let these youngsters clamber to the top of the greasy pole while they're still wet behind the whatsits – if that's not mixing our metaphors too much.

The ancients got it right. Tribal elders. You never hear of any proper civilizations being built by tribal youngers do you? And there's a very good reason for that. Wrinklies are better at everything. All the important stuff anyway.

When some buffoon goes and bankrupts his bank by dodgy dealing it's always someone who looks like he hasn't started shaving yet.

When you go on a spiritual journey to seek some yogi living in a cave who is supposed to have the meaning of life at his fingertips you don't want to be greeted by a teenager in a pair of jeans and a Ché Guevara T-shirt do you?

When you finally receive your long-deserved knighthood or damehood you don't want to get it from some junior member of the royal family who's just got back from a night's clubbing, you want to be tapped on the shoulder by someone with more lines on their face than you've got. Dignity. Gravitas. Seniority. Stuff like that. In other words, The W factor.

How To Be A Wrinkly

People think it's easy, but it so isn't – as your younger family members might say.

They think it's simply a case of getting older. Just start young and let Mother Nature do the rest. No, being a wrinkly is as much a state of mind as it is the state of your body. For example:

Dress

The accent is on comfort. No more tottering around in high heels or showing off hectares of bare flesh. Especially if you're a bloke.

Interests

You've had all the excitement you need in your youth thank you very much, so now it's time for a bit of dull. You should now be getting up at around the same time as you used to go to bed as a teenager.

Friends

Friends are people you share interests with, but true friends are people who never remind you how old you are. Probably because they're the same age. It's a sort of unwritten wrinkly pact.

Outlook

When you grow out of the challenges of family, job, etc you have to invent new challenges. Being able to stay awake through an entire film at the cinema for example, or being able to crouch down to pick something up and then stand again without holding onto anything.

Role

As it is the teenager's role in life to be a flaming nuisance, so it is the wrinkly's role to disapprove. The wrinkly's disapproval does not of course have to confine itself to teenagers, it can include: declining standards of broadcasting, almost any change or modernisation, and the tops of medicine bottles being impossible to unscrew.

History

A wrinkly does not fully live in the present. Perhaps three quarters of a wrinkly's existence is spent in an imaginary golden past where young people were polite and respectful, where you didn't have to choose between 170 TV channels, when smoking wasn't harmful and beer was tuppence a pint.

The star of this vintage newsreel is our wrinkly, who as a younger person was a model child, a sensible teenager, and an industrious young adult who could work out the cost of 27 aniseed balls at a farthing a half dozen without the aid of a calculator.

Tastes

Music: not too loud; food: not too spicy; decor: not too bright (or dark); company: not too long.

Exercise

Exercise must be entirely incidental. None of this 'going to the gym' nonsense. Put biscuits on top shelf in kitchen for stretching exercises. Walking to kitchen for biscuits is about as cardio-vascular as you want to get at your time of life. Lifting your own body weight out of the armchair to walk to kitchen is weight training in anyone's book. Sorted.

If The World Was Entirely Peopled By Wrinklies...

What a wonderful world it would be! Yes, Sir Harry Secombe should have sung a song about it. If we ruled the world, every day would be pension payout day, every day would be free of horrible booming music, every day would be full of people being polite to one another. OK, it doesn't quite scan as well as Sir Harry's version, but the sentiment's there.

Too much in the world today is centred around young people and what they want. Yes, we were all young once (though we're pretty sure we didn't get up to half what the youngsters today get up to), but the fact is that the majority of the population are over 40. Over 80% of the cash in the UK is in the hands of the over 50s (where's my share then, we hear you ask).

So, if we just take this a smidgeon further to an imaginary world entirely peopled by wrinklies we'd have:

- No more burglary (the average age of a burglar is 16 to 24 – bring back national service at once!)
- No more boy racers on the roads.
- No more 24-hour drinking, late night partying, and general din.
- Lovely quiet pubs without big screens, thumping music and young bar staff who don't know a gin and it from an egg nog.
- Proper queues at bus stops instead of a brawling rabble of foul-mouthed schoolchildren.
- Decent radio stations with proper music.
- Nice TV shows without swearing.

- No more dreadful offspring of celebrities in the paper all the time or so-called supermodels, footballers, daft pop stars, etc.
- People talking properly instead of in this ghastly yoofspeak.
- Proper clothes shops with suits and dresses and other smart attire (jeans may be all right for doing the gardening in, but...)
- Restaurants where you can order a sandwich without having to choose between submarines, wraps, ciabattas, baguettes, and all those other bizarre concoctions.

Of course, there may be some drawbacks to a world entirely people by wrinklies. For instance:

- The pin-ups in the paper might not be quite so alluring.
- Would you want your laser eye surgery to be performed by someone whose hands were shaking?
- The Olympics could be a bit dull.
- The bin men would be even slower.
- Our overseas fighting forces would be like *Dad's Army* (without Pike).
- YMCA would have to change its name to the WMCA.
- The Rolling Stones would be considered a boy band again.
- Who would you get to sort out your computer problems?
- There'd be no more toyboys or dollybirds available when you won the lottery.
- Who could you blame the state of the world on?

Real-Life Wrinkly Achievements

Never, in the field of human achievement, has so much been done by so many wrinklies. Sorry, Winston, for paraphrasing one of your greatest speeches, but it neatly sums up what it is to be a wrinkly today.

Once upon a time, you were over the hill at 40, on the scrapheap at 50, and virtually invisible by the age of 60. Once you'd reached retirement you were expected to eke out your last days in an armchair on a diet of tea and biccies and listening to *Mrs Dale's Diary* on the wireless. Not now though – we've got daytime TV!

No, all joking aside, the modern wrinkly is a force of nature – hang gliding, windsurfing, marathon running, writing novels, climbing mountains, swimming with dolphins, learning Chinese, mastering the Internet... quite a busy weekend all in all.

And famous wrinklies don't retire or give up. They just carry on doing what they've always done, but slightly slower.

Rock & Roll

Take the Rolling Stones. Between 2007 and 2009 their Bigger Bang tour grossed over half a billion(!) dollars, the biggest in history. At the time the combined age of the band was around 4,002 (allegedly).

Sex Symbols

Even famous beauties just carry on regardless – Sophia Loren (born 1934) can still show these young bimbos a thing or two, and Joan Collins (one year older than La Loren), and Honor Blackman (another eight years older than Joanie, but who's counting?) can still set the pulses of men racing. Though for wrinkly men that can of course be rather dangerous.

And the women still seem to like the cut of the jib of blokes like Clint Eastwood and Sean Connery (both born 1930), Michael Caine (1933) and Robert Redford (1936).

The fact that they also have quite a lot of money of course is absolutely nothing to do with it, all you cynics out there!

Arts, Fashion, etc

Michaelangelo was still working on churches in his eighties, Pablo Picasso was still painting at the same age, Coco Chanel was still running her fashion empire as an octogenarian, and at around the same age Pablo Casales was playing cello concertos... It just goes to show, if you've got an 'o' at the end of your name it's a passport to longevity.

Mind you, if your name's George you're in with a chance too. Playwright George Bernard Shaw was still writing in his nineties, actor George Burns worked until he was almost a hundred, and King George II was still going into battle at the age of 60 which, taking age inflation into account, is probably about 102.

Inventions

In 1996 at the grand old age of 59 Trevor Baylis won the BBC Design Award for his invention, the clockwork radio. People thought it was a wind-up, and it was, but in rather a good way.

In 2010 'veteran' 'renegade' (fill in your own epithet) ex-MP Tony Benn revealed that at the age of 85 he had invented the 'seatcase', a sort of suitcase that incorporates a nifty chair for people who need to sit around en route. Was it a coincidence that it was announced in the middle of a BA strike? With wrinklies in mind though, how about a 'loocase'? Just a suggestion…

Showbiz

From Tony Benn to Tony Bennett (was he originally known as Anthony Wedgwood Bennett we wonder?) Of 1926 vintage the Bennster is still singing, painting, and variously not giving a fig about his age. Good on him.

Likewise Bruce Forsyth (born 1928) who, in his eighties, found a new generation of fans by hosting Have I Got News For You.

Just when you thought he'd be spending more time with his golf clubs. All together now: good gameshow, good gameshow!

Politics

Politics, which someone once described as 'showbiz for ugly people', has always had its fair share of wrinklies. Winston Churchill was 65 when he took over as war leader in 1940 and Menzies 'Ming' Campbell was around the same age when he took over the leadership of the Lib Dems in 2006.

Some members of the House of Lords are believed to be some of the oldest people ever to have lived, putting their remarkable longevity down to lots of champagne, foie gras, and plenty of sleep (on those nice comfy red benches).

Sport

True, there aren't many wrinklies in the England football squad, so caps off to Brazilian professional Pedro Ribeiro Lima who scored his first goal at the age of 58 for his club Perilima in 2007.

Tennis player Martina Navratilova won the US Open mixed doubles in 2006 just before her 50th birthday and she won the Ladies Invitation Doubles trophy with Jana Novotna (41) at Wimbledon in 2010.

George 'The Fossil' Blanda played professional American football until the grand old age of 49 in 1976. Somehow it's quite comforting to know that someone else was being called a fossil at that relatively young age.

And if you play golf you won't be considered a fossil for quite some time. The oldest person to play in the PGA championships was Jerry Barber who was just a couple of months short of his 78th birthday at the time.

Tough stuff

It's usually younger people who climb mountains, but who takes them up? That's right, bony old grey-haired Sherpas.

In 2004 George Burnstad (what is it with these Georges?) swam the channel at the age of 70.

There simply isn't room to list all wrinkly achievements, but rest assured, they've done the lot. Whether it was John Glenn going up in the space shuttle Discovery at the age of 70 or Kirk Douglas becoming a blogger at 92 or Methuselah simply making it to the age of 969, it's pretty impressive. A wrinkly thumbs up to all concerned!

The Seven Habits Of Highly Effective Wrinklies

You may have read those motivational books about how highly successful people live their lives, and the things they all have in common that have made them the successes they are. Hell, you may even be one of those highly successful people! What they don't tell you though is how to be a highly effective wrinkly.

This is a separate skill in its own right, and here for the first time anywhere, are the secrets that you must be aware of to be a highly successful wrinkly.

1) Embrace wrinklyhood. There's no point in going into denial. Say it loud, you're wrinkly and you're proud!

2) Try something new. There's nothing worse than being a wrinkly in a wrut, sorry, rut. Go clubbing, show those youngsters a thing or three!

3) Learn a martial art. Muggers see wrinklies as an easy target. Thanks to CCTV your heroics may even end up on YouTube.

4) Buy a walk-in bath before you actually need one, then it'll look like you don't really need one when you do need one (if you see what we mean).

5) Sell your house now and live in luxury in a rented room – why leave it to those ungrateful relatives/ government?

6) You know how there's always someone worse off than you? Well there's always someone older too. Be their young friend!

7) Compared with the future you, you're relatively young – hold on to that thought!

The Official Wrinkly-Way Code (aka The Wrinklies' Guide To The Road)

Wrinklies are to the road as confused tourists are to the Angel of the North – slightly bewildered, a bit dumbstruck, and wondering where the nearest toilet is.

We don't really do roads very well do we? Everyone whizzing around far too fast, too much noise and pollution and confusion reigning all around us.

For many wrinklies the road from A to B is more likely to feel like it could be the road from A to A&E. The quicker we're back in our comfy houses the better. Which is why we sometimes cut corners, ignore a few of the niceties of road usage and try to get the hell out of there. Who can blame us? It's dangerous out there.

So, here are a few Wrinkly rules of the road:

- All road users under the age of 50 are idiots – treat with extreme caution.
- When crossing the road the little green man always starts flashing when you're halfway across, so ignore him and step out whenever you feel like it.
- Road signs showing old people are ageist and should be pulled down or blown up by all self-respecting wrinklies.
- Speed limits are only guidelines so if you feel safer going at 15mph then ignore all those idiots behind you tooting their horns – even if you are in the fast lane of a motorway at the time.

- Motorised scooters are not cars so none of the rules of the road applies to them. Have fun!

- Road signs are all very well if you've got 20/20 vision, but unless they start printing the letters a bit bigger how the dickens are you supposed to follow them?

- Same with sat nav. However many times you say 'speak up a bit dear', she just carries on regardless. No wonder we get lost.

- Going slow is fine. Remember: overtakers end up at the undertakers.

- Remember the wrinklies' green cross code: stop, look, turn up your hearing aid.

- If you get too close behind a large vehicle he can't see you in his rear-view mirror, so that's the perfect time to give him a V sign for getting in your way.

- If you get stopped by a policeman asking for your licence, first feign deafness, then spend ten minutes rooting round in the glove box for your reading glasses, before beginning the search for your licence. Eventually he'll get fed up and leave you alone.

- When walking, always take a stick, then when you want to cross a busy road simply hold up your stick and dodder about on the kerb till someone stops. Why faff around looking for proper crossings?

- The Highway Code says the correct stopping distance when travelling at 30mph is 23 metres. However, as most wrinklies don't think in metres, let's call it about the length of the downstairs hall and halfway down the kitchen.

Songs For Wrinklies To Sing To Grandchildren At Bedtime

'The Wheels On My Chair Go Round and Round'

'Wee Willy Wrinkly'

'Necks, Shoulders, Knees and Toes (and Other Rheumatic Places)'

'Pop! Goes My Back Again'

'Zippered His Doo-dah (Poor Old Grandad)'

'If you're Happy and You Know It, You're Not a Wrinkly'

'There's a Hole In My Pension'

'Bah, Bah Humbug, Christmas Costs Too Much'

'One, Two Buckle My Shoe please, I can't Reach That Far Anymore'

'Skip To The Loo'

'There Was An Old Lady Who Swallowed a Fly (That'll Teach Her to Fall Asleep When She's Out For a Drive)'

'This Little Wrinkly Went to the Hypermarket (Where the gin's only a fiver a bottle)'

'Incy Wincy Pension'

'Wrinkly Had a Little Lamb (Have you seen the price of it these days?)'

Wrinklies With Attitude

When you reach wrinklyhood - and it comes to us all
– you may get a bit of flak. Particularly from younger
members of your family and friends. Jokes about bus
passes, forgetting things, walking sticks... All good
knockabout stuff.

But you also get a bit of aggro from shop assistants, bus
drivers, checkout staff and so on.

They seem to think that grey hair on your head equals
no grey matter inside it.

They seem to think that your inability to immediately
find your loyalty card on demand at the checkout is due to
the fact that your age is the equivalent of quite a good golf
score.

Patronising gits!

Even politeness grates. Do you want my seat on the
bus? What, because I wear bifocals? Do I want help
crossing the road? Listen, Sunny Jim, I've been crossing the
road by myself since you were in nappies. What do you
mean, 'exactly, grandad'?

Ooh, it makes your blood boil doesn't it? And no jokes
about blood pressure, if you don't mind.

The fact is, that when you become a wrinkly (and
when exactly is that, by the way? Are you totty one day,
and tottery the next?) you have to build up some defence
mechanisms, a bit of a tough skin.

In other words: a wrinkly with attitude. And here
are a few examples of how to handle yourself in certain
situations:

On the buses

When you try to swipe your library card instead of your freedom pass and the driver tuts while you look for your reading glasses just remind him how lucky he is that you're not still driving – then he'd really have something to complain about.

In the shops

When the checkout person asks 'do you want any help packing?', just say, 'I can pack my own groceries thank you very much, and I can pack a punch as well if necessary'. It usually works.

In the pub

When the barman makes a sarcastic comment about you making half a pint of bitter last three hours politely remind him that it takes roughly three hours to 'earn' enough state pension to pay for his overpriced beer in the first place.

At home

When someone comments about how unsocial it is for you to nod off during family gatherings ask them if it's any more social to be texting, listening to iPods, playing computer games or playing virtual tennis on an electronic gadget that sounds like a slightly unpleasant bodily function.

Kids

When kids ask you about the war, gently tell them you can just about remember the Falklands, and possibly Vietnam, and no, you have no direct experience of dinosaurs either.

Wrinklies Through History

As you lie down in your bed for the night, why not consider the achievements of the wrinkly ancestors who have gone before you!

The Missing Wrink

It has often been wondered how, in evolutionary terms, a happy-go-lucky 30-something can suddenly turn into a wrinkly. Scientists and anthropologists believe they have now found the answer. A skeleton has been found in the chalk hills of Dorset which appears to be the missing link between the two sub-species. The Missing Wrink, as he has been dubbed, has one over-developed hand, a result of writing letters of complaint to various tabloid newspapers and commercial organisations, one deaf ear that can be turned towards those he does not wish to listen to, and a comfy cardigan.

The Cave-Dwelling Wrinkly

He hunted for bargains with his club card and he invented the wheel... Well, the wheelchair. He was also the first person in human history not only to discover fire but also to complain about a winter fuel payment from the government to help keep it going during the cold months.

Wromulus and Wrinkmus

According to legend, the twins who originally founded the city of Rome. Wromulus was however left to do most of the heavy lifting involved in establishing the city because his ageing brother Wrinkmus was suffering from a bit of gyp in his back at the time.

Wrinklius Caesar

Under his rule, the Roman Empire fell. The Roman Empire then had to phone a special emergency number and wait until someone came to help get it back up again.

Attila the Wrinkly

Rampaged across Europe in the fifth century AD causing death, destruction, and rather a lot of complaints about people parking outside his house. He famously went up and across the Alps sitting on the back of an elephant or, as he described it, on an early design of stairlift.

Wrinkly the Conquerer

William's lesser-known brother who got lost on the way to Hastings and ended up a bit further over to the west. Here his wrinkly invasion force took over several south coast seaside resorts and made damn sure there were plenty of nice tea rooms, conveniently placed benches and disabled parking bays.

Wrinkhard The Lionheart

Early recipient of transplant surgery.

King Wrinkly VIII

Had six wives whom he treated appallingly badly. None bore him a son and heir so he bored them to death with tales of his wartime exploits, his love of single gauge steam railway trains and a non-stop diatribe against the failings of the local council's rubbish collection 'service'.

William Wrinkspeare

Very nearly the most famous writer in the English language. Unfortunately he never got round to composing a single play or line of poetry because he spent his entire career composing letters of complaint to the local paper.

Napoleon Wrinklyparte

A man who moaned so much about the way things were being run by the local council that he somehow ended up as Emperor with much of Europe under his command. He then attempted to invade Russia but gave up when he found there was no disabled access to the country. He was ultimately defeated at Waterloo, the name of which put him at a severe disadvantage. At the height of battle he kept feeling like he needed to find the nearest gents. He spent the last few years of his life stuck on the remote South Atlantic island of Saint Helena. Historians now believe this was as a result of buying an ill-advised timeshare property.

Ludwig Van Wrinkhoven

Wrote nine symphonies and every movement of every single one of them is slow. When people suggested that his music would be more popular if he occasionally speeded it up a bit, he always gave the same response: 'Pardon?'

Albert Wrinklestein

Formulated the Theory of Relatives: the more they visit, the more they are hoping to be left lots of money in your will.

Gypsy Rose Wrinklee

Ageing striptease artist and burlesque dancer who appalled audiences worldwide with her act which left nothing to the imagination, though many wished it had. 'Get 'em off!' her audience would cry at the start of her act before changing their tune abruptly a few seconds later and yelling in horror, 'Put 'em back on again!'

Wrinkly Churchill

No relation to our great wartime leader of course, but a stout defender of the rights of wrinklies everywhere with his stirring speeches such as 'We shall fight on the beaches, on the landing, down in the front room, in the fields and on the streets, and if the buggers try to put us into old people's homes we shall never surrender.'

Tim Berners-Wrinklee

Invented Ye Olde Worlde Wide Web to keep wrinklies in touch with one another worldwide. Some of the innovations wrinklies have him to thank for include: Social nitpicking sites, online carbon-dating (to determine the real ages of prospective computer dates), and an online marketplace for selling and swapping ill-fitting false teeth – ebaygum. He invented several other things as well but unfortunately although he had invented them they turned out to be a bit too complicated for him to be able to get them to work, and so they were lost to the world.

Things That Go Wrinkly In The Night

Are you suffering from things going wrinkly in the night? Your curtains, sheets, pyjamas or nightie? Or is it the contents of your pyjamas or nightie that are revealed in the light of dawn as slightly more wrinkly than you remembered them looking yesterday?

How can this be?

We are regularly advised that in order to keep looking young and beautiful, we should try and get as much sleep as possible. But, like all advice that we are ever given by other people, this is clearly complete rubbish!

Young people never sleep. They're up every night drinking, taking drugs, having sex, dancing until dawn and chronicling the whole hideous experience on Facebook. And yet despite their complete lack of sleep, young people still look young.

We wrinklies however usually spend most of the day looking forward to toddling off to bed the moment that the clock strikes ten in the evening. Often we look forward to this highlight of the day from the moment we get out of bed in the morning. And yet despite spending our entire lives either asleep or looking forward to getting back to sleep, we still look old.

If only nature was a bit fairer. If only we really did look and feel younger as a direct result of the total amount of sleep we had had during our lives.

That way the older you became the more young and beautiful you would begin to look.

As a result of the cumulative amount of sleep experienced over a lifetime, a 60-year-old would end up looking youthful and gorgeous. Twenty-year-olds on the other hand who had not yet lived long enough to experience sufficient amounts of beauty enhancing sleep would look haggard and dreadful.

Old people would look young while young people would look old!

Surely that's got to be a fairer system!

Of course there is an obvious reason why older people are wrinklier than the young. The old have all clearly made the mistake of having once been young.

The wrinkles and jutting mounds of sagging flesh that have come to the surface in later life are in fact the remnants and reminders of parties and drinking sessions from years before.

The young may chronicle all their exciting experiences on Facebook but really there's no need. In a few years they'll have an abundance of unsightly protuberances and lines etched into their ageing flesh to remind them instead.

Each sign of age is a little message posted from the past!

The dark lines under your eyes are like a Twitter message from your younger self telling you what a great time they were having at an all night rave. The lines on your face are like a text you posted a few decades earlier to tell your ageing self what fun you were having at a 24-hour orgy.

OK, in retrospect it might have been better if you'd just kept a diary instead!

Wrinklies' Bedtime Routine

To keep healthy it is important for us wrinklies to follow a very strict bedtime routine every night (n.b. when we say strict, we don't mean getting someone dressed as an old fashioned school teacher to bend you over the bedstead and cane you within an inch of your life).

Nevertheless following a regular routine as you prepare yourself for bed will help you relax, unwind and enjoy the full eight, nine, ten or twenty three-and-a-half hours sleep your body now requires each night.

Firstly remember that eating late in the evening will give your stomach insufficient time to digest your food. Disturbed slumber will then result either from indigestion, burping in your sleep or the duvet being repeatedly blown off by the noxious guffs exuding from the bottom of your pyjamas.

Instead it is recommended that you eat your main meal as early as possible in the evening – preferably the night before. You should also avoid late night barbecues – particularly after you've got into bed.

Next avoid any activities during the evening that are likely to over exert your system and cause your heart rate to dramatically increase. For most people these side effects might result from participation in extreme sports, rampant sex and/or drug taking.

We wrinklies however are able to save time, effort and money because we are able to dramatically increase our heart rates just by walking up the stairs a bit too quickly.

Of course it can be difficult to avoid going up the stairs at bedtime (unless you live in a bungalow or have really given up on life). This is why wrinklies often end up having a stairlift installed in their homes. Thanks to stairlift technology, wrinklies can get up the stairs to bed without setting their pulses racing so fast that they are left unable to sleep for the rest of the night.

Don't forget also that a closed door will prevent a fire from spreading during the night. So if you find a fire blazing in your living room just before you go to bed, pick it up using a large shovel and put it in the cupboard under the stairs until morning when you can take it out and put it back in the living room again. So in conclusion:

- You must go to bed at exactly the same time every single night.
- You must follow the same strict routine as you prepare to sleep.
- You must secure your home against night-time intruders, burglars, murderers, arsonists and hoodlums.
- You must prepare for bed in exactly the same way every single night.
- You must then lie in bed in the same position as the night before whether you really want to or not while putting all thoughts of intruders, burglars, murderers, arsonists and hoodlums out of your mind.

Once you have done all these things it will be possible for you to finally relax and enjoy a good night's sleep!

Wrinkly Thoughts About Health, Diet And Exercise

- Being healthy is of course the slowest rate at which it is possible to die. And if you eat and drink sensibly as well, this will make the time pass even more slowly.

- Stay healthy as you get older but try not to look too good because otherwise younger people will never do anything to help you.

- If you manage to maintain a perfect physique into later life, after a certain age others will no longer regard you as being healthy but a freak!

- When people tell you 'you're extraordinary for your age', this is usually only a good thing if you are under 20 or over 70 years old.

- You wouldn't think that a small piece of cake could possibly hurt you – the name 'Death By Chocolate Cake' is a bit of a hint though.

- Don't forget that no pain equals no gain. So that's a handy way to remember how to avoid pain.

- Healthy versus wealthy: if you are healthy it doesn't matter if you aren't wealthy (because if you're healthy you can rob other people and run away in time).

- You can always say that you are allergic to health food.

- Chew each mouthful at least 20 times. After one mushroom you'll be exhausted.

- Look on the bright side! As long as you've got your health, you should have no trouble getting to the off licence and back.

The Wrinkly Guide To Staying Healthy

Get plenty of exercise:

One way for a wrinkly to do this is to spend years eating as much as possible thus becoming grossly overweight. The overweight wrinkly will then have to expend considerable effort and thus get plenty of exercise just by lugging his or her own enormous body around the place!

Take up jogging:

It would be unwise for a wrinkly to try jogging too far at first. Start off with quite short distances, for example to the biscuit tin and back. Remember, if you try jogging to the kettle and back you will probably spill your cup of tea on the return journey.

Eat your five-a-day:

There are lots of ways for wrinklies to get their five portions of fruit and veg a day: Jaffa Cakes, tomato sauce, cheese and onion crisps, strawberry jelly or, to get all five daily portions of fruit in one handy pack, a packet of Fruit Pastilles! But yes – that does mean you're not allowed to leave the green ones!

Give up drinking and smoking:

Of course if you don't drink and smoke to begin with this will mean you have to start by taking them both up.

Get one of those computer game/workout things:

With a Wii console or similar, it is possible for the average wrinkly to work up a considerable sweat. And that's just from trying to wire the thing up and getting it to work.

What Your Night Drink Says About You

Hot chocolate	Choco-holic
Glass of scotch	Alcoholic
Cup of tea	Tea-aholic
Horlicks	Horlic-aholic
Ovaltine	You are likely to burst into the Ovaltiney song at any moment. 'We are the Ovaltineys, Little girls and boys...' See! You've started already!
Hot milk	You've forgotten to buy any cocoa powder, haven't you?
Hot water	Not only did you forget the cocoa powder, you forgot the milk and sugar as well – or did you get a bit mixed up and pour a mug full of hot chocolate into your hot water bottle by mistake?
Cold water	Bloody hell! The electricity's gone off now!
Triple espresso	If you can get to sleep after drinking this, you really must be knackered
Several large scotches	You have such an excess of energy, you need to be completely sedated last thing every night in order to stop you careering around the place. So it's either this or your spouse has to shoot you with a tranquiliser dart
Can of energy drink	Unless you consume 800x your daily recommended allowance of caffeine, you can't muster the energy to get up the stairs to bed

The Wrinkly's Guide To Fad Diets

The F Plan Diet:

You eat a bit of roughage with everything. So it's obvious what the 'f' stands for - the Fart Yourself Thinner Diet!

The Raw Food Diet:

You can eat whatever you like as long as it's raw! This will definitely help you lose weight. Eating a single raw potato for example will take up much of the day while requiring a considerable amount of energy in the process. You will therefore not only lose weight but gain a highly developed jaw muscle. You can then move on to try and eat a raw cow.

The Cabbage Diet

You eat absolutely nothing except cabbage. Not only will you lose weight, you will also lose the will to live.

The Grapefruit Diet:

You eat endless amounts of grapefruit. This helps you lose weight because you are constantly being blinded by the grapefruit juice squirting up into your face when you plunge your spoon in. As a result of this temporary loss of sight you will be incapable of finding the biscuit or cake tins.

The Atkins Diet

You are only allowed to eat people with the surname Atkins. Also known as the Cannibal Conviction Solitary Confinement Prison Diet.

Ways To Avoid Going Quite So Wrinkly In The Night

A guide to natural remedies that can be applied over night to help reduce fine lines (or alternatively to fill in great canyon-like wrinkles like yours).

Cucumber over the eyes

These are traditionally used to hydrate the area around the eyes and to prevent dark oily patches forming. Another way to stop dark oily patches forming is to avoid spending each night lying in your driveway beneath the back axle of your car.

If you choose to place cucumbers over your eyes, remember to use sliced cucumbers. Don't lie there with two full grown vegetables on your face. If you do it will be extremely difficult to lie still for the entire night balancing a cucumber sticking up from each eye socket.

The danger will also exist that if you sit up suddenly during the night, you may catch a cucumber on your bedstead and put your eye out. This would prove that cucumbers aren't so good for your eyes after all.

Also the sight of you lying with two full grown cucumbers sticking up from your eyes may give your spouse a nasty turn if they wake up during the night. Seeing you in the half light, your spouse will be sure to assume that some horned figure from hell is occupying the other side of the bed rather than you squinting like mad to hold a pair of 12 inch cucumbers in your eye sockets.

So instead carefully place a slice of cucumber over each eye. Dangers may still exist however. In particular you may wake up, open your eyes, see nothing but a pair of enormous cucumbers and shriek in terror believing that you have fallen into a enormous vat of salad during the night.

Once morning comes don't forget to remove the cucumbers before you get up or they will be perceived by others as a new pair of humorous novelty spectacles and by yourself as an alarmingly sudden development of light green cataracts.

Tea bags over the eyes

You can try putting tea bags over your eyes instead of cucumbers. This may however cause a slight burning sensation particularly when you pour some hot water from the kettle over them to brew up.

Carrots up the nose

This ploy, similar to that of cucumbers over the eyes, is used by wrinklies who wish to avoid bags and oily circles forming under their nostrils.

Be careful however. If you sneeze during the night a carrot may be fired from one or other of your nostrils and spear your cat like an enormous orange dart.

Elastic bands

Wrinkles form as the result of a loss of elasticity. Sadly nature does not provide replacement elasticity. However your local stationery shop does! Why not try stretching a few elastic bands round your face to pull out the wrinkles over night? Or, alternatively, large strategically placed paper clips may do the trick.

Egg yolk over the skin

Rubbing egg yolk, lemon juice and olive oil into your face may help reduce dry rough skin.

Plus if you go to sleep with this mixture splattered over yourself and wake up with the sun shining directly onto your bed in the morning, you may find a sizzling pancake cooking on your face ready for your breakfast.

Pineapples on the wrinkles

Applying slices of pineapple to your face will help reduce visible wrinkles. It is however quite difficult to keep it balanced there and when you walk down the street you may attract comments along the lines of: 'Why is that wrinkly old person wandering around with bits of pineapple stuck all over their mush?'

For really deep wrinkles, hollow out an entire pineapple. Then stick your head inside it. Remember to make a couple of eye holes first.

Lemon juice in the wrinkles

Rubbing squeezed lemon juice into your wrinkles may make them magically disappear over night. Or alternatively it might make them extremely sore. Then when you wake up the next morning your wrinkles will not only still be there but they will be standing out better than ever because they are glowing bright red!

And if you do fill any particularly deep wrinkles with lemon juice don't forget there is then the possibility that next time you grin or grimace, this will cause citric acid to squirt sideways from your face thereby blinding those standing around you.

Yoghurt

Plain yoghurt smeared over the face is used in many exotic beauty regimes. Just slap a large tub of yoghurt all over your wrinkly chops until you look as though a passing emu has shed its load on you during the night.

If you don't have a plain yoghurt then why not use something else from the fridge? A 'fruit corner' yoghurt for example has the advantage that you can put the yoghurt over your cheeks and the fruit over your eyes.

This mix should then be left overnight after which skinflint wrinklies can try and scoop it back into the plastic pot again ready for that night's dinner.

Eating the mixture after it has been sitting on your face for an entire night is obviously rather disgusting and unhygienic. So try to fix it so your spouse ends up getting it for their pudding instead of you.

Two beef burgers, a portion of chips and a couple of doughnuts on the face

Not so much a beauty treatment as a late night snack. The food is laid out on the face (in the absence of a plate) making it both easier to locate in the darkness and easier to consume without having to completely wake up.

This treatment may help the skin on your face to tingle and glow but this will only occur if the food is applied to the cheeks straight from a hot frying pan.

A Book At Bedtime

In theory we wrinklies can read a book at any time, especially if we're retired wrinklies, but the bedtime book is something else entirely. It's a sleeping tablet in book form. Just read a few pages and zzzzz – you're fast asleep.

This probably means that to be truly effective as an aid to sleep your bedtime reading matter should be as boring as possible. *The Political Diaries of Geoffrey Howe* perhaps, cooking for vegans with nut allergies maybe, the history of cross-stitch...

But sometimes you don't want to nod off after just a couple of pages, especially if you've gone to bed at a wrinkly-friendly 9.30 pm.

You want to plump up your pillows, get the hot water bottle into exactly the right position to warm your wrinkled toes, have your bedtime drink placed within the required optimum range of your outstretched arm and get a couple of chapters under your pyjama rope belt before you enter the land of nod.

On the other hand you don't want to be over-stimulated by hair-bristling horror stories, steamy sex novels or by the spine-tingling and frankly shocking fine print of your pension plan.

Like most things in life, it's a fine balance.

Yes, the wrinkly book at bedtime is ideally the literary equivalent of a mild curry. Something that will tickle the taste buds rather than throttle them to death and something that will satisfy the appetite without laying on the stomach like a house-trained brontosaurus and leave one wanting more, but not just yet, thank you very much.

In fact, there may be publishers out there who could see this as a possible gap in the market. Like everything else these days, books are all too often aimed at youngsters – i.e. people under 50.

Bookshops always seem to be selling biographies of young slips of things who've been on some dreadful reality TV show and then feel compelled to write their 'entire' life story at the age of 19, or chick lit or lad lit or some other daft thing aimed at people who probably can't even read anyway.

No, what we need is old git lit. We don't want to read about 20-somethings called Lucy and Katy and Jake and Tarquin who all work in advertising agencies and drink skinny lattes all day. We want to read about people of our own age, people who've lived a bit, possibly who've died a bit too, people whose idea of a bit of excitement is finding a new crisp flavour at the supermarket.

We don't want doorstop blockbusters about crazed serial killers, we want nice autobiographies by celebrity gardeners. We don't want sex and shopping novels, just the shopping is fine, if it's all the same to you.

There's a whole, vast, untapped market out there for some enterprising publisher. Imagine the titles: *The Girl With the Dralon Tattoo*, *The Bus Traveller's Daughter*, *Captain Corelli's Ear Trumpet...*

Goodnight wrinklies everywhere! (Hope that exclamation mark didn't wake you up).

Rip Van Wrinkly And Other Role Models

Rip Van Wrinkly

The world of fiction is full of role models for wrinklies.
Take Rip Van Wrinkly for example, Rip Van Winkle's lesser-known brother. He slept for a hundred years, then woke up and sued the local health authority who prescribed his super strength sleeping tablets. That'll teach 'em.

Chubb-locked Homes

The brilliant detective who never had a single case to solve because he joined his Neighbourhood Watch team and encouraged everyone in the locality to have locks on every door, window, skylight and catflap to keep the thieving beggars out.

Pilly Bunter

What's the use of free medical care if you don't use it? You've paid in all your life, so now it's time to take something out. You can get pills to help you sleep, pills to wake you up, pills to help you eat, pills to keep off the weight, pills to make you go to the loo… well, you get the picture.

Long Johns Silver

At a certain time in our life we don't want to be wearing skimpy underwear. Too skimpy, and it might even get lost under the rolls of fat and defeat the object of wearing any at all. No, on reaching wrinkliehood the only option is several yards of cotton that will cover everything, dangling or otherwise. And if you happen to be a limb-deficient pirate, the all-covering underwear will also disguise the fact that you have a wooden leg.

Harry Chamberpotter

Who wants to go stumbling around in the dark at the dead of night? You wake up at three o'clock sweating from a terrible dream about being stuck in a lift with an earnest young politician and you have an uncontrollable desire to rush to the toilet. Rushing, these days, is not in your repertoire so a quick feel under the bed and out comes the old faithful 'gazunder'. Perfect.

Robinson Creosote

Not for him the idling around at weekends so beloved by the younger generation. No, there are a thousand and one little jobs around the house that can be found if you put your mind to it. And if you ever think you've run out of little jobs you can always creosote the fence, or the shed, or anything else in the garden made of wood. The Devil makes work for idle hands and all that. This person is not to be confused with Robinson Crusoe who got somebody else to do all his little jobs for him.

Peter Pan-acea

Aches and pains to the wrinkly are what cats and dogs are to the vet – they come with the territory. The big mistake most wrinklies make is to start to enlarge their medical cabinet to a size that Damien Hirst might consider to be a suitable installation for the Tate Modern's Turbine Hall. No! Far better to take a panacea, such as a nice box of chocolates, a drink or two, or even a crafty fag.

The Da Wrinkly Code

The Da Wrinkly Code is a little-known series of clues woven through literature to let wrinklies know the meaning of life.

In 2004 an author by the name of Dan Brown published a book entitled *The Da Vinci Code* which has no connection whatsoever with the Da Wrinkly Code.

One of the classic books to contain clues for the Da Wrinkly Code is *Alice in Wonderland*. Many wrinklies have a bottle of sherry on the sideboard which has the invisible words 'drink me' written on it.

When a wrinkly gives up work (or vice versa) and has a bit more time on his or her hands, the words 'drink me' seem to take on an almost supernatural luminosity.

Whereas at one time the cork would not be popped until the sun was over the yard arm, or at least until the six o'clock news had started, in the timeless half-life of retirement one hour merges into another so that before you know where you are you're having a quiet tipple with your cornflakes.

Alice in Wonderland also contains a metaphor for ageing: that of the shrinking person. As the years roll by wrinklies find that not only are policemen getting younger, they're getting taller as well! This can be simultaneously comforting and rather disconcerting.

In Charles Dickens' *A Christmas Carol* the wrinkly will find the ultimate role model in Ebeneezer Scrooge. Not for him the shallow pursuit of pleasure, the sunny nature, the modern obsession with dishing out money to layabouts, ne'er-do-wells, and charities for people who should lift themselves up by their own bootstraps instead of sponging off others. He has the old fashioned virtues of thrift, hard work and clipping kids round the ear if they get out of hand.

But some clues in the Da Wrinkly Code are harder to spot than others. Have you ever been on a stairlift? Close your eyes and you may experience a sensation similar to that of flying. Just like Peter Pan!

Neverland is of course retirement, Captain Hook is the Chancellor of the Exchequer, wickedly keeping your pension low, Tinkerbell is the personification of wrinkly charities such as Help The Aged, and the Lost Boys are those wrinklies who end up on park benches drinking strong cider out of cans. It all makes perfect sense now doesn't it?

Look through your bookshelves and find your own clues in the Da Wrinkly Code. Once you start you'll be amazed at how many there are.

1984: Winston Smith battling against an overweening state which has CCTV cameras everywhere and ministries that do the opposite of what they're supposed to; *Brave New World* where everyone's obsessed by sex and you're over the hill at 60; Kafka's *Metamorphosis* where you wake up and find you've turned into a giant insect – yet another wrinkly metaphor!

Yes, once you start to look, you'll find clues in the Da Wrinkly Code everywhere from Noddy to Godot.

Books To Read At Bedtime

Don Quixote – Miguel de Cervantes

An inspirational book for wrinklies everywhere. Retired 50-something wrinkly decides life is a bit dull and goes off in search of adventure. Sensibly, Don Quixote doesn't go off to fight dragons or anything dangerous like that; he has a pop at something not likely to fight back – windmills.

Pride And Prejudice – Jane Austen

The marvellous thing about reading the classics is that you've seen so many films, TV adaptations, pop-up books and so on that you can skip the boring bits and still know what's going on. P&P also won't be so exciting that you can't nod off eventually.

Ulysses – James Joyce

A 'stream of consciousness' book that with a bit of luck will result in a stream of unconsciousness from you if you're finding it hard to get off to sleep. One sentence alone is over 4,000 words long, so who knows, you may not even get to the end of that before drifting away.

Dr Zhivago – Boris Pasternak

Simply imagine that he's your doctor, and you're running through your usual little list of ailments. You'll be sleeping like a baby in no time. It also has the advantage of not boring your usual doctor to death with all this stuff too.

The Picture of Dorian Gray – Oscar Wilde

The concept of a picture in your attic that ages while you stay eternally young should be of great appeal to wrinklies everywhere.

Books Not To Read At Bedtime

War of the Worlds – H.G. Wells

Surburbia should be a place of sanctuary for wrinklies. It's bad enough when you get hoodies invading your peace and quiet, but Martians in Woking? It's hardly conducive to a good night's kip is it?

Moby Dick – Herman Melville

After reading about someone being attacked by a whale it would be terrifying to find in the night that your amply-proportioned other half has rolled over you and made you feel as if you were reliving the fate of Captain Ahab.

Brighton Rock – Graham Greene

Although you may once have associated Brighton with Mods and Rockers having punch-ups on the beach, it may now well be the sort of place you'd go to for a nice day out. You may not sleep so easy in your bed though after reading about Graham Greene's low-life gangsters going round murdering people.

Les Miserables – Victor Hugo

Reading the book shouldn't be a problem, but if you've seen the musical and it keeps prompting you to break into song every few pages then you won't be popular with your spouse, your neighbours, or any music lovers who are within earshot.

The Gruffalo – Julia Donaldson & Axel Scheffler

How old are you exactly?

Opening Lines Of Novels That Wrinklies Can Identify With

A Tale of Two Cities – Charles Dickens

It was the best of times, it was the worst of times – my daughter-in-law baked us some lovely scones but I can't find me teeth.

Pride And Prejudice – Jane Austen

It is a truth universally acknowledged, that a single man in possession of a good fortune, must be in want of a wife and that if he finds one he won't be in possession of a good fortune for very much longer.

Lolita – Vladimir Nabakov

Lolita, light of my life, fire of my loins, get your clothes back on and pretend to carry on cleaning.

Mrs Dalloway – Virginia Woolf

Mrs. Dalloway said she would buy the flowers herself. Well, it's her funeral so let the silly old cow do what she wants.

1984 – George Orwell

It was a bright cold day in April, and the clocks were striking thirteen – so all in all a typical morning waiting for a train in our wonderful country!

A Portrait of the Artist as a Young Man – James Joyce

Once upon a time and a very good time it was there was a moocow coming down along the road and this moocow that was coming down along the road wasn't stopped outside Waitrose for five minutes before a traffic warden slapped a ticket on its backside.

Fahrenheit 451 – Ray Bradbury

It was a pleasure to burn down the town hall when they put my council tax up again.

Rebecca – Daphne Du Maurier

Last night I dreamt I went to Manderley again, but of course this morning it was just the bottle bank and the library as usual.

To Kill a Mockingbird – Harper lee

When he was nearly 13 my brother Jem got his army badly broken at the elbow. And even now, at the age of 65 he still says it was me who pushed him out of that tree.

The Old Man and the Sea – Ernest Hemingway

He was an old man who fished alone in a skiff in the Gulf Stream as it was actually cheaper than trying to buy fresh fish in his local supermarket.

Anna Karenina – Leo Tolstoy

Happy families are all alike – teach your grandchildren to play a decent game like Bridge or Gin Rummy.

I, Claudius – Robert Graves

I, Tiberius Claudius Drusus Nero Germanicus This-that-and-the-other (for I shall not trouble you yet with all my titles) do solemnly declare that I shall tell the truth, the whole truth and nothing but the truth regarding the non-payment of my council tax due to the inadequate provision of disabled parking bays in the borough…

The Hobbit – J.R.R. Tolkein

In a hole in the ground there lived a Hobbit. Probably had to sell his house in order to fund nursing care, I shouldn't wonder.

Bedtime Stories For Wrinklies To Tell Their Grandchildren

Goldilocks and the Three Wrinklies

Once upon a time three wrinklies lived in a little wrinkly house in the woods. Mummy wrinkly, Daddy wrinkly, and a wrinkly little baby.

One day, a young girl named Goldilocks was walking through the woods when she stopped at the house. She saw on the door a picture of a ferocious looking Alsatian dog with the words 'I live here' on it. She saw the Neighbourhood Watch sticker on the window and the sign reading 'all visitors must show their ID'. She then noticed the burglar alarm on the wall and the sign reading 'no hawkers, circulars or beggars'. She then noticed a wrinkly face peeking out from behind the net curtains and saying 'clear off!' Goldilocks took the hint and decided to go to the three bears' house instead.

Little Red Riding Hoodie

Little Red Riding Hoodie was bunking off school one day, and she decided to go and visit her grandmother to see if she could blag some money for cigarettes and lip gloss.

When she got to her grandmother's house the door was open. 'Typical!' she thought to herself, 'Someone's already turned the place over and nicked Gran's money so I'll have to go shoplifting instead.'

But out of curiosity she looked inside, and there was a little hunched up figure sitting in her grandmother's armchair. But there was something odd about her.

'Blimey, Gran!' exclaimed little Red Riding Hoodie. 'What's occurring with your eyes? They're like, ginormous! And look at your teef - they're well out of order!'

It was then that Little Red Riding Hoodie remembered her grandmother didn't have any teeth, and she whisked off the shawl from her head.

'April fool!' shouted Gran from behind her. The daft old cow had dressed the dog up in her clothes.

The Three Wrinkly Goats Gruff

Once upon a time there lived three wrinkly goats gruff. One day the three wrinkly goats wanted to cross the river to get to another field where the grass was greener. The only problem was that on the other side of the bridge lived a troll. That's right, it was a troll bridge.

'What if he eats us?' asked the smallest of the wrinkly goats. He won't eat you,' said the middle-sized wrinkly goat, 'you're too small.'

'He won't eat either of you,' said the biggest wrinkly goat gruff. 'It's me he'll eat because I've got most meat on me.'

So the little wrinkly billy goat gruff went across safely and the middle-sized one did too.

The big billy goat gruff hesitated as he saw the troll waiting on the other side of the bridge.

Then the troll shouted out, 'You're all right mate I wouldn't want to eat a wrinkly if you paid me, I'm off for a pizza.'

The Three Little Wrinkly Pigs

Once upon a time there were three wrinkly pigs who lived in houses that were too big for them after their piglets had grown up and left home. Also, they were finding the council tax a bit steep so they decided to sell up and move into something smaller and cheaper.

The first wrinkly pig made himself a house out of straw but a bad wolf easily broke in and ate him up.

The second wrinkly pig built himself a house out of old walking sticks, but the bad wolf easily broke into that too and ate him up.

The third wrinkly pig was a bit cleverer and built himself a house made of bricks. And sure enough, the bad wolf couldn't get in.

However, an even badder council tax official turned up at the door and told him he would have to pay even higher council tax than he had before.

The moral of this story is: if you think getting eaten by a wolf is bad, don't mess with the council.

Wrinkly Rapunzel

Once upon a time a beautiful young girl named Rapunzel was locked in a tower by a wicked witch.

For many years Rapunzel lived in the tower despairing of ever being freed. She got older and older and her long golden locks turned to grey and as even more years passed by she gave up hope of ever being released.

Then one day, a handsome young prince stopped at the tower and called out: 'Rapunzel, Rapunzel, let down your hair!'

So Rapunzel leaned out of the tower and threw down her hair.

The prince caught the wig in his hand, looked up at the bald Rapunzel and rode off never to be seen again.

And he, at least, lived happily ever after.

The Wrinkly's New Clothes

There once lived a very wrinkly old man and every time he went to the local swimming pool, people laughed at his wrinkly old body.

So he went to a special shop for wrinklies that provided lifelike body suits without a wrinkle in sight.

The old man put the suit on and looked proudly at himself in the mirror. Not a single wrinkle! He turned this way and that and from whatever angle he looked all he could see was lovely smooth skin.

Later that day he went to the swimming pool, donned his wrinkle-free body suit and dived confidently off the top board.

As he did so, a young child cried out, 'He hasn't got any clothes on!'

Yes, the silly old wrinkly had put on the body suit all right, but had forgotten his swimming trunks. His case comes up next week.

Wrinkly Bedside Bits & Bobs

We all know it is prudent to keep certain items on your bedside table. These may often include a lamp, an alarm clock and maybe even a book or magazine to read.

That's not enough for wrinklies though. Over the years, wrinklies have built up a much more detailed and extensive itinerary of items that are vital to have within arm's reach during the night.

A small bedside table will never be enough for the average wrinkly. They will instead require some form of significantly sized storage unit with drawers, cabinets, a broad worktop, several bookshelves, possibly a few secret compartments and a small medical centre. It would probably be possible to open some wrinklies' bedside cabinets as small department stores.

Wrinklies have an obvious requirement for various medical supplies at their bedside. When the drawer of the wrinkly's bedside cabinet opens, it does so with a maraca-like rattle as several hundred pill bottles shudder into view. The wrinkly's bedside table is nothing short of a small pine effect life-support system. The addition of a small compartment in which a midget pharmacist could sit would surely be a welcome addition.

There are then various over-the-counter lotions, potions and of course the in-bedside-cabinet chiropodist's department. Here the wrinkly will store a range of items to help trim, smooth and pick bits off themselves should the need to do this suddenly arise at any time during the hours of darkness.

There will also be a phone on one side or the other of the wrinkly bed. Possibly both. This would thereby make it theoretically possible for the wrinkly on one side of the bed to call up the wrinkly on the other side to tell them to stop hogging the duvet.

In-bed entertainment will be another feature. No, not that sort of in-bed entertainment! There will however be a radio and a CD player somewhere on this vast bedside cabinet.

There will also be a remote control handy for the enormous but slightly outdated television that was moved from the living room a year ago (in order to make way for an even larger model) and which is now precariously balanced on the dressing table opposite the end of the bed.

And let's not forget the teasmade. This incredible machine sits on the bedside table and can be programmed to sound an alarm to wake you up and then present you with a freshly brewed cup of tea. Wrinklies will probably also have various other foodstuffs readily to hand.

Wrinklies are clearly working towards a point where they will have everything necessary to sustain life at their bedside: food, drink, medical supplies, TV, radio, communication systems with the outside world! Why bother getting out of bed again?

If only the whole set up could be made mobile so wrinklies could tootle down to the shops while still lying in bed.

Or is that the reason the bed has casters?

Essential And Less Essential Items For The Wrinkly Bedside

Bedside Essentials	Bedside Less Than Essentials	Maybe A Bit Over The Top To Have At The Bedside
Teasmade	Cappuccino maker	Fully licensed bar
Radio	CD player	DJ turntables plus dance area with mirror ball
Nail clippers	Callus knife and other implements to remove hard skin	Full hospital operating theatre equipment
Telephone	Mobile telephone	Switchboard operating system
Pills and other drug items prescribed by the doctor	Non-prescription/ illegal drug items	Extensive chemistry set with test tubes, a Bunsen burner and a white-coated assistant
Dry skin cream	Creams for every conceivable skin condition	Enough lotions to preserve an Egyptian mummy
An emergency contact telephone number	Telephone number for an emergency chiropractor	Hotline to your local Member of Parliament
Television	Surround sound cinema system	A small group of repertory players
A half read library book	A pile of books and magazines	A small branch of W H Smiths
A packet of biscuits	Microwave oven	Barbecue

Everything You Ever Wanted To Know About Beds

In ancient times only the very rich could afford beds. The poor were therefore not only poor but permanently quite tired although they did have an excellent opportunity to rob from the rich while the rich were snoozing away on their expensive beds.

The first bed raised off the ground was introduced around 3,400 BC. Coincidentally it was around this time that DFS started their sale which, as we all know, is still going on to this day.

In *The Odyssey*, Odysseus's bed is described as being made of a woven rope. A rope would however be extremely difficult to balance on for an entire night particularly if you fell asleep at any stage.

An additional danger associated with the rope bed was that an intruder could pull on the ropes during the night and thus use them to catapult you out of your bedroom window.

Mattresses were originally stuffed with straw. The effect must therefore have been like trying to get to sleep balanced on a giant Weetabix.

The expression 'sleep tight' is said to come from tightening the ropes used to support mattresses during the 16th century. Or alternatively it means falling asleep because you're blind drunk.

Beds are still popular to this day. They are used by most people for sleeping and procreation purposes and by wrinklies as places beneath which they can keep lots of stuff they have bought but which they never seem to use.

Breakfast In Bed Wrinkly Style

Breakfast in bed is a much overrated luxury which inevitably results in spilt drinks and bits of food all over the sheets.

But then it is called breakfast in bed isn't it?

It also invariably leads to bouts of indigestion as a result of wrinklies attempting to eat and drink a large number of items in rapid succession whilst reclining in a semi-prone position without adequate back support.

The other reason breakfast in bed is a dubious pleasure is because it requires someone to get out of bed, go downstairs, prepare the sumptuous repast and carry it all back up the stairs balanced precariously on a small tray. They will then probably trip over the cat and unload the feast all over their partner who has remained snoozing in the bed.

Once again, it is literally breakfast in bed!

An amazing device was invented to save wrinkly marriages. This was the teasmade. This state of the art invention was designed to sit by the bedside and wake the wrinkly couple up each morning with a freshly made cup of tea. This would then be ruined by the addition of milk which had curdled after being left out by the bedside all night.

Ironically the teasmade in fact may have led to many divorces among wrinkly couples. Well, if you could get a machine to make you a cup of tea each morning very little reason seemed to remain for some wrinklies to stay with their partners.

Wrinklies Bedside Essentials: The Speaking Alarm Clock

Just what the sleepy wrinkly needs first thing in the morning. An alarm clock that wakes you up with an appropriately phrased message (spoken quite loudly in case you're a bit hard of hearing).

Choose from the following wrinkly wake up call messages:

- 'Come on! Get up! If you can hear this you are still alive... theoretically!'
- 'Attention! It is now time for you to wake up! This therefore means that everything that happens from this point on is no longer a dream but reality!'
- 'Wakey wakey, wrinkly wrinkly!'
- 'Get up, you lazy wrinkly! Hurry up and start moving or distant family members will begin staking their claims to your savings!'
- 'Get up! Shake a leg! Though at your age you better not shake it too vigorously!'
- 'It's a brand new day! There's a whole new world out there! It's time for you to get up and start moaning about things!'
- 'Good news and bad news for you this morning: the good news is that it is possible for you to smooth the wrinkles out of your bed sheets...'
- 'Wake up! Get out of bed as quickly as you can without risking giving yourself a heart attack!'

The Ultimate Wrinkly Bed

So what special features might the world's ultimate bed for wrinklies boast? How about:

Bizarrely misshapen mattress to exactly fit the contours of a wrinkly's bizarrely misshapen back.

Alarm built into bed covers which will sound if either of the wrinkly bed occupants tries to claim more than their fair share of the duvet.

Miniature beds along the bottom of the bed for the use of any wrinkly pets that share the bedroom.

Volume control knob on headboard to turn down the nocturnal noises produced by your wrinkly bed companion.

Gently vibrating mattress to send you to sleep at night before going into a more vigorous shaking cycle to wake you up in the morning.

Guttering round edge of bed to carry away any night-time dribble coming from sleeping wrinklies' mouths.

Thermostatic control attached to electric blanket to make sure wrinkly bed occupants' feet never drop below a certain temperature.

Microphone on bedstead attached to loud hailer on outside of house to directly address miscreant youths gathering in street outside, irritating neighbours arriving home late etc.

Small machine gun turret at end of bed in case of night-time intruders unexpectedly turning up in bedroom.

Bedtime Checklist

Going to bed as a wrinkly is not simply a case of walking up the stairs, it's like the planning of a military campaign. Dunkirk? Agincourt? Glastonbury? Mere child's play. A place for everything and everything in its place. But you need never be caught out again with this wrinkly bedtime checklist.

1) Bedtime drink. Whether it's malty and milky or malty and 70% proof just make sure it's nowhere the glass with your teeth in it – you could have a nasty shock.

2) Bedtime reading. Nothing too exciting now. You don't want your loins girded just before you try to get to sleep do you?

3) Cat out? There's nothing worse than being woken in the middle of the night by a great furry lump rubbing up against you and purring – and it's just as bad if it's the cat.

4) Doors and windows locked? The odds of getting murdered in your bed are probably about the same as Elvis crashing his UFO into your house, but best be on the safe side.

5) TV off? TV on standby uses as much electricity as cooking your morning toast. And if your other half finds you've been wasting electricity again you'll probably be toast.

6) Milk bottles out? You don't want to have to rush out at 5am in your dressing gown do you?

7) Torch handy for night-time loo excursions?

Goodnight wrinklies everywhere!

How To Adapt When Not Sleeping In Your Own Wrinkly Bed

Sleeping in a strange bed in a nice yet reasonably priced hotel can be a disarming experience for a wrinkly.

The following points should therefore be kept in mind:

Hotel beds may be loaded with six pillows or more. Do not attempt to spend the night with your head balanced precariously at the top of these unless you have a neck like a giraffe.

The bedding on hotel beds will be turned down ready for you in the evening in case you get confused about how to climb in. Your bed at home will be turned down ready for you because you didn't get around to making it that morning.

Hotel beds have crisp clean sheets. Maybe the reason you're so wrinkly is not because you're getting older but because you are covered in imprints from all the creases in your infrequently changed bedding at home.

Hotel beds may have a button at the side to press for room service. If you wish to have one of these installed at home, have it attached to a buzzer on the opposite side of your bed. You can then use it to wake your wrinkly partner to do your bidding!

Wrinklies should remember to remove the chocolate left on their hotel pillow before sleeping otherwise they will wake up with a large brown blob stuck firmly to the side of their heads and presume they have contracted some form of melanoma.

Wrinklies Bedside Essentials: The Teasmade-Cum-Defibrillator

A handy new invention for the wrinkly who might be having a bit too much of a lie in.

A nice cup of tea brewed by the teasmade machine at the side of the bed is usually enough to get anyone up and out of bed in the morning. Often this is because the tea made by the teasmade tastes so horrible they are forced to get up and go down to the kitchen to make themselves a proper drink instead.

However for those of us who sometimes need just a little more impetus to get up in the morning comes the teasmade cum defibrillator!

Yes, if the tea doesn't get you going, the hot plates from beneath the kettle and teapot double as defibrillator pads. Simply remove the tea crockery and put it in a safe place then pull out the defibrillator pads from the teasmade and attach them to the chest.

Then just flip the switch on the teasmade to the 'boil' setting and 1,000 volts will flow through the sleepy wrinkly's chest cavity. It should be just the jolt he/she needs to get out of bed in the morning!

And after this emergency cardiac arrest treatment, what could be nicer than to relax with a cup of tea heated up on the same electrically charged pads?

And remember this is the only defibrillator currently on the market to have a handy 'snooze' function setting!

Wrinkly Pyjamarama

If wrinklies had their own country, pyjamas and dressing gowns would be the national dress.

Pyjamas are loose, comfortable garments with elasticated waists thus making them ideal for wrinklies.

Pyjamas were first brought back to Europe from the Far East by the explorer Vasco Pyjama, a manager at a branch of Marks and Spencer, who had been out there for a sleepover.

When pyjamas were first introduced in the 18th century, people wore them at all times of the day. This tradition is maintained to this day by wrinklies.

Pyjamas are nowadays usually worn for sleeping. Wrinklies wear them during the day because they may fall asleep at any time.

A dressing gown is so called because if you are wearing one it means you don't have to bother dressing.

A smoking jacket is similar to a dressing gown, the only difference being that the smoking jacket has recently been ironed using too high a setting.

Children's pyjamas are often emblazoned with the image of a well loved cartoon character such as Winnie the Pooh or Spiderman. Popular designs for wrinklies' pyjamas include ones printed with pictures of Dame Vera Lynn, Winston Churchill, Mrs Thatcher and the man who invented Viagra.

Other popular patterns for wrinkly pyjamas include tartan, stripes, polka dots and varicose veins.

Pyjamas are usually highly unfashionable in design. They therefore will not clash with other items in the typical wrinkly's wardrobe.

Pyjamas are often garishly coloured or patterned which makes them easier to find if their wearer's eyesight isn't what it used to be.

Pyjama trousers offer very little to get in your way if you need to get to the toilet quickly. Again this proves pyjamas must have been specifically designed with the wrinkly wearer in mind.

Pyjama jackets usually have a single breast pocket specially designed to hold your handkerchief, glasses and teeth safely during the night.

Other forms of nightwear are available with erotic elements of design such as the peek-a-boo nightie or various crotchless items of apparel. Pyjama manufacturers were quick to respond to this demand with the non-buttoning wide open pyjama trouser fly.

The open trouser fly on a pair of pyjamas trousers makes them terrifying to others. This helps ensure that when pyjamas are worn in public, few people will bother you. Once again this makes them particularly attractive to wrinklies.

If you go to the shops wearing your pyjamas you will often be brought home by the police. This can save you a fortune on bus or taxi fares as well as providing a nice young man to carry your heavy shopping for you.

Nightwear For Wrinklies: Not Recommended

The following are probably inappropriate forms of nightwear for a wrinkly:

- Peek-a-boo nightie (particularly for male wrinklies)
- Anything with the word 'crotchless' in its title
- Anything with the word 'micro' in its name
- The form of night apparel described as 'au naturel' is also not recommended for wrinklies (it's probably best for wrinklies to stick to 'au completely artificial' these days)
- Anything too silky (when the wrinkly climbs into bed they will fly straight out of the bottom of the duvet like a piece of soap)
- Anything labelled 'see through' (that's not because wrinklies don't have beautiful bodies – of course they do! It's just that because of the poor state of their eyesight, if a wrinkly lays an item of see through nightwear down anywhere, they will probably never be able to find it again)
- Anything made from rubber (squeaking and farting noises will probably keep a wrinkly awake all night. And that's before we even get onto the noises produced by their rubber pyjamas)
- Anything made from acrylic material particularly when combined with nylon sheets (it will be like a lightning storm in the bedroom every time the wrinkly climbs into bed – on the other hand the resulting electrical charge might unexpectedly re-invigorate the wrinkly making them feel suddenly younger and more energetic)

Nightwear For Wrinklies: Recommended

The following forms of night apparel will probably look a bit more appropriate on a wrinkly and prove less distracting during the wee small hours:

- Warm comfortable sensible flannelette pyjamas or nightdress of course!
- A long nightshirt and pointy nightcap or bonnet. This outfit should preferably be set off with a burning candle standing on a little candle holder held in one trembling hand. Basically if a wrinkly ends up looking like something straight out of a Dickens novel that's probably about right. This form of nightwear has the added advantage that if any youths or local miscreants come knocking at the door after nine o'clock in the evening, the wrinkly can pretend to be a ghost and frighten them away!
- Anything with a blue check pattern (to match the patterns of a wrinkly's varicose veins).
- Eye mask and ear plugs and anything else that might blot out the awfulness of the modern world. Don't forget though if nose plugs are inserted as well these may cause asphyxiation.
- A dressing gown so thick, soft and cuddly it is possible for a wrinkly to trip over and bounce down the stairs while wearing it and not injure themselves in any way.
- Pyjamas with stripes that make a wrinkly look like an inmate at a maximum security prison.

The Wrinklies Guide To Bedtime Snacks

Bedtime snack	Reasons it might be inadvisable
Cheese and biscuits	Cheese! Before bedtime! You might as well make it hallucinogenic drugs and biscuits!
Piece of toast	Eat this in bed and afterwards it will be like trying to get to sleep while lying on a gravel pathway
Beans	Remember to open all windows and extinguish any naked flames
Breakfast cereal with milk	If you want to leave a pebbledash effect over your bed covers that's your business
Chips	Don't forget to have a range of clothes ready for the morning that are all two sizes larger than the ones you were wearing today
Pancakes	Your digestive system will spend the night making noises not unlike the opening of a Jean Michel Jarre album
Takeaway	Are you worried you're going to starve to death during the night? By morning your indigestion will not only have burnt right through your oesophagus, it will have singed a hole in your mattress as well
Dried fruit	We suppose it will get you up and out of bed nice and quick in the morning. Alternatively the build up of gas during the night may be sufficient to propel you from the bed like a circus performer fired from a cannon

Wrinklies Bedside Essentials: Luminous Dentures

These days we all know the importance of being green and counting the pennies. Well, why not do both?! Yes, you can save the energy and cost of expensive night-lights by getting yourself a set of luminous dentures! New Dentaglo ™ dentures are at the biting edge of tooth technology. Simply pop them into a glass of water at bedtime and leave on your bedside table. Their eerie dentalescent glow will then light up your bedroom throughout the night providing sufficient illumination to get you to the toilet and back as many times as you need. And as we all know that can be quite a lot of times!

> 'When I wake in the night it's as though there's always someone there smiling at me in the darkness.' *Mr P, London*

> 'It's like having the reassuring presence of the massive teeth of a ghostly Bee Gee beaming at you from the side of your bed.' *Mrs B, Devizes*

> 'I bought a set of Dentaglo ™ luminous dentures and people soon began to notice the difference. Particularly when I smiled at them during a temporary power cut.' *Mr S, Portsmout*

And that's not all! Dentaglo ™ luminous dentures can also be used as a small portable torch available at any time of the day or night. Looking to see if your car keys have fallen under the sofa? Simple! Just get down on your hands and knees and grin into the darkness!

Night-Time Prayers
For Wrinklies

Bedtime is the time when you get down on your knees and say your prayers. Wrinklies should however be careful when attempting this acrobatic feat. Make sure your panic alarm is to hand. Otherwise you might get down on your knees and discover that you can't get back up again afterwards.

You would then be left in a praying position for the entire night and by morning would have achieved a state of utmost serenity. Or hypothermia as it's sometimes known.

At least you'd be in the right position to pray for someone to come and help you. Failing that shouting and swearing at the top of your voice until assistance arrives is probably more effective, although less serene. Shouting and swearing will however probably involve frequent references to the deity.

Even if you are able to spring nimbly in and out of a kneeling position, wrinkly prayers may not always be conducted in quiet contemplation.

The praying wrinkly may intend to look back and give thanks for the day just gone. Unfortunately the day just gone has probably contained its fair share of frustrations and irritations. Before you know it, the wrinkly's prayer of thanksgiving has become a series of muttered curses on those who have crossed him/her during the day.

Nevertheless wrinklies are often looked upon as religious and spiritual leaders. Jobs such as Archbishop of

Canterbury or Pope are seldom given to those in the first flush of youth.

After all who would want to see his holiness come out on the balcony in St Peter's Square dressed in a hoodie, with a piercing in his eyebrow, showing off his new tattoo and doing a double thumbs up to the crowd by way of a blessing?

No, religious leaders tend to be the wrinkliest of the wrinkly. The more wrinkles you have, the more likely you are to get the job!

This is why you are very unlikely to see the leader of the Greek Orthodox Church fronting an advertising campaign for Oil of Olay or the Chief Rabbi turning to camera and saying the words, 'Because you're worth it!'

But why are we wrinklies perceived as being so holy that it seems that any of us might be given a job as leader of one of the world's great religions apparently at random?

Perhaps people believe we have lived so long we have reached a deep understanding of life. They obviously fail to notice that we have never even managed to reach a deep understanding of how the video recorder works. Perhaps they have just mistaken an other-worldly sense of the sacred for our tendency to nod off at the slightest opportunity.

Alternatively it could just be that the people who are appointed Archbishops and Popes are just the ones who have managed to outlive all their main rivals for the posts.

But what sort of prayers should a wrinkly say before bedtime and are there any modern alternatives?

Do's And Don'ts Of Saying Your Night-Time Prayers

Do: commence your night time prayers by giving thanks for all the good things that have happened to you during the day.

Don't: commence your night time prayers by screaming the words 'why me?' over and over again at the top of your voice.

Do: use religious language when talking to your God.

Don't: swear or make obscene bodily gestures.

Do: adopt a kneeling position with your hands held together in prayer.

Don't: do star jumps while waving an angry fist at the heavens.

Do: address your God humbly and respectfully.

Don't: use the expression, 'Hey you up there! Are you listening to me, pal?'

Do: share your day's troubles and blessings with your god in a period of quiet meditation before going to bed.

Don't: share your day's troubles and blessings with your neighbours in a period of drunken shouting and swearing from your bedroom window.

Do: make your peace with all those with whom you have disagreed during the day before going to bed.

Don't: challenge them all to a massive fight to the death at dawn.

Do: list the people you want to pray for.

Don't: list all the people you would like God to strike down with botulism.

Things A Wrinkly Has In Common With God

- They are both of a similar age.
- They have both seen many changes during their time.
- They both have quite set ideas about the way things should be in the world.
- Others find it very hard to imagine what could have existed before they came along.
- Fewer people talk to them these days than used to be the case.
- They are both known for being a bit judgemental.
- Both of them avoid direct intervention in current world events if this can possibly be avoided.
- People still turn to them in times of crisis (although in wrinklies' cases this tends to be younger family members looking for a cash hand out).
- Young people are only ever nice to them if they want something in return.
- People often preface things they have to say to them with the words: 'Can you hear me?'
- They have both sent their children out into the world but were not entirely delighted with the reception they were given.
- They both live somewhere nice and peaceful at a bit of a remove from the world.

The Wrinkliest Characters In The Bible

Methuselah

Patriarch mentioned in the Book of Genesis. He lived to the ripe old age of 969 years, this being the oldest age given for any figure in the Bible. Known to many wrinklies today as 'The Kid'.

Adan

Lived to be 950. Like many wrinklies, he had a very nice garden. Unfortunately as a result of meddling by his wrinkly wife, he lost access to this and the pair had to move out (presumably into sheltered accommodation). Even more typically for a wrinkly his kids (Cain and Abel) didn't get on and one of them had to go and live in the Land of Nod (or, for wrinklies, The Land of Nodding Off). Overall Adam and Eve were said to have had 33 sons and 23 daughters. This would obviously have made it a nightmare when they all came to stay at Christmas but luckily for them Christmas hadn't yet been invented.

Noah

Lived to the age of 930. A typical wrinkly male. Keen on DIY, woodwork and collecting an assortment of different pets. Famously had a spot of bother with his local water supplier.

Job

A nipper at just 210 years old. Lost his wealth, his health and his children. The story of many a wrinkly.

Jared

Lived to 962 years old and is thus the second oldest person recorded in the Bible. But who remembers that now? It's all Methuselah this, Methuselah that, isn't it? Jared must have been absolutely gutted. He was pipped to the title of oldest person in the Bible by Methuselah who was just 7 years his senior! Presumably he might have lived that little bit longer if only he'd gone to the gym a bit more often and given up smoking a few years earlier.

Moses

Lived to be 120 and so, in biblical terms, died young. Led his people to the Promised Land without even having to use a sat nav. His wrinkly descendants still complain to this day saying, 'If he'd turned right rather than left when he came out of Egypt, we'd have got the oil!'

Seth

Adam and Eve's third son who lived to be 912 years old. Was born when Adam was 120 years which is a heck of an age to be lumbered with a baby again. Seth's son was born when he was 105 thus further lumbering Adam with babysitting duties when he was 225.

Deborah

At 130, the oldest female wrinkly mentioned in the Bible. Still performing as lead singer of Blondie to this day.

Abraham

Lived to 175 years. It sounds old but it's only 25 in dog years!

Thoughts For Wrinklies To Contemplate

- All you can do in this life is be true to yourself – on the other hand, look where that's got you up to now!
- Laugh and the world laughs with you although the world will probably be thinking, 'What's that idiot laughing for?'
- Learn from your mistakes. If you'd started doing this earlier, you'd be a genius by now!
- It requires more muscles to frown than it does to smile – so frowning will provide you with better exercise.
- Remember, the wrinklies attitude to strangers: there are no strangers in this life, just idiots who haven't annoyed you yet.
- You are what you eat – so after all these years just think what the ingredients list for you must look like.
- If you can keep your head when all those around you are losing theirs, you must be on exceptionally strong medication.
- You learnt all you know today at the school of hard knocks – particularly as regards the best way to treat bruises.
- A smile costs nothing – oh yeah? Tell that to your dentist.
- In the kingdom of the blind, be exceptionally careful when crossing the road no matter what the traffic signal says.
- If you can't think of anything good that happened today, console yourself with this thought: at least it was better than tomorrow's going to be!

Biblical Plagues To Call Down On All Those Who Have Crossed You During The Day

The Bible can be a source of great wisdom and solace for wrinklies. Not only that but it's full of plagues and other fantastic ideas which wrinklies can pray will befall all the people that have annoyed them during the day just gone:

- How about a plague of locusts on the green grocer who sold you that rotten veg this morning?

- For the bin men who emptied rubbish all over your driveway, a plague of flies? After all they left you with one.

- A plague of boils for that sulky supermarket checkout assistant? Oh no. He had already been hit by one, hadn't he?

- And if you see that builder who did that shoddy work for you, get your trumpet out and give him a Jericho-like encounter with the wall he's currently building.

- How about a biblical flood to pour down on the man from the water board who informed you that you still have to pay your bill even though the travellers' camp next door is currently getting its supply from an illegal connection attached to your water meter?

- And the doctor who keeps giving you all that dietary advice can be turned into a pillar of salt (which of course you then won't be allowed to eat).

Oh yes, when wrinklies refer to the Bible there is sure to be a weeping and a gnashing of teeth (or should that be gums).

Getting To Sleep And Staying There

Since the dawn of time scientists have been coming up with theories about why we sleep. One of the more popular of these is that it's because we're a bit knackered at the end of the day and there's nothing worth watching on the telly.

But why do we need to sleep at all? Much scientific research has been devoted to this question. Ironically if you try and read any of this, it will quickly make you feel extremely drowsy.

There could be many benefits if we could survive without sleep. For example we would be able to rent out our bedrooms because they weren't being used any more.

Young people seem to need very little sleep. Instead they spend their nights dancing like maniacs at all-night raves while off their faces on Lucozade or Sherbet Dib Dabs (or some similar sort of stimulating substance).

Wrinklies on the other hand are shagged out all the time. You would think that by their time of life, wrinklies would be experts at getting to sleep. Unfortunately they often have great difficulty in doing this. This may partly be due to a lack of physical exercise or poor digestion or alternatively because they are kept awake by the all-night rave organised by the young people living down their street.

Wrinklies can sometimes make getting to sleep look easy but they usually do this while they are watching something they particularly want to see on television.

Prime Minister Mrs Thatcher used to boast to journalists that she hardly slept at all at night, like Dracula. This lack of sleep clearly did her no harm or cause her to lose her grip on reality or develop a pair of bulging red rimmed unblinking eyes.

For most of us though it is important to get a good night's sleep each night and perhaps during the day as well.

Scientists have now identified that our sleeping pattern moves through several cycles. Sleep experts have named these stages rapid eye movement, non-rapid eye movement and dribbling.

The rapid eye movement (or REM) stage is the time when most people dream. The time when wrinklies most often dream is however defined as during any brief lull in a conversation.

Non rapid eye movement is like rapid eye movement but with less rapid eye movement. Wrinklies often experience prolonged periods of non rapid eye movement during the night and periods of non rapid everything else movement during the day.

Sleep is believed to serve a number of cognitive purposes including memory processing. Basically if you don't sleep enough your memory will eventually get so bad that you won't be able to remember where your bedroom is. So potentially it's a vicious circle.

As far as is known, all living animals need to sleep. It is not however advisable to let them all share the bed with you as this will be unhygienic, uncomfortable and the cumulative sound of snoring will be ear shattering.

The Wrinklies Guide To Getting A Good Night's Sleep

Try to relax and let your mind become completely blank – this will become increasingly easy as you get older.

Forget all your earthly desires – again this will become increasingly easy as you get older.

Don't do anything in bed that might suddenly raise your heart rate – this is getting a bit repetitive now isn't it?

Empty your mind of all thought – this can usually be achieved by watching anything broadcast on television during the prime time schedule.

Achieving a restful state can also be helped by having a nice bedtime drink – a mug full of a hot milky beverage should do the trick although a few cans of something stronger can also reduce you to a condition of complete rest fairly quickly (or possibly to a condition of complete paralysis which is quite similar).

Consider all the good things that have happened to you during the day just gone – don't start feeling sorry for yourself when you realize the highlight of your day was the chocolate HobNob you had with your elevenses.

Stroking a pet may also help reduce your stress levels and heart rate – it will also reduce your breathing rate if the animal settles down for the night on your face shortly after you've nodded off.

Wrinklies Theories of Sleep

We need to sleep each night because our body needs a period of time to rest and recuperate after the exertions and stresses of the day. This is a brilliant theory but obviously someone should tell your body about it.

Unfortunately the theory doesn't explain why your body decides to keep you keep awake each night by fidgeting, making odd noises and requiring numerous visits to the toilet.

You need to rest each night to allow your body to repair and rejuvenate itself so you stay looking healthy and young. One glance at yourself in the mirror would suggest that you can't ever have slept a wink in your life.

Overall you spend about a third of your life asleep. So if you haven't had quite enough sleep so far there is a genuine danger you may suddenly drop off and keep snoring away for an entire decade or two.

In your dreams you are able to do all sorts of outrageous and incredible things that you could never do in real life. This is why wrinklies spend most nights dreaming of repeatedly bending over and touching their toes.

You sleep to restore order and balance to your mind and body. Well, you would if your bed didn't have that wonky leg.

There are many theories of why we sleep but no-one knows the real reason.

In fact now you've started thinking about it, the problem is probably going to keep you awake all night!

Wrinklies' Dreams And What They Mean

Everyone is fascinated by dreams aren't they? Everyone, that is, with the small exception of everyone else on the planet who didn't have the dream themselves.

So in other words, everyone is fascinated by their own dreams but extremely bored by everyone else's. In fact if someone starts telling you about the amazing dream they had last night, it will probably be so boring it will send you straight off to sleep.

This does however mean that the moment they shut up about their dream, you can wake up and get your own back by telling them about the dream you yourself were just having as a result of being bored to death by their dream.

The imagery of dreams was analysed by the celebrated bald, bearded wrinkly Sigmund Freud. Freud was the father of psychoanalysis and also of several children (the majority of whom were also bald and bearded).

Freud believed that our dreams are all about wish fulfilment, although eating too much cheese before bedtime may come into it as well.

Freud published his book *The Interpretation of Dreams* in 1899. This was a 500-page tome in which Freud expressed his theory of why we dream. In fact the book just has the words, 'It's all about sex innit?' printed on every page. Or was that just in one particularly poorly translated edition that was quickly withdrawn from sale?

But do wrinklies' dreams mean exactly the same as they would to a normal person?

Dream Image Or Event	What It Signifies To A Normal Person	What It Signifies To A Wrinkly
Flying	Sex	I must check if there's any package holiday bargains on the internet at the moment!
Water	Sex	Perhaps a cruise would be nice instead!
Falling	Yet more sex	Maybe I should get one of those emergency alarm buttons to go round my neck!
Lighthouse	Phallic symbol of a sexual nature	I must remember to buy some new light bulbs from the supermarket tomorrow!
Bushes	Full frontal sex	Time to spray the rhododendrons!
Entering a tunnel	Let's face it – it's sex again isn't it?	Has my Senior Citizens' Railcard run out?
Nudity in a public place	Sexual desire, exhibitionism, sex, sex, sex and more sex	Damn it! I took all my clothes off again when I went to the shopping centre this morning didn't I?
Sex	Hugely perverse kinky sex	I really must write a letter of complaint to the *Daily Mail* about that filthy television programme I saw on BBC2 last night!

Things A Wrinkly Can Count To Help Get Off To Sleep (If You Want To Irritate Yourself)

- The number of times you have been asked to participate in a telephone survey during the past week.
- The number of times petrol has gone up in price over the past few days.
- The number of youths you have seen over the past week with their trousers half way down their backsides exhibiting a couple of inches of their Calvin Klein underpants in the process.
- The number of pills prescribed by the doctor that you have to take every day.
- The number of charity collection bags you have had stuffed through your letter box in the past week.
- The number of buttons you have to press in order to speak to a human being when you call your bank.
- The number of advertising leaflets that fall out of your TV guide when you pick it up.
- The number of TV cookery shows you have seen in the past 24 hours.
- Your wrinkly friends coming up to you one by one to tell you about their latest health problem.
- The number of individual aches and pains you have flashing around your wrinkly old body.

Things A Wrinkly Can Count To Help Get Off To Sleep (If You Want Something A Little More Entertaining)

- Flashy sports cars being overtaken on the dual carriageway by you in your old banger.
- Cold-calling salesmen coming to your front door and being electrocuted when they press your specially booby-trapped doorbell.
- Politicians losing their parliamentary seats on election night.
- Bankers being lined up and told one by one that they are going to lose their annual bonuses.
- Hoodies being given ASBOs.
- Bits dropping off the house of an irritating neighbour.
- Simon Cowell being repeatedly kneed in the groin by every *X Factor* auditionee he's ever been rude to.
- Telling all your unwanted telephone callers to bugger off one after the other!
- All the 4x4s in the neighbourhood going into a pile up on the local dual carriageway.
- Local troublemakers being chased by their own pit bull terriers.
- A highly tattooed upstart of a celebrity having his tattoos removed one by one with an industrial sander.

Counting Wrinkly Sheep: The Best Way To Get To Sleep... Or Is It?

Counting sheep is a method frequently used by those wanting to get off to sleep. There is however little or no evidence that this system really works. After all:

- Are shepherds notorious for falling asleep after a few minutes surveying their herds?
- At livestock auctions, do the auctioneer and spectators pass out as soon as a few sheep walk round the ring in front of them?
- When performing surgical procedures in hospital operating theatres, do doctors ever attempt to put their patients to sleep with a brief demonstration by a recent winner from the TV series *One Man And His Dog*?
- When a stage hypnotist wishes to put someone into a deep sleep, doesn't he usually dangle a pocket watch in front of them... not a sheep!

There is however one thing worse than counting sheep and that is counting wrinklies. Yes, you have probably seen so many of your fellow wrinklies during the day that their balding or blue rinsed images are now permanently burnt into your mind.

However counting these wrinklies attempting to jump over a five-bar gate will not help you get to sleep. Instead you will lie awake all night working yourself up into an apoplectic rage while muttering, 'Jump, you stupid old wrinkly! What's the matter with you? It's only a small gate! You'll never get over it shuffling at that speed! Put your Zimmer frame down and jump!'

Wrinklies' Night Time Fantasies

The Tropical Island

You find yourself washed up on the shore of an idyllic tropical island where the beautiful and naked inhabitants are all eager to do anything at all for anyone who can bring them up to date on the latest events in Coronation Street, Eastenders and/or The Archers.

The New Neighbour

A new, highly attractive, young neighbour moves in next door to you. You invite them round for afternoon tea and are surprised to discover that for them Werther's Originals seem to have a strong aphrodisiac quality.

The Celebrity

You receive an unexpected call asking you to re-pot some geraniums for a top celebrity after whom you have always secretly lusted. The celebrity returns home and discovers you in their garden shed. Seeing you with your sleeves rolled up, up to your arms in potting compost, they suddenly become unable to control themselves.

The Most Romantic City In The World

You meet a gorgeous young member of the opposite sex who tells you that their dream has always been to see the sights of Paris while sitting on the back of a mobility scooter.

Save The World

Humanity is doomed unless scientists can find an aged person who can teach young people how to make love properly again.

How To Tell Your Dreams From Reality

You are trying to run away because someone is chasing you, but find it difficult to make your legs move.

Experiencing difficulty in moving your legs while running is a common element in many peoples' dreams. For wrinklies it is also a common element in reality, particularly if you have just got up out of a chair a bit too quickly.

The clincher is the fact that someone is taking the trouble to chase you. If you are being chased by a scantily clad member of the opposite sex, it is probably all a dream. If however you are being chased by someone wanting you to switch your gas and electricity supplier, it is probably reality.

You are naked in a public place.

Are you feeling chilly and can you hear the sound of giggling and/or sirens approaching in the distance? If so, it's reality so put your cardie back on quick!

The Queen has come to your house for tea.

This was once said to have been a commonly experienced dream. It is of course unlikely that Her Majesty would wander into your house unannounced and demand you get the PG Tips and HobNobs out. On the other hand, she's getting on a bit herself so maybe she does stroll into peoples' houses in a state of confusion. Better get the best china ready but avoid giving her an old chipped mug issued to commemorate any of her children's failed marriages.

You discover that you unexpectedly have to sit an extremely difficult exam paper for which you have done no preparation.

This is another common dream. Congratulations if you ever have it! You could lie in bed at night recalling your happy childhood memories: the long hot summers, having fun with your friends, your first ever kiss…

But no!

Instead you've decided to have a dream about everyone's least favourite part of childhood: going into a dingy great hall, sitting trembling at a desk and spending three hours sweating like a pig while attempting to do an exam on a subject you have no interest in or knowledge about whatsoever.

It might however be worth checking the exam paper you see in front of you. If a glance at the top of the paper reveals that it is not an exam after all but a tax return or a passport application form, bad luck! It's probably grim reality once again!

You are in a large building desperately trying to find where the toilets are located.

This is a common dream. It is also how we wrinklies spend every minute of the day once we leave the comfort of our own homes.

There is therefore very little possibility of being able to tell whether this is a dream or reality other than to find and use the toilet facilities.

If you later discover your bed sheets are damp, it was a dream.

Lullabies for Wrinklies

'Rock-a-bye Wrinkly'

Rock-a-bye wrinkly, in the tree top,
When the wind blows, the wrinkly will drop,
Down comes the wrinkly and suffers a thoracic disorder,
All because he tried to prune his own leylandii border.

'All Through The Night'

Out of bed and along to the toilet,
All through the night,
Tramping downstairs, turn the kettle on and boil it,
All through the night.
One more cup of tea to help quench your thirst,
All through the night,
Lying back in bed with a bladder fit to burst,
All through the night.

'Hush Little Wrinkly'

Hush little wrinkly, don't say a word
Mama's gonna buy you some lemon curd
And if that lemon curd don't taste
Mama's gonna buy you some curry paste.

And if that curry tastes like stew
Mama's gonna buy you a vindaloo
And if that vindaloo ain't strong
We're all gonna know your tastebuds have gone.

'Hinkly Wrinkly'

Hinkly Wrinkly sat on a wall,
Hinkly Wrinkly had a great fall,
A lawyer took the wrinkly as one of his cases,
And sued the wall's owner on a no-win-no-fee basis.

'Wrinkle, Wrinkle Little Pa'

Wrinkle, wrinkle little Pa
How I wonder what you are
Sitting in your favourite chair
Without a tooth or single hair.

Up above, your hand held high
A Double Diamond helps time fly
Wrinkle wrinkle little Pa
In your favourite corner of the bar.

'Silent Night'

Silent night, noiseless night
The snoring cure has turned out right
Up each nostril there's a plug
You're so quiet I could give you a hug
'cos I can sleep in pee – eace
At last I can sleep in peace.

Silent night, blissful night
Not a sound since we turned out the light
Though you're now verging on comatose
You can't have died I suppose?
But if you have I can be sure – ure
It's the last I'll hear of your snore.

Can't Sleep?

What should you do if you can't sleep? This is the terrible problem many of us face every single day. And it's even worse if it happens while you're lying in bed at night.

There are a range of sleep disorders to choose from these days. These include insomnia, sleep apnea or depression, delayed sleep phase syndrome and not being able to get comfy.

Wrinklies can have difficulty sleeping as a result of many different things. In fact wrinklies are endlessly inventive as regards things that will keep them awake at night.

A wrinkly can be kept awake by any one or any combination of the following:

> any twitch, itch or pulse anywhere about their own person; the sound of their own breathing; any aches or pains they have; the slightest movement, snoring or sharp inhalation of breath made by their wrinkly bed companion; the need to go to the toilet (either now or within the next few hours); pets moving about anywhere in the house; noises produced by the central heating system; any creaks, squeaks or odd noises; people anywhere nearby communicating in anything more than a whisper; any vehicle driving past; any television or music being played nearby at any volume; young people doing anything at all; a firework going off anywhere within a 20-mile radius;

304

murderers smashing their way in through the French
windows downstairs, etc.

Yes, you name it – a wrinkly will be kept awake by it.

If they gave out prizes for innovation in the field of
insomnia, wrinklies would sweep the board.

Wrinklies are the world experts at not being able to get
sleep. They have lived so long that they know everything
that can possibly keep them awake. And if these things
don't happen, wrinklies will instead lie there worrying that
they're about to happen at any moment.

Basically we wrinklies almost never get a wink of sleep.
This explains a lot about our appearance and character.
Anyone who got as little sleep as we do would look and
act like a wrinkly. They would be grumpy, they would
have bags under their eyes and they would spend their
days moaning about everything.

Also of course, wrinklies have lived so long that they
now have particular expectations of sleep. They refuse to
be fobbed off with any old sleep. Wrinklies demand a good
sleep. They need a proper night's sleep. They want top
quality, luxury, Taste The Difference sleep every night of
the week.

And if they don't get it, they will give everyone they
meet the next day a detailed critique of the disappointing
sleep they had.

So how can a wrinkly make sure of getting a good
night's sleep without disturbance?

Do they need to invest in earplugs, eye masks and
enough drugs to sedate an elephant?

Or is it too much to ask that the rest of humanity could
just try to stay quiet for a few hours every night?

Things Wrinklies Should Try Not To Think About At Bedtime

Things That You Should Avoid Thinking About At Bedtime	Why You Shouldn't Worry
The thought that the house might burn down in the night	No need to panic. You perform an impromptu test of your smoke alarm every day when you make a piece of toast… or has doing that worn out the batteries?
The threat of burglars and murderers breaking into the house in the middle of the night	No need to worry! You've got so many locks and security fittings on all the doors and windows they could never possibly get in! Of course, if they've already managed to slip in during the day while you weren't looking, you'll never manage to get the door unlocked in time to escape!
The scary programme that you have just watched on TV before going to bed (e.g. a documentary about health, the news or *Crimewatch* – which always rubs it in with its final message directed specifically at wrinkly viewers: 'don't have nightmares!')	Don't worry! It's only the television! It's not real! Oh no, hang on! The news, a documentary, *Crimewatch*! It is all real!! Panic!!!
That other scary thing you saw just before bedtime	In future remember not to look downwards when climbing out of the bath

The trauma that results from being told that an acquaintance is not well or even not long for this world	Now you're a wrinkly you'll hear this kind of thing every single day of your life! You'll soon get used to it and instead of being traumatic, it will become a source of endless fascination
The fear of an earthquake occurring in the middle of the night	Well, it's been a while since you've had the opportunity to ask your partner, 'Did the earth move for you?'
The worry that the chimney stack will fall over through the roof and down on top of your bed during the night	Don't be ridiculous! That chimney stack has been standing there since before you were born…! Oops! Maybe it would be best to move the bed a few inches to the right. Or alternatively, switch sides with your spouse whenever it's windy
The thought of dying in your sleep	Look on the bright side! If this happens you'll get a really good lie-in in the morning
The fear that your house might be haunted	You have now lived so long, you are probably older than most ghosts. Any ghosts will probably therefore be more scared of you as well as looking slightly healthier

Composing Imaginary Ripostes And Letters Of Complaint

Why do so many of us wrinklies start mentally composing imaginary ripostes and letters of complaint when we go to bed? Why does the part of us that is most grumpy and quick to take offence wake up when the rest of our wrinkly old bodies are trying to get to sleep?

Once this grumpy bit of us wakes up, it starts analysing all the impertinences and lack of consideration we have encountered from others during the day.

These didn't bother us at the time. At the time we remained polite and calm in our dealings with the series of ill-mannered buffoons life found to throw at us.

They came to us during the past 24 hours doing, saying and/or emailing the most incredibly annoying things. But then, as we wrinklies know, that is what other people have been put on this Earth to do.

When our wrinkly heads hit the pillow however, the irritable little person inside us wakes up.

This little fellow inside our heads spends hours during the night examining the maddening things people have said and done during the day just gone. He then goes on to painstakingly work out carefully worded responses that, come the new day, we should give or send to those who have vexed us.

This then is the process of composing imaginary ripostes and letters of complaint! It is one of the most efficient ways available to stop wrinklies getting off to sleep easily.

You lie for hours in bed devising arguments so carefully and brilliantly worded that, hearing them, those who annoyed you over the past 24 hours would immediately see the error of their ways and fall to their knees begging you to pardon their foolishness.

But it's a waste of time! You're in bed! All the idiots who tormented you during the day have gone away!

Apart that is from one of them!

A wrinkly bed companion may be lying close at hand. This makes them ideally placed to receive your complaints and withering put down lines as soon as you think of them (and whether or not they were the ones who provoked them in the first place).

Otherwise you have to commit everything to memory and type up your letters of outrage and complaint in the morning. You can try typing them in bed but this really will keep you and your partner awake.

Perhaps what we wrinklies need is some sort of computerised dictation program wired up to our beds. This would transcribe our nocturnal pronouncements as we angrily mutter them from our pillows.

Ideally this program would then go on to put our night-time rants into emails which it would then automatically dispatch to their intended recipients.

By the time we woke up in the morning those who had annoyed us during the day just gone would have our full and frank assessment of their behaviour waiting for them in their in-boxes.

What could possibly go wrong?

Things You Should Really Try Not To Worry About While You're Lying In Bed

Money problems

There's no use lying awake worrying about this. There's not much you can do to make money while you're in bed is there? OK there is one thing but that sort of career change is probably inadvisable at your time of life.

The weight you've put on

Are you lying awake worrying that you've put on weight? Well, try and get to sleep and dream that you're out jogging! Of course this sort of weight loss regime will probably be more successful if you jog while you're awake and then spend all night dreaming of eating cakes. On the other hand, as we all know, if you do dream you're eating a big cake, you will wake up in the morning to find that your pillow has mysteriously disappeared. If however you are worrying about the weight you have put on and you are unable to sleep because your bed keeps collapsing, your worries may have some justification.

Losing your looks

This is never going to be a problem when you're asleep. Think about it. What's the worst that can happen? You'll dream you're making an advance on a gorgeous member of the opposite sex only for them to rebuff you with the words, 'In your dreams!' You can then respond quick as a flash, 'Exactly!' This will leave them with no choice but to fall into your arms.

Getting older

You should not worry about getting older while you're asleep. We're all getting older and we're all doing this at roughly the same rate as each other: one second per second.

It is therefore very unlikely that you will go to bed looking beautiful and young and wake up in the morning looking hideous and old. This does occasionally happen in the following situations: you go to bed caked in lots of make up which all comes off in the night; you go to bed and the plastic surgeon whose bill you haven't paid breaks into your house in the night and removes his handiwork; you stay asleep for several decades.

Most of these ways to age suddenly and terribly in the night are fairly unlikely to happen although a similar effect can also be achieved by the following method: look at yourself in the mirror without your glasses on immediately before going to bed and then in the morning look at yourself with your glasses on.

Dying in your sleep

What are you worried about? Waking up, finding yourself dead and the shock being almost enough to kill you?

What you should be worried about is falling into such a deep sleep that people can't tell the difference and decide to bury you anyway. It is therefore always a good idea to keep your mobile phone in your pyjama pocket at night. Then in an emergency you can phone someone to come and dig you back up again.

Wrinkly Ghosties And Wrinkly Ghoulies

Skeletal figures, ghastly pale faces and constant wailing. That's wrinklies for you.

But what about the ghostly apparitions that might be found in a run down spooky old house. Could they be wrinklies as well?

Evidence seems to exist that ghosts are in fact all wrinklies. Well, they spend their time hanging round in run-down, old houses don't they?

Ghostly wrinklies walking through the walls

These are believed to be the spirits of wrinklies who died unable to find their spectacles and who are now doomed to wander the earth in a state of myopic confusion and frustration unable to find either the door frame or their car keys.

The headless wrinkly

These figures are often seen holding their decapitated heads under their arms. Some say they are the ghosts of wrinklies who died after making an over forceful attempt to correct a crick in the neck that had developed during the night. Alternatively they may be the ghosts of wrinkly men who were desperate to examine the bald spot on the back of their heads in closer detail.

A ghostly figure looking in through the window

Clearly the ghost of a wrinkly who has forgotten to take his/her keys when they went out of the front door.

Poltergeists

They go round the house smashing crockery. They are undoubtedly the spirits of wrinklies attempting to carry a tray of tea things from the kitchen to the living room.

The sound of chains rattling and moaning

The ghost of a wrinkly who has died on the toilet and who then spends the rest of eternity moaning that there isn't a fresh roll of toilet paper handy.

Is anybody there?

When conducting séances, a medium will often have to call, 'Is anybody there?' several times before a reply is received from the spirit world. This suggests that the spirits must be slightly deaf and therefore quite possibly wrinkly as well.

Ghostly knocking on the walls

This is the sound produced by a wrinkly ghost checking his cavity wall insulation during the middle of the night.

A shrouded ghostly figure

A ghostly figure in a white sheet? Is it a rubber sheet? If so it could be the ghost of an incontinent wrinkly.

Weird noises in the middle of the night

The ghost of a wrinkly with tummy trouble.

Terrifying Wrinkly Nightmares And Explanations To Help Put Your Mind At Rest

Wrinkly nightmare	Possible explanation
The sound of ominous creaking somewhere in the house	It's your own creaking old bones moving as you breathe in and out
The sound of an eerie wind blowing	Again you probably don't have to to look very far for the source of this
A strange distant disembodied voice calling your name over and over again in the darkness	You forgot to hang up the phone earlier after calling your cousin in Australia, didn't you?
Weird ethereal coloured lights floating just outside your window and shining in through your curtains	You haven't got round to taking down the Christmas decorations this year
The sound of someone moving around downstairs in the middle of the night	You live in a flat
The silhouette of a small devil with pointed ears sitting at the end of your bed looking at you	You shouldn't let the cats sleep in the bedroom with you
Slow ominous footsteps coming up the stairs towards you	Your spouse is turning in for the night at last
Heavy breathing in the darkness as though from some strange and terrible brutish creature	Your spouse has managed to get up the stairs, into bed and is now lying next to you
A light appearing above your head and a ladder descending towards you	Your spouse has got up again in the night and, in a moment of confusion, has gone up to into the attic

Bad Bedtime Habits For Wrinklies

If a wrinkly wishes to enjoy a good night's sleep, the following activities may be inadvisable just before bedtime:

- Calling everyone you know and leaving messages on their answer phones to call you back no matter what time they get in;
- Giving yourself a night-time treat of a family size pack of liquorice novelties washed down with a flagon of prune juice;
- Making an attempt on the world record for the number of barrels of water a single individual can drink in under an hour;
- Inviting a suspected local serial killer round for a nightcap and then telling him to see himself out when he's finished;
- Partaking in an extensive late night espresso coffee sampling session;
- Renting your spare room out as rehearsal space for the thrash metal band formed by members of the local insomniacs self help group;
- Practicing your fire eating act while sitting in bed;
- Conjuring up some evil sprits using your handy bedside ouija board set;
- Unnecessarily raising your heart rate by going up the stairs to bed as fast as you can on a pogo stick followed by half an hour's trampoline practice on your mattress.

Wrinkly Bed Companions

Wrinklies may not share their beds quite as often or with quite as many companions as the oversexed younger generation. On the other hand wrinklies do have their own bed companions. There is often a wrinkly partner and possibly a wrinkly pet hidden somewhere about the bedding. This means that many wrinklies can still boast to their friends that they enjoy a threesome every night!

But when you get to our time of life, the attractions of sharing your bed with others are perhaps less obvious. It's difficult enough to get to sleep with your own wrinkly old body twitching, fidgeting and sniffling away all night while accompanying the whole performance with a series of peculiar noises. If you've got a second wrinkly body crammed in next to yours doing the same thing, isn't that twice the amount of distraction?

Ever since that bloke broke into the queen's bedroom at Buckingham Palace in the 1980s, we have known that Her Maj and her husband don't sleep together. Presumably Prince Philip was being kept awake each night by the sound of his wife's crown on the pillow next to him tinkling away as she breathed deeply in her royal sleep.

Nevertheless there are probably lots of reasons why other wrinklies should continue to share their beds.

Obviously one of the main reasons you still share a bed with your wrinkly partner is for all those long nights filled with non-stop, rampant, passionate sex. No, thought not.

Like many wrinklies you perfected the art of lovemaking years ago, didn't you? That's why you decided to retire from this art form when you were still on top (as it were) and leave your wrinkly partner with unspoilt memories of ultimate ecstasy.

Besides if you tried that sort of thing, think of the appalling squeaking noises that would be produced. And your bedstead would probably make a bit of a racket as well.

No, these days if any of your friends tell you they're a 'bit of a five times a night man', this probably just refers to the number of nocturnal visits they make to the bathroom.

You could say that by sharing a bed, you help keep each other warm at night. Unfortunately even this isn't true any more. These days your circulation is so bad, you and your partner keep each other cold at night and set each other shivering if either of you accidentally comes into contact with the other's ice cold extremities.

But at least it should be possible for you to demonstrate enduring affection with a brief cuddle. Unless, that is, one of you then experiences a sudden hot flush which leaves the pair of you sweating and gasping for breath at opposite ends of your steaming mattress.

But what makes the ideal wrinkly bed companion? What is it that we do to annoy them and is there anything else we can do to make sure that we get the bed all to ourselves?

Celebrity Bed Companions And Why They Wouldn't Suit A Female Wrinkly

Tom Cruise	You'd be kept awake all night by the light reflecting off his great pearly teeth
Russell Brand	He's probably not going to come up to bed at a sensible time is he?
Mick Jagger	When you're a wrinkly, the last thing you want in your bed is someone with extra wrinkles to spare – on the plus side he would make you look quite young
David Beckham	Presumably if you wanted to sit and read, he'd just sit there stuck for something to do
Simon Cowell	Just think of the critical comments you'll get for the cup of cocoa you took him
Arnold Schwarzenegger	Every single time he went to the toilet during the night, he'd tell you, 'I'll be back!'
Andy Murray	He moans, he grunts, he shouts and swears – it would be just like spending the night with your usual wrinkly old bed partner
Ant & Dec	A bit small – we suppose you could use one as a pillow and the other as a hot water bottle
Russell Crowe	He'd definitely get a bit cross if you stole the covers off him
Tom Jones	The wrinkly female's ideal man – but if that's the way he sounds when he sings, imagine what his snoring must be like
Prince William	He's probably a nice young man but he won't be used to putting the cat out and making sure the back door's locked himself, will he?

Celebrity Bed Companions And Why They Wouldn't Suit A Male Wrinkly

Kylie Minogue	Too small – you'd keep losing her in the duvet
Madonna	Too muscular – if you get into a pillow fight with her, you're very unlikely to win
Jordan	It will be cheaper just to buy yourself a new pair of big pillows
Posh Spice	Too small a surface area to plant your feet on so you can warm them up on a cold night
Britney Spears	All very nice I'm sure but is she going to take turns to make a nice cup of tea in the morning?
Mariah Carey	Unlikely to be satisfied by your electric blanket and teasmade
Any supermodel	If you try and cuddle up to them in bed they will snap in half plus they will never make you a decent fry-up for breakfast
Nigella Lawson	The perfect bed companion for a male wrinkly except for the fact you would never get to bed because you'd permanently be in the kitchen stuffing yourself on her cooking
Joanna Lumley	Again a wrinkly's ideal but if you get involved with her the Ghurkhas will surely be after your guts for garters
Angelina Jolie	Just imagine the cold sniffy look she will give you when she sees you in your tartan design pyjamas
Lady Gaga	She is bound to take up more than her fair share of space in your wardrobe

How To Avoid Upsetting Your Wrinkly Partner In Bed

Don't steal the bedclothes

Who says wrinklies don't get enough exercise? Wrinkly couples spend many nights playing tug-of-war with one another. This is played in the wrinkly couple's sleep using the duvet in place of a rope. This game of physical skill is played by wrinklies during much of the colder periods of the year (which to wrinklies usually means the entire year apart from the first week of August).

No, nothing annoys your partner more than having their bed covers stolen during the night. Even heaving them to one side in order to fit a younger more attractive companion next to you in their stead will annoy them less.

After a certain age they will regard this not so much as an affront to their dignity than as an extra source of warmth during the cold winter nights (n.b. the authors cannot accept legal responsibility if you choose to follow this advice and then discover your partner's reaction is not quite as described).

However if they wake up and find themselves lying exposed to the Arctic wind blowing through your bedroom and suffering the first symptoms of frostbite while you are wrapped up in the entire duvet like an enormous sausage roll, they are likely to be displeased.

You should also particularly avoid stealing the bedclothes from your partner if they are now estranged from you and live in a different house to which you do not have legitimate access.

Don't warm your feet on your partner's back

During the day wrinkly wives will frequently complain to their wrinkly husbands that they feel less supple than they used to. After the passage of years their joints are now painful and stiff and are difficult to bend.

During the night though, it's a completely different story.

Suddenly a wrinkly woman's leg joints become as flexible as those of a 20-year-old. This flexibility is not of course exhibited as part of any pleasurable bed-based activities.

No, instead the wrinkly husband discovers that his wrinkly wife's joints have been mysteriously rejuvenated when he becomes aware that she has managed to lift her legs right up in order to plant her freezing cold feet flat on his back.

Often a wrinkly man will have a permanent imprint of a pair of size 6 feet on his back. This marking has been indelibly left by a process similar to the freeze branding of identification marks on farm animals.

Why do wrinkly women's feet go cold from the 1st of September until the following May? Perhaps it is the first sign of the changing seasons. Perhaps it is because these days her feet spend much of the day shaded from direct sunlight. No-one really knows.

So, wrinkly men, this is the real reason your partner prepares a nice hot drink for you just before bedtime. As far as they are concerned what they are doing is filling up their hot water bottle for the night.

Don't keep your partner awake all night by snoring

A wrinkly may not care for the noises (verbal or otherwise) that emanate from their wrinkly partner during the daytime. During the night however they will find themselves subjected to a sonic performance that is even less welcome.

Wrinklies will often spend much of the night producing some of the most disgusting noises to have ever emerged from the upper half of a living creature. During the hours of darkness they will lie producing a bizarre low frequency rumbling. This is accompanied by the sound of gargling and guttural oscillation from various parts of their internal tubing.

The whole effect is akin to lying in the middle of a swamp full of bullfrogs and walruses, several of whom seem to be performing Swedish massages on each other. If your central heating system were making this racket each night, you'd apply for a boiler scrappage payment after evacuating the building for health and safety purposes.

You might assume that the noise if not the physical vibration produced by this aural extravaganza would be sufficient to wake everyone in the vicinity including the wrinkly producing it. But no! The wrinkly responsible for this soundscape sleeps on completely oblivious of his or her guttural dexterity.

Various devices can now be used to reduce the sound of snoring. A clip over the nose may help. Or, if you want a more permanent solution, try several very strong clips over the nose, nostrils and mouth.

The Dangers Of Multiple Wrinklies In One Bed – A Wrinkly Physicist Explains

The presence of one wrinkly man and his wrinkly wife lying in bed together inevitably means a lot of wrinkles in a small confined space. This is particularly the case if their sheets and blankets are also quite wrinkly.

The possibility then exists for all the hundreds perhaps thousands of individual wrinkles contained together in the bed to combine during the night. This can eventually lead to the formation of what scientists describe as a super-massive black wrinkle.

This resulting cosmologically huge wrinkle would be so enormous it would be capable of drawing everything in the surrounding area into itself.

It's a wonder that wrinkly couples don't wake up in the morning to discover that their bedside cabinets, their bedside lamps, their teasmade, dressing table and entire double bed have all disappeared as a result of being consumed by a super-massive wrinkle in the night.

This is the real reason why wrinklies can't find items such as their slippers or glasses when they wake up.

The super massive wrinkle would potentially affect all space and time around it. This is why wrinklies' bedrooms often have a retro look and seem to be filled with items dating from some lost period of time.

Even at the border of the region of space surrounding the wrinkly bed there will be an effect and the walls will be decorated with wallpaper which appears to have come from a previous century.

The Wrinkly Sutra

Positions for wrinklies to adopt in bed to help ensure that hanky panky is not only unlikely but probably physically impossible as well!

The Missionary Position

The lady wrinkly lies flat on the bed waiting while the gentleman wrinkly sits downstairs in the living room with the vicar who has unexpectedly popped by for a chat and a cup of tea.

The Doggie Position

The gentleman wrinkly lies facing upwards on one side of the bed. The lady wrinkly lies facing upwards on the other side of the bed. Directly between the gentleman wrinkly and the lady wrinkly lies their great hairy pet Labrador snoring away contentedly.

The Sixty-Nine Position

As everyone knows this position gets its name from a reference to a Chinese takeaway menu. After enjoying a takeaway earlier in the evening, the gentleman wrinkly and the lady wrinkly bend over. This is because they are now not feeling well and are both poised over the toilet bowl.

The Spoons Position

The gentleman wrinkly and the lady wrinkly both bend over the cutlery drawer and engage in several minutes hard polishing with the Brasso.

The Lotus Position

This is not advisable for wrinklies. The Ford Focus
Position, the Vauxhall Astra Position and the Rover 200
Position may all be better suited to wrinklies but probably
not the Lotus Position.

Suspended Congress

The gentleman wrinkly stands with his back to the lady
wrinkly and begins talking to her. When he turns round
he discovers that his lady wrinkly partner must have left
the room a little while ago and that he has therefore been
talking to himself for the last ten minutes.

The Golden Shower

The gentleman wrinkly returns home and discovers that
his lady wrinkly partner has had an ostentatious new
bathroom suite installed without his knowledge.

Annual Sex

Frequently subject of a very unfortunate misprint in a
number of widely available sex manuals. As wrinklies
know it should of course really be 'annual sex'.

Karma Suture

A sexual position in which things go disastrously wrong
thereby resulting in the need for immediate surgical
treatment.

Karma Chameleon

Being put off sex by the thought of Boy George.

The Wrinkly's Guide To Why Sex Is An Overrated Pastime

- Anything that young people like can't be much good.
- Everyone is obsessed with sex these days but general election results show how misguided the majority view can be.
- Sex was all right back in the good old days (when the wrinkly's generation invented it) but the over exposure it gets now has spoilt it for everyone.
- Sex was specifically invented to produce other people. And if there's one thing that irritates wrinklies it's other people!
- Modern day sex seems to involve a lot of moaning. Wrinklies are capable of moaning but with much less fuss and effort.
- There are plenty of more constructive ways for a wrinkly to put his or her back out.
- For wrinklies it's a bit like the pop music of their youth. It's probably still fun but the equipment necessary to enjoy it may require some servicing or a complete upgrade.
- Sadly it is necessary for wrinklies to avoid any strenuous bed based activities these days as the guarantee on their mattress has probably run out.
- A wrinkly can get quite enough sex for one day just by reading a magazine or newspaper or by watching an evening's television.
- Two words to sum up why wrinklies and sex shouldn't go together: Peter Stringfellow.

Here Are Some More Bed Companions For You

Even wrinklies who sleep alone get to share their bed. And not in a particularly nice way!

A used mattress may contain anywhere between 100,000 to 10 million dust mites. So looking on the positive side, you should never be lonely at night.

According to the *Wall Street Journal*, 'The average mattress will double its weight in ten years as a result of being filled with dust mites and their detritus.'

And do you know what these dust mites are feeding away on? Yes, on you!

These miniature bed companions spend their lives chomping away at dead skin cells. Dead skin cells are of course what wrinklies are mainly made up of. So when a wrinkly climbs into bed, there's a good chance they might be completely eaten away during the night by their own mattress.

If you wake up in the morning and find your wrinkly partner has disappeared listen very carefully. You may hear their muffled call for help from within your mattress. They may have been dragged inside the mattress by 10 million dust mites who were all feeling a bit peckish.

If your mattress has turned man (or wrinkly) eater it may be time to get a nice new one. If your wrinkly partner is still trapped inside you could release them before taking the old mattress to the tip.

Or you might just like to get a nice new partner to go with your nice new mattress.

Wrinkly
Wresolutions

You might think that at a certain time of life – all right, let's spell it out: wrinkliehood – you wouldn't need to make any more resolutions, or even wresolutions.

All that stuff's for younger people. People who still feel they've got something to prove. Wrinklies however, have been there, done that and got the wrinkled T-shirt.

But that's where you'd be wrong.

Wrinklies have to keep on top of things. You may be retired, you may have finally got the kids off your hands, but there are a thousand and one things to occupy your time.

In fact, you wonder how you ever found the time to fit in a job and a family and all that other stuff.

From the moment a wrinkly wakes up and has to make their first decision of the day (tea in bed, tea at the breakfast table, or tea in the garden), to the last one at night(cocoa, Ovaltine, or perhaps something a little stronger) it's go, go, go.

The first peek through the bedroom curtains presents the wrinkly with a multitude of choices too.

Has that flipping paperboy chucked the newspaper in the porch again like some dreadful American child from a 1950s sitcom? Have the dustmen left half the rubbish strewn behind them like participants in a wastepaper chase? Have the sparrows been at my silvertop again?

Already the wrinkly is writing imaginary letters of

complaint. Already the blood, which has simmered down overnight to a lukewarm sludge, has begun to boil.

Oh yes, and this is before the sun is barely over the horizon.

And then there are the health issues. The wrinkly wakes to find a strange stiffness in the left knee joint. That wasn't there yesterday, says the wrinkly to him or herself. Let's see if it passes before I make a doctor's appointment.

That twinge in my tooth – how can it be? It's a crown for goodness sake. That strange lump on the back of my hand – has it always been there? Oh yes, here's one just the same on the other hand. That's all right then.

Then there are the hundred and one decisions of what to do today. Do I need to renew my library books? Oh God, they've changed the system at the library to self-service and I don't know whether I can go through that again.

Should I speak to the next-door neighbour about their cat doing its business in my vegetable patch? How many times do I have to explain to them that cat poo is not manure? Perhaps I'll leave it as I want to borrow their strimmer later on.

Breakfast. I need to lower my cholesterol, but what is the point of being able to have the time for a leisurely wrinkly breakfast and then just have a piece of crispbread with low fat spread.

Sod it, I'll have a fry up again.

Things You Can Safely Put Off Until Tomorrow

One of the joys of being a wrinkly is having that little bit of extra time on your hands. You might be retired, you are probably not putting quite so much effort into trying to meet members of the opposite sex, and unlike younger people, you may not find it quite so necessary to be constantly phoning, texting, emailing, and updating your social networking websites.

But somehow, you're quite busy. What you need is WTM or Wrinkly Time Management.

This means deferring the not so pressing tasks, commitments and other flipping nuisances that clutter up your day.

The diet

George Orwell said, 'At 50, everyone has the face he deserves.' He could have added, 'and the body too.' Let's face it, if you've gone this long without adhering to a diet it's hardly worth bothering now is it?

Saving for a rainy day

The rainy day, my friend, is already here in the form of wrinkliehood. Spend it while you can!

Tidying the loft

The loft is the upstairs equivalent of under the carpet, but on a bigger scale. Instead of hiding bits of fluff and so on, it is the convenient receptacle for all the things that might 'come in useful one day'. Which may in theory be true, but only if you could remember what the hell was up there in the first place. It can wait.

Trying to find out what's in fashion

Without naming names, we all know the kind of shops wrinklies like to buy their clothes from. Reliable, trusted chains that don't have any truck with 'cutting edge' fashion.

But that doesn't mean to say the wrinkly wants to look like either Darby or Joan just yet. Shopping at High Street, Middle England means wrinklies don't have to think about fashion at all. They can be suited and booted in safe, vaguely contemporary attire without consulting Vogue. Perhaps we need our own fashion magazine called Fogue?

Cleaning the house

What was it Quentin Crisp said? Something about not bothering to dust because after six months it doesn't get any dustier? He's got a point. Plus of course, you can't build up your bodily resistance if you're living in a clinically clean environment can you? Well, that's our excuse anyway.

Mowing the lawn

Do you think Adam possessed a lawn mower in the Garden of Eden? Precisely. It's unnatural. It would also be interesting to see if Mr Crisp's dictum held true for grass too? After a certain time does the grass simply not get any higher? It's probably all academic anyway, as after a while you'd never be able to find the lawn mower out there.

Learning another language

You've lasted this long with *deux bierres s'il vous plaît*, so why bother?

Things You Should Have Done Today But Didn't

But enough of these trifling things that you will defer to another day. What about those really important things that you should have done but never quite got around to?

Written that novel

Well at least, starting it. You read somewhere that everyone has a novel in them. If only you could come up with perhaps a title or even an idea for a title. But no, as the sun sinks down again over that unmown lawn the unwritten novel stays unwritten.

Eaten your five a day

You know it makes sense, you know it's good for you and you really should have but you haven't quite done it again have you? But surely the currants in your garibaldis count, and the leaves in your tea, and the lemon in your gin and tonic, and the grapes in your wine…

Done your exercise

You know it's important after a certain age to keep your body in trim, and you've still got that magazine article you cut out about gentle exercise for the over 50s, but you haven't quite got round to it yet have you? Yes, we know that in your humble opinion it isn't gentle enough, but walking from the TV to the fridge simply isn't enough exercise – even if you do do it 20 times a day.

Recycled

You put your rubbish in the proper bins on rubbish day, but the rest of the time you're about as green as a radish.

Yes, you have good intentions, but life's too short to wash your baked bean tins isn't it?

Learned how to text

Your children virtually forced you to buy a mobile phone, and that, as far as you were concerned, is about as modern and up to date as you were prepared to get. Then you started to get texts from your grandchildren saying things like 'thnx 4 mi xmas prezzie' and you're expected to text back.

What's the point of being a wrinkly if you're going to act like a 12 year-old?

Fitted your panic alarm

Another of your kids' bright ideas, and still sitting in the box it came in.

Checked your blood pressure, cholesterol, etc

There comes a point in a wrinkly's life when you feel like a car that's having a daily MOT test.

Most old bangers manage to chunter on quite nicely without them most of the time – and cars do too.

Invited the neighbours in for a drink

You keep meaning to, but by the time you've had breakfast, then elevenses, and lunch, it's time for a little nap, then Countdown, then it's dinner, and 40 winks in front of the box, and blow us down, it's bedtime again! Where does the time go?

Counting Your Wrinkly Blessings

It's so easy to look on the downside of wrinklyhood isn't it?

Well, to be fair, there are one or two things you might not be over the moon about, but let's not dwell on those; let's look at the upside.

You're not dead

Being dead does have its advantages of course: no more tax, no more aches and pains, and no more ear-bashings from your wrinkly other half.

But it's not ideal by any means. So, you're a bit older than you used to be but so is everyone else, and you're still here to tell the tale.

You're not young

Youth is overrated. Would you really want to spend all your waking hours either texting people or reading texts, or worrying about who hasn't texted you?

Would you want to be self-confined to the house for a fortnight because you had a tiny little spot on your nose? Would you really want to try to walk with your trouser waist perched just above your knees because it's fashionable?

You possess wisdom

Yes, young people like to think they know it all, and they may have a slight advantage when it comes to fixing your crashed computer, but do they know which cutlery to use first at a wedding reception? Do they know how to spell any word of more than one syllable (or sometimes just one syllable)?

Do they remember what the government before last was like and know not to vote for them? Can a Kentucky fried chicken fly?

You have fewer worries

With a bit of luck your mortgage is a dim and distant memory. You may even be in profit if you're charging your teenage and adult children rent!

You don't care what you look like. Well, up to a point. Even wrinklies have some pride. But you're not a slave to fashion, and you won't be devastated if the postman catches you in your jim jams (some hope with the modern postal system!)

You are at the end of your working life

Even if you're still working, the end is in sight! No more clocking on, bunking off, trying to invent new excuses for throwing a sickie, having to go to leaving parties of people you don't even like, contributing to collections every time someone gets married, has a baby (not necessarily in that order) or runs a half marathon. Freedom!

You don't care any more

'Beyond dignity' might be putting it a bit strong, but frankly, who cares if anyone laughs at your dress sense, talks behind your back, questions your sexuality, calls you a racist, flashes a V sign because of some minor motoring misdemeanour or other such trivialities.

Mind you, if they said your garden looked a bit on the untidy side you would of course be well within your rights to give them a sock on the jaw.

How To Look Good Wrinkly

These days there is absolutely no shortage of role models for the wrinkly gorgeousness aspirant. Did we mention somewhere else in this book such names as Joan Collins, Sophia Loren, Helen Mirren, Raquel Welch, Jane Fonda, Sean Connery, Harrison Ford, Clint Eastwood…?
So, what's their secret?

No artificial help

Never mind the Botox. What's the point of being, ahem, of a certain age, if you look like a box-fresh Barbie doll? Actors everywhere adhere to that dramatic dictum: 'you can't emote with a face full of 'Bote."

Besides, people will be highly suspicious of an actor playing say, Moses, if he looks about 12.

A few million dollars

Yes, regular, unlimited access to fabulous food, designer clothes, expensive gyms and tanning salons can help – so keep filling in those lottery tickets!

Great lighting

Actors have the advantage of being able to dish out official photos, taken in subdued lighting with perhaps a Vaseline smeared soft-focus lens. Then there may be a bit of jiggery pokery with some clever photographic software to enhance those lined, and frankly southbound, features.

So for us non-thespian wrinklies that probably means having a life-size professional photo taken, and then wearing it like a mask at all times.

False Memory Syndrome

Somehow we have a fixed idea in our minds of actors at
their peak regardless of how old they've got, or even look.
In our mind's eye they are still just as they were when
we first set our caps at them. Perhaps this is why Mickey
Mouse never looks any older, despite being the wrong side
of 80. But actors, and famous rodents aside, what else can
the wrinkly do to keep the years at bay?

Bare flesh

It's all right for the doctor to see you in the buff. He's
probably bound by a Hippocratic oath or something not
to breathe a word about what's baggy, saggy or wrinkly
about your body, on pain of being struck off.

Not so your friends. Keep your wrinkles under wraps.

Fancy dress parties

If you restrict your socialising purely to fancy dress parties
then you will be able to cover up the worst of what the
years have done to you. This might explain why certain
ageing fashion designers always appear to be in fancy dress.

Good works

Have you noticed how many retired people start doing
good works – helping out at charity shops, taking old
people out for the day, that sort of thing? There is of
course a philanthropic element to all this, but it has the
marvellous side benefit of making the helper look younger
in contrast to the helpees.

Who wouldn't look quite perky next to a
nonagenarian?

What You Intend, And What You Actually Do

We wrinklies like our resolutions. What we don't like so much is actually sticking to them. For example:

Intention: I'm not going to end up like my father/mother.
Actuality: You get mistaken for them by even older, and perhaps slightly confused members of the family.

Intention: I'm not going to become a grumpy old man/ woman.
Actuality: Your tongue is feared and dreaded more widely than that of a venomous snake.

Intention: I'm going to keep myself fit.
Actuality: If you moved any less in an average day you would probably be dusted by anyone cleaning the room.

Intention: I'll try to keep up with all this modern technology.
Actuality: You thought broadband was a type of margarine.

Intention: I'd like to do a bit of travelling.
Actuality: It's all such a hassle. Even preparations for a trip to the supermarket stop just short of injections, passports, and travel pills.

Intention: I'm not going to get stuck in a rut.
Actuality: You're still watching the same TV programmes that you did 30 years ago, but now it's on oldies TV channels and DVD.

Intention: I'll try to keep up with the latest clothes fashions.
Actuality: They don't seem to do the latest fashions in a 44-inch waist.

Intention: I'll start doing something useful for the local community now I've got a bit more time on my hands.
Actuality: I'm writing more letters to the local paper about dog mess, fly tipping, and the outrageous council tax rises.

Intention: I'll try not to have the first drink of the day before the sun's over the yard arm.
Actuality: The sun is over the yard arm somewhere in the world by 11am isn't it?

Intention: I'll try to keep up with younger bands and their music.
Actuality: Tribute bands are usually quite young aren't they?

Intention: I'll research my entire family tree now I've got the time.
Actuality: How do you get this computer going again?

How To Live Cheaply

Wrinklies can often find themselves a bit short of cash what with retirement, redundancy, and possibly several other words beginning with 're'.

It is therefore essential that wrinklies have a few tricks and tips up their cardie sleeves to eke out those sparse coppers in their later years.

It is rather a shock to the system when your spending goes from huge to Scrooge, but as always, the wrinkly will bear it all with characteristic fortitude, forbearance and dignity.

Eating the cat's food

When you look at the labels on cat food these days you start to think 'wait a minute, this animal's eating better than I am!' Tenderloin of beef, trout with mixed vegetables, ocean fish, chicken breasts with vegetables and brown rice. What's going on here?!

Now we're not suggesting of course that you open a tin of cat food and consume the contents yourself, tempting though this may be. No, you cook yourself the tenderloin of beef, trout or whatever and let the cat have the leftovers. The money you save on not buying this ridiculous cat food will enable you to eat like a king.

Turn off the heating

Even with your wrinkly winter fuel allowance it still costs an arm, a leg, and probably several other parts of your anatomy to heat the house during the cold weather.

The trick is to arrange with your wrinkly friends that they will all come to your house on, say, Monday, then you turn off the heating for the rest of the week while you go to another wrinkly's house on Tuesday, then a different one's on Wednesday and so on.

You will cut your heating bill by 85%, you will be having a house party every day of the week, and you may even be in profit from your Winter fuel allowance. Fantastic!

Run your own postal service

With the price of a first class stamp now approaching the equivalent of the national debt of a small African country it is time for wrinklies everywhere to unite.

What with sending postal orders and presents to grandchildren, writing letters of complaint to various companies, and of course your ongoing correspondence to newspapers national and local, your postal bills are now quite sizeable. But help is at hand!

Wrinklies all over the country have free local travel. It should not therefore be beyond the wit of man for wrinklies to form a national network that passes mail on from one wrinkly's local area to another.

Before long the entire country would be one vast postal system with letters and parcels passing from hand to wrinkled hand.

It should be possible to get a letter from Land's End to John O'Groats in less than a week which may actually be quicker than the current second class 'service'.

Wrinklies of the world unite! You have nothing to lose but your chain letters!

New Year Resolutions You Might Keep

Just after your two weeks of gluttony and over-consumption, otherwise known as Christmas, you will probably start thinking about how you will reinvent yourself in the New Year so you become a better wrinkly and generally all round wonderful human being.

To make things easier for yourself and so you don't fall short of your high expectations you should only make New Year resolutions that you have a hope in hell of keeping. For example:

Slowing down a bit

Taking the law of unintended consequences to its logical conclusion, you will slow down whether you want to or not. As long as you don't actually grind to a complete standstill it's nothing to worry about.

Giving up something

People always make the mistake of resolving to give up something they enjoy. What's the point of that? It's so much easier to give up something you don't enjoy, e.g. eating offal, or cleaning out the cat litter, or being polite to double-glazing salesmen on the doorstep.

Not running the marathon

It's all very well to get into the record books for being the oldest person to run the marathon, or the fastest pensioner, but you don't want to be in there for the wrong reasons, e.g. the shortest distance ever covered before collapsing in a heap.

New Year Resolutions You Probably Won't Keep

Oh, if you really must. Go on, make a fool of yourself. Make a great long list of all the wonderful things you're going to do come January 1st; all the things you're going to give up; all the ways you're going to be a model citizen, a paragon of virtue and all that other stuff. But don't come crying to us when it all goes pear-shaped, or more likely when you go all pear-shaped after your diet comes to a sticky (and probably sweet) end on January 2nd.

Here are the ones you probably won't keep (though congrats all round if you do):

The diet

If you've been resolving to lose weight every year since about 1971 and failed what hope do you think you've got now? And why should you care anyway? If you were meant to lose weight why did they invent expandable waist trousers?

Smoking

Ditto smoking. If you were going to give it up you would have done so by now. And if you're prepared to shell out the six quid a packet or whatever it costs these days you must be pretty determined to carry on puffing.

Cutting down on drinking

Considering you've probably never accurately evaluated your weekly alcohol consumption it's going to be quite difficult to determine whether you've actually reduced your intake. Which is probably exactly what you'll argue next time someone 'twists your arm' to have just one more.

Life, The Wrinklyverse And Everything

When lying in their beds at night, wrinklies will often contemplate the meaning of life. Well, first they might contemplate the gas bill they received that morning and where to go for their holidays this year. Nevertheless eventually they will get onto the great questions of existence.

What is the meaning and purpose of life? What answers can science provide us? Are there great secrets which are deliberately being withheld from us by the government?

What's it all about?

Wrinklies are very concerned by these big questions. For a start they can't believe they have lived as long as they have and still not managed to crack them.

Failing that couldn't they have found a way of cheating to get hold of the answer? Couldn't someone have surreptitiously slipped the solution to them by now or at least given them details of a website where you could look it up?

Unfortunately if a wrinkly ever knew the meaning of life, it now seems to have slipped their wrinkly old memory. Wrinklies are thus left sitting in the exam hall of life feeling as though they have done insufficient revision to pass. Nevertheless others will inevitably regard wrinklies as sources of great wisdom.

By their time of life wrinklies should resemble great gurus or venerable ancient philosophers. They should all wear great flowing gowns. They should have enormous grey beards and big bulging bald heads. Possibly male wrinklies should have these as well.

All wrinklies should look like solemn thinkers cogitating on the deepest insights of which man is capable.

This is not however what wrinklies usually look like. Wrinkly men are often balding and pot bellied and dressed in flat caps and beige zip up jackets. Wrinkly ladies often have curly permed hair and dress in comfortable slacks and nice cardies. Neither of these images tend to spring to mind when people hear the phrase 'great philosopher' but perhaps they should.

Because of their age and experience, wrinklies rightly believe that they should be regarded and valued as elders of their community. Many people do regard and value wrinklies as elders. This is why they refer to them by names such as 'Grandad', 'Grandma' or 'You old dear'.

Nevertheless the fact that they either don't know or have forgotten the answers to life's great questions remains a source of potential embarrassment for wrinklies.

Wrinklies fear young people will come to them demanding to know what the meaning of life is and they will only be able to respond with statements such as 'Always remember to wear sensible shoes' and 'A little of what you fancy does you good.'

So when put on the spot what can wrinklies say or do to make themselves look a bit wiser and more inscrutable?

Indeed could the secrets of being a wrinkly be a key to the secrets of life itself? Perhaps we are all living not in a universe but in a wrinklyverse!

How To Look Like A Wise Old Wrinkly Who Might Possibly Know The Meaning Of Life

Do: sit puffing slowly on an old Meerschaum pipe in order to cultivate the air of an ageing academic.

Don't: sit blowing bubbles from a brightly coloured plastic pipe in order to cultivate the air of a complete idiot.

Do: wander around in a long flowing gown like an ancient philosopher.

Don't: wander around in a long flowing gown open to reveal your backside like a patient who has escaped from a secure unit.

Do: give carefully considered answers to those who come to you with life's great questions.

Don't: wander up and down the high street shouting at anyone who passes by.

Do: sit cross-legged surrounded by your disciples.

Don't: sit cross-legged surrounded by your disciples while repeatedly raising your left buttock to break wind.

Do: sit slowly stroking your chin while contemplating life's mysteries.

Don't: sit slowly scratching your groin while contemplating the fungal infection you have recently developed.

Do: sit dispensing words of wisdom.

Don't: sit dispensing the words of Norman Wisdom.

Wrinkly Conspiracy Theories

The Moon landings were faked by wrinkly actors in a film studio: that's why the astronauts appear to move so slowly and clumsily on the Moon surface. One of the astronauts even resorted to playing golf on the Moon thereby clearly revealing himself to be a wrinkly.

A UFO landed at Roswell, New Mexico in 1947; pictures of the autopsy performed on the Roswell alien show an odd looking bald figure with a protuberant veined skull. Clearly the Roswell alien was a wrinkly from another galaxy who had come to make contact with wrinklies on Earth. The story therefore had to be hushed up by young people.

Elvis Presley faked his own death: Elvis 'died' aged 42 years old. Exactly the time when he would have been turning wrinkly! Obviously it was all a hoax to stop him wiggling his pelvis before he put an artificial hip out.

The world is governed by a secret all-powerful organisation: well, they certainly never tell us wrinklies what's going on.

Shakespeare didn't write the plays commonly ascribed to him: this is a conspiracy theory put about by young people who cannot believe that a wrinkly slaphead like Shakespeare could have written his plays and that they must therefore have been written by someone younger with a full head of hair like Christopher Marlowe.

Global warming is a hoax: this is a tall tale clearly perpetrated by the government in an effort to cut winter fuel payments to older wrinklies.

Feng Shui For Wrinklies

Feng Shui is the wise and ancient Chinese art of where to put stuff. Wrinklies are also wise and ancient and spend much of their time wondering where to put all the rubbish they have accumulated during their lives. So which of the essential principles of Feng Shui specifically apply to wrinklies?

Avoid placing a mirror opposite your front door

This is good advice for wrinklies because otherwise every time they walk through their front door they will be terrified by the sight of the shrivelled old person standing opposite them and this may cause them to drop their shopping.

Hallways should be bright places

Your front door should open into a bright well-lit hallway because otherwise wrinklies' photochromatic varifocals can be slow to react causing them to immediately be plunged into darkness and fall over.

Beware of straight roads leading to your front door

The front of your house should not face a straight road. Wrinklies should pay particular heed to this advice especially if the brakes on their wrinkly old cars need attention or their reactions are a little slow. Otherwise the Ford Focus will end up parked for the night in the living room... again.

Positioning your bedroom at the end of a long corridor is unlucky

This is because wrinkly house guests may wander in during the middle of the night thinking they have found your bathroom and you will then wake up the next morning feeling slightly damp.

Wind chimes around your garden will make you popular

Or maybe they'll just make so much racket you won't hear the neighbours shouting at you to take them down.

Exposed overhead beams are sources of bad energy

Or more to the point they are sources of dirty great bruises on your wrinkly bonce. To diffuse the bad energy, hang a wind chime from the beam. The irritating tinkling sound will then alert you to the fact that you have just bashed your head on the beam as well as helping to drown out the shouting and swearing that follows a moment later.

Don't hang mirrors in the bedroom

Otherwise they will keep shattering every time you get undressed in front of them. And that's just from the sound of the high pitched screaming that usually follows.

The ratio of windows to doors in a room should not exceed 3:1

Otherwise there is a corresponding 3:1 chance that a forgetful wrinkly will attempt to leave the room via one of the windows. This advice is particularly important for wrinklies living in high rise flats. One door and one window per room at least gives you a 50/50 chance of survival every time you pop out to put the kettle on.

Keep the toilet door closed

Particularly while you're in there and you have guests in the house.

Wrinklies' Universal Scientific Laws

The following are the fundamental scientific laws
underlying the wrinkly universe:

- For every action there is an equal and opposite pain in
  your knee joints.
- A body will remain in a state of rest or at least it will
  until its wrinkly bed partner tells it to get up and
  make a cup of tea.
- The speed of light in a vacuum is constant but the
  speed of your vacuum depends on the depth of your
  shag pile.
- The energy in a closed system remains constant unless
  it's just got back from the shops when it will feel a bit
  tired.
- Every particle in the universe attracts every other
  particle but the older wrinklier particles tend to get
  less of a look in.
- The likelihood of bumping into someone you know
  when you go out is inversely proportional to how
  much you want to see them.
- The speed at which people move away from you in
  the high street is in direct proportion to whether they
  think you noticed them or not.
- Computers will keep on getting smarter but they will
  never get so smart that they won't mess up your direct
  debit payments.
- If you let Archimedes use your bath, you'll end up
  with water all over your bathroom floor.

- A watched kettle never boils (Boil's Law).

- Simon Cowell earns more money than you do (Susan Boyle's Law).

- Your sleeve will always catch on the door handle (Hook's Law).

- Things are more difficult than they should be (More's Law).

- Grated carrot and cabbage in mayonnaise goes nicely with a salad (Coles Law).

- If an apple drops out of a tree onto your head you'll run round in agony for several minutes (Newton's Law of Motion).

- I'm not certain where I left my keys (Heisenberg's Uncertainty Principle).

- Your lottery numbers will win the jackpot the week you don't buy a ticket.

- If you are looking for an item in the supermarket, someone will appear and stand in front of it at the precise moment you finally locate it.

- Mechanical and electrical appliances will break down the day after the guarantee runs out.

- If you are looking for an item in the supermarket and finally give up and ask an assistant, you will then discover that you are in fact standing right next to it thereby making yourself look like a complete idiot.

The Wrinkly Universe

If you're ever feeling a bit old, just think how the universe itself must feel. The universe is currently about 13.5 billion years old (and probably by the time you read this, it will be slightly older). The universe is therefore only slightly less old than you feel. No wonder it's in the state it's in. Not only that but no-one ever remembers its birthday.

The universe is therefore the ultimate wrinkly. Like other wrinklies the universe doesn't seem to be doing quite as much as it did in its earlier days, it seems to be moving slower than it used to, it's feeling colder, it's looking more dishevelled and it's a very very long time since it enjoyed a Big Bang.

Also like other wrinklies not only is the universe extremely old, it has been steadily increasing in size since the year dot. So if you ever feel depressed about putting on weight, just think of the universe.

When it began, the universe was about the size of an atom and now look at it! Even with the most stringent diet, the universe is clearly going to have some considerable difficulty getting back to its original size!

Many wonder whether, like its fellow wrinklies, the universe still has any particular purpose any more. Some fear the day is approaching when the universe will finally collapse.

Nevertheless, like many other wrinklies, the universe seems to carry on regardless with its regular routine day after day.

The planets in our solar system are around 4.5 billion years old. Yes, we know you remember the day some of the newer ones formed.

At 4.5 billion years old the planets are clearly a bit wrinkly. Nevertheless the universe must see them as young upstarts and thus regard them with suspicion. Planets however even look wrinkly being covered in craters and having dry, cracked surfaces. Planets are surely crying out for a bit of Oil of Olay.

And to further prove planets are wrinklies: they are often grey-looking; they spend their days wandering round in a circle while being battered with all that the universe can throw at them; they fear falling into black holes; and many of them are shrouded by atmospheres in which a lot of people would find it difficult to breathe.

Yes, the planets might as well all go round the sun on planet-sized Zimmer frames!

It is therefore clearly a wrinkly universe.

In fact when you think about it, the entire future is wrinkly.

By the time the future arrives today's young people will be old. Also thanks to advances in medical science there will be an ever increasing number of wrinklies around.

The inevitable fate of the universe is therefore not that it will be full of glamorous young astronauts zipping around the galaxies but that it will gradually fill up with wrinklies.

Those may not be stars twinkling in the sky but the grey heads of an infinite number of wrinklies!

Frequently Asked Questions About Life On Other Planets

Is there life on other planets and if so why can't we see it?

We never see any signs of life when we look at other planets in the universe. This is because we are only able to use telescopes to look at other planets at night-time when it is dark. Clearly at night-time wrinklies have all gone to bed or are sitting in the back room watching television. The reason we have not detected life on other planets is therefore because all extra-terrestrial beings must be wrinklies.

What do aliens look like?

Large balding heads with protuberant veins. Withered looking limbs. They're wrinklies! (see Wrinkly Conspiracy Theories p.155)

Why are UFO sightings only ever reported in remote areas where few people live?

Remote locations with few people around are exactly the sorts of places a wrinkly might go for a short break or day out. UFOs that visit Earth must therefore be piloted by alien wrinklies. We can thus deduce that the insides of UFOs must have a tartan rug on the backseat and a little nodding dog and a box of tissues on the parcel shelf at the back.

Why does it seem that messages we have sent out into space have not been picked up by alien civilisations?

Because it's all wrinklies out there. They're all a bit deaf. They probably didn't hear any of our messages.

Why have alien civilisations not made more attempt to contact us?

That's wrinklies for you. They like to keep themselves to themselves.

Are alien civilisations greatly more advanced than our own?

Alien civilisations are vastly more scientifically and technically advanced than us. Unfortunately the wrinklies who live in these alien civilisations have probably never been able to take advantage of the scientific and technical advances available to them. This is because the instruction books that came with all their advanced scientific and technical technology had a lot of small print and were a bit complicated to read. This is another reason why we don't receive regular communications or visits from alien wrinklies.

Why would aliens come to our planet?

If they're wrinklies, mainly for medical treatment on the NHS or to visit National Trust properties.

How long would aliens take to travel to Earth?

If they travelled from Proxima Centauri, the nearest star to us after the sun, their journey would take 76,000 years. So even if they weren't wrinkly when they set off, they certainly would be by the time they got here. It is possible aliens may have more advanced spaceship technology. This will not however speed up their journeys because, being wrinklies, they will need frequent toilet stops and get a bit lost travelling round unfamiliar solar systems. Also, being wrinklies, they might just decide to leave the spaceship at home and come here by bus instead.

Wise Utterances For Philosophical Wrinklies

- Life is what you make it. Your excuse can therefore be that no-one ever gave you a proper set of assembly instructions.
- Life is a sexually transmitted disease. And you weren't even the one who got the sex.
- Life is a lottery so look on the bright side. Even getting the booby prize is fun!
- Life is like a box of chocolates. When you get to a certain age, there's less to choose from, they're all coffee creams and the ones you've had up to now have rotted your teeth.
- Life is a series of things going wrong and the biggest thing going wrong happens right at the end.
- Life is like having a ticket to the greatest show on Earth but you'll probably spend all your time trying to find somewhere to park.
- No-one can tell you the precise meaning of life although many will try and palm you off with a misleading translation.
- Not only is life not fair, there isn't even a complaints desk.
- Life is the sum of all your choices. This may cause you to ask how can I have been wrong that often?
- Life is like an annoying neighbour with a big car. It goes past far too quickly and invariably fails to acknowledge you.
- Live your life as though each day is your last although this will mean that friends and family will become increasingly annoyed to see you again each morning.

The Wrinkly Whisperer

You've heard of amazing animal experts such as the horse whisperer, the dog whisperer, the cat whisperer and the slightly less successful three-toed sloth whisperer.

These people seem to have an extraordinary ability to understand what animals are trying to tell them although this is usually along the lines of, 'Could you speak up? I can't hear what you're saying because you keep whispering!'

Wrinklies also have a great affinity with other species (with the notable exception of young people that is). But what would different animals say to a wrinkly?

Animal	What They Would Say To A Wrinkly
Cat	I am your master and you will feed me, look after me, clean up after me and do everything I command from this day forward!
Budgie	And that goes for me too!
Dog	I've noticed that when we're out for a walk, you seem to need a wee about as often as I do.
Goldfish	So tell me, what's it like living with such a poor short-term memory?
Tortoise	Is that really the fastest you can go?
Snail	Don't worry. I'll go on ahead and tell the tortoise to wait.
Lion	It's OK I'm not going to eat you. Not when you're clearly so far past your 'Best before' date.
Skunk	Can you smell something funny in here?
Cow	Blimey! I thought mine hung a bit low!
Elephant	Blimey! You're more grey and wrinkly than I am!
Cat (again)	So are you getting me my dinner or what?

Tomorrow's World

When you're a wrinkly today increasingly seems like tomorrow. Every day seems to bring some bewildering change, technological or otherwise, that seems bizarre, baffling, or just plain daft.

Once upon a time, not so long ago, you had things called records, that you played on record players. These had been around since you were a tot, and probably since your parents were tots too.

OK, your mum and dad probably had to get used to the vast cultural shift of 78 rpm records being jettisoned in favour of those little 45s, and having to plug the record player into the wall rather than using one of things like a starting handle (note to younger readers: that was what you used to start your car with back in the day when Churchill was a politician and not a talking dog).

But essentially, a record was a record regardless of what speed it revolved at!

Then came cassettes and CDs, and yes, CDs were sort of like mini records that came in miniaturised cases that mimicked ye olde album covers.

Now they're going too. To be replaced by what?

Nothing! Nothing, you ask? Now you have to 'download' your favourite tunes via a computer (what if you don't have a computer?) and put it on your iPod, whatever that may be. It sound like an awful lot of faffing about, and you don't even get a record cover to hold in your grubby mitts.

And they charge you for this. Ee, it's like buying thin air as your granny might have said.

Now they're talking about digital TV, and how we'll all have to change our TV sets – and our radios too.

Isn't it strange, that while TV is still broadcasting *Coronation Street*, and radio still has *The Archers* and *Desert Island Discs* and the shipping forecast and all those other shows from the mists of time we suddenly need all this new-fangled equipment to watch or listen to them on?

And don't even get us started on videos. What a boon it was when they invented the video and you could record *Eastenders* while you were at the bingo or in the pub.

Then some bright spark decided it was too simple, too convenient, and we'd need DVDs instead. Only problem was, you couldn't record on them to begin with.

Then they brought in something called blu-ray. What's that when it's at home? Is it related to bluetooth? And what's HDTV? Why do they have to keep changing things? Progress, they say.

But no, we wrinklies have been around long enough to know that all this talk of progress and technological advancement is just moonshine.

Tomorrow's world will be just like today's world but they'll just have more scientific excuses when it all goes pear-shaped.

Inventions Wrinklies Are Waiting For

"Build a better mousetrap and the world will beat a path to your door" is what Ralph Waldo Emerson has often been credited with saying.

These days it would probably be: "Build a better mousetrap and you might not get the mickey taken out of you on *Dragon's Den*."

What we really need though is a sort of *Dragon's Den* for wrinklies. If such a programme existed this is what we'd like to see on it:

Large print road signs

You know what it's like, you're driving along and you see one of those road signs with a big exclamation mark warning of some terrible hazard, but the writing underneath is minuscule. Well, minuscule for the average wrinkly anyway. And if that means giant road signs with other road signs warning you to look out for them so be it.

Pill-dispensing cuckoo clocks

Frankly it's a faff. You have to remember to take your little blue pill at breakfast time, your little pink pill at half past eleven, two yellow pills at 3.30pm, a white pill with your evening meal and your disgusting brown ones just before bed. If you're taking even one of those pills to help your memory then you're on a loser from the start. What you need is a clock, a bit like a cuckoo clock, but instead of a wooden cuckoo popping out you get a little man in a white coat carrying your pill du heure. What could be simpler?

Walk-in cars

It's all very well getting in and out of cars if you're a
sprightly young thing but when your age is fast heading
towards the national speed limit and your joints are in
more need of oiling than your car then it's not such a piece
of cake. They invented a walk-in bath for people who
don't bend in the right places, why not a walk-in car too?
There's a fortune to be made by some lucky person.

Proper sized telephones

Some of these phones nowadays aren't much bigger than a
Mars bar. By the time you've picked them up and fiddled
around trying to find which button to press, the caller has
rung off.

An exploding handbag

Old ladies with handbags full of pension money are seen
as easy targets by some criminal elements. This bag would
explode within ten seconds of being snatched by a simple
'tug reaction' mechanism. They might have to work on
how to avoid your pension money being blown to bits as
well though...

Ride-on supermarket trolleys

At a certain time of life we don't want to be pushing
trolleys full of HobNobs and cat food around the
supermarket. What we need are ride-on trolleys. They
would have to be for the exclusive use of wrinklies though;
you wouldn't want boy racers with trolleys full of cheap
lager cutting you up on the corners. The other advantage is
that people would no longer be able to accuse you of being
off your trolley.

The Wrinklies' Guide To The Modern World

Who was it who said the past was a foreign country? Well, they obviously hadn't seen the future, or what is now known as the present.

We wrinklies were brought up on Dan Dare and other space exploring heroes. We were led to believe that by the 21st century we would all be walking around skyscrapered streets in space suits, flying down to the shops using our jet-packs and having pet robots doing all our chores for us. Ha! Tosh and nonsense!

The nearest we get to a space suit is a shell suit and the prospect of getting a stairlift is hardly an adequate replacement for our long promised jet packs.

Surely we're due some sort of compensation for the future we were promised but never got. Instead we've got a future nobody expected!

What nobody imagined was people of a certain age – all right, wrinklies – walking around in jeans, T-shirts and trainers like superannuated James Deans. We had no idea that the morning post would be delivered in the afternoon or that our fifteen minutes of fame would be on CCTV.

Oh it's a rum place all right, this modern world. For example:

Coffee

Well for a start there's no such thing as 'a coffee' any more. It's a latte, or a cappuccino, or an Americano, or a Mocha or some such daft thing. Whatever it is, it certainly isn't our cup of tea.

And you can't get a small one, it has to be 'regular' (dreadful Americanism meaning large) or large (meaning huge) or possibly grande (meaning it's served in a bucket and will keep you in the toilet for the rest of the day). Then they serve this concoction in a cardboard cup and ask you to stump up almost half a week's pension for the privilege!

Friendship

Once upon a time you met people and they became your friends – or not, as the case may be. Now you have to have friends on social networking websites. People you've not met. People you're never likely to meet. But they're your 'friends'. If you can't invite them round for tea they can't be proper friends can they?

Technology

What's a Blackberry for example? You hear of people who can't live without their Blackberries. Maybe it's some sort of pacemaker or dialysis machine?

Twitter. For the birds. Well it sounds like budgie food. Skype. Something like Sky Plus maybe? The problem is that when you reach wrinklyhood you're constantly bombarded with all this new technology day in, day out.

Hardly a day passes without some new bit of kit coming onto the market that we all 'must have'. How long before we're all expected to walk around with a Hadron collider in our pocket? iPad – it sounds like something the doctor would give you to put over your peepers after your cataract operation.

Other annoying things

And what's this new fashion for giving everyone daft nicknames? Jennifer Lopez became J-Lo, Boris Johnson became BoJo, and Susan Boyle became SuBo. Does this mean that if your name is Susan Moore you have to be SuMo or that if you were unluckily christened Boris Zonk, you're going to be BoZo?

So-called entertainment

Have you watched *Question Time* lately? Unfortunately it's no longer a simple case of watching it; you can 'push the red button' if you're watching digitally, follow it on Twitter, email in your comments, phone, or even write in using ye olde postal system. If you miss it you can watch on the iPlayer whatever that may be.

In the old days, if you missed a programme you missed it. 'End of!' (as soap opera characters annoyingly tend to say these days). Radio programmes are available as 'podcasts' which sounds like some unpleasant plaster of Paris support around your nether regions. It's impossible to miss anything! Even if you really don't want to watch it!

Even more technology!

Nothing's simple anymore is it? Whenever you phone anyone it's a rare treat if you actually get through to a human being straight away.

More likely it's the answerphone or voicemail, or a multichoice switchboard. Press one for this, and two for that and three to top yourself. Then when the call finally goes through to someone with a welcome ringing tone it suddenly cuts to piped music.

Is this what happened to all those robots we were promised? They don't do your housework for you but you do get to speak to them whenever you phone any large institution. For ten minutes, an android will boss you around telling you which button on your telephone keypad to press next. Weren't they supposed to obey us?

Has anyone ever calculated the number of man hours wasted every year listening to this garbage? It would probably be enough to rebuild Hadrian's Wall, put up the third terminal at Heathrow, and solve the meaning of life – with enough time left over to work out whether the title of *Britain's Got Talent* is a statement or a question.

Yes, the modern world is a strange land indeed, and the wrinkly is like a time traveller variously marvelling at and being repulsed by it all.

The great advantage for the wrinkly though is he or she can mentally travel back in time to 'the good old days' when the post was delivered three times a day, when the only person wearing a hoodie was Father Christmas, when tweets were the dawn chorus, and when a financial crisis was the pound being worth less than four dollars.

If you told the kids of today how marvellous life was in your wrinkle-free youth they wouldn't believe you. Not that they'd hear you anyway; they'd have some electrical device plugged into their ears and by the time they'd got it out you'd have forgotten what you were saying.

The Ideal Things For Wrinklies To Wake Up To

Probably the best thing to wake up to would be not being a wrinkly, but hey, you can't have everything, and if you did, as comedian Steven Wright once noted, where would you keep it anyway?

Wrinklies enjoy their little luxuries. After a lifetime of work and bringing up kids, not for them the lights and the sights, but a bit of gentle relaxation. For example:

A bit of peace and quiet

As soon as you wake up you hear the rumble of traffic, the clatter of milk bottles and the paperboy's squeaky bike. As the day goes on there's more and more unwanted noise. Older people aren't actually hard of hearing, they voluntarily go a bit Mutt 'n' Jeff to avoid all the racket.

Not 5.00am

Why is that when you get older you need less sleep? If you're retired it's sometimes hard enough to fill the day with useful things to do even if you wake up at nine o'clock.

Tea in bed

Why can't they extend the Meal on Wheels service to tea in bed? They could call it Char by Car. OK, it would probably mean a bit more on your council tax but ooh, wouldn't it be lovely?

A time lapse

If it can happen on the TV series *Life on Mars*, why not in real life? Just as long as you don't end up in the 70s or 80s. The Swinging Sixties might be nice, or those reliable old black & white 50s (after rationing finished of course). Just imagine waking up and looking out of the window and not seeing a car in sight, or a bollard, or a yellow line... bliss.

A gorgeous other half

Millionaires do it every day. Even if they're ninety years old. As long as they've got enough noughts on their bank statement they seem to have beautiful young members of the opposite sex swarming round them. Noughty but nice.

To find that it's all been a dream

Yes, you've just had this horrific dream that you're past your prime, you've got more lines than BT, your body's stiff in all the wrong places and your entire life savings might not even be quite enough for a new set of garden furniture. Then you wake up to find you're a 23 year old millionaire snoozing on your yacht in the Mediterranean.

Proper music on the radio

Music with tunes, singers who can actually sing – it's not much to ask is it? It comes to a pretty pass when even Radio 2 is playing some dreadful racket with people shouting and swearing and Reith knows what. We can get all that at home thank you very much.

Microchips With Everything

Whatever you buy these days seems to be computerised. They're even putting microchips into your wheelie bins now to keep an eye on what you're throwing away. Whatever next? Chips in your chips to make sure you don't eat too many?

And whoever thought you'd have microchips inside your pets?

Your dog has a microchip so he doesn't get lost. Your cat has a microchip so she's allowed in through your super duper state of the art cat flap.

Perhaps even your goldfish will have a chip soon. Or in other words – fish and chips.

Then there are phones. If you'd told Alexander Graham Bell that one day you'd be using your phone to take photos with he'd have had you locked up.

Nothing's simple any more. You try going to a phone shop and asking for a phone that you can just make and receive phone calls with and they'll look at you as if you're a fruit cake.

They say that before long your washing machine will have a chip in it which phones the manufacturer itself when it breaks down to call out a repair man. But you know what? They'll still say that the repair man will come 'any time between 8am and 6pm' next Tuesday, and you'll wait in all day, and the buggers still won't turn up.

No, progress is all very well, but we wrinklies prefer our chips with salt and vinegar thank you very much.

Original Things To Moan About Tomorrow

The wrinkly has certain subjects which he or she is
duty bound to moan about: the weather, young people,
bewildering modern technology, bad manners, modern
'art', incorrect use of the English language, slovenly dress,
swearing, etc etc.

When two or three wrinklies are gathered together the
subjects for discussion will more often include one, or
possibly all, of the above. But! To keep life interesting and
to avoid boring the XL pants off your wrinkly friends,
perhaps it is time to think of something original to moan
about.

SETI

Or the Search for Extra Terrestrial Intelligence. For the
past goodness knows how many years scientists have been
scouring the airwaves of the universe looking for aliens.
As all wrinklies know, the aliens have been smuggling
themselves into the country on containers without being
spotted. What a colossal waste of money!

Five Boys Chocolate bars

Desperation, pacification, expectation, acclamation and
realisation. If you're not a wrinkly you will have no idea
what any of the above is about, but why oh why oh why
can't you buy this wonderful chocolate bar anymore?

The Hadron Super Collider

If you had to invent a sure-fire way of wasting taxpayers' money you couldn't do much better than this: a vast machine lodged under the Swiss Alps or somewhere, firing particles around to see what happens. They might as well be firing £50 notes around, or just building a giant bonfire of them. Madness!

Floral clocks

Once upon a time many a trip to the seaside would be enlivened by the serendipitous discovery of a floral clock. Where are they all now? Gone digital we suppose.

Tectonic plates

Fancy building countries on top of tectonic plates! No wonder we have all these earthquakes and volcanoes and things. It's like building your house on a pile of Pontefract cakes with minds of their own.

Elephants

You go to a zoo, you expect zoo animals. Any fool can open an insect house in their spare room, but you try finding an elephant at London Zoo – you've got more chance of seeing a policeman!

Human statues

Now you don't mind slinging a few coppers into the hat of someone who can dance or sing (as long as it isn't Streets of London again), but some of these jokers expect you to stump up for watching them standing there doing nothing. Scandalous!

Fibonacci numbers

And any of that other mathematical stuff that ordinary people don't understand. So, you get a Fibonacci number by adding together the previous two. So what? Let's invent a new one: you get a Wrinklati number by adding together the previous three: 0, 1, 1, 2, 4, 7, 13, 24, 44... now can we have a Nobel prize?

Songs To Help Wrinklies Through The Day

Pop music is of course made for young people, and those old records from your youth were made for young people too. That means that there are precious few songs out there for the wrinkly. We have therefore suggested a few slight adaptations of classic songs for you to sing as you dance round your dining room, leap about in your lounge or boogie in the bedroom.

'Wrinkly The Best' – Tina Turner

'Olden Years' – David Bowie

'Stairlift to Paradise' – George Gershwin

'I Want Your Specs' – George Michael

'Take the Werthers With You' – Crowded House

'Walking Frame In Memphis' – Marc Cohn

'The Not So Young Ones' – Cliff Richard

'I Can't Get No Sanatogen' – Rolling Stones

'Give Me Sheltered Accommodation' – Rolling Stones

'My Degeneration' – The Who

'Denture the One That I Want' – John Travolta & Olivia Newton-John

'Freedom Pass' – Wham

'Beyond the Se-nile' – Bobby Darin

'Magic Carpet Slippers' – Mighty Dub Katz

'Middle-aged Spread Your Wings' – Queen

'I Bet You Look Good on the Darts Night' – Arctic Monkeys

'Get Ur Free Prescription' – Missy Elliott

'Can't Get Out Of My Bed' – Kylie Minogue

'I Predict a Riot Of Colour from My Spring Plantings' – Kaiser Chiefs

'Chasing Sidecars' – Snow Patrol

'I've Got Flu Babe' – Sonny & Cher

'A Lighter Shade of Ale' – Procol Harum

'Sad Gran's Disco' – Scott McKenzie

'Money's Too Tight in My Pension' – Simply Red

Headlines That Wrinklies Would Like To See In Their Morning Paper

Doctors Find Miracle Cure To Combat Ageing

Read all about it! Yes, you can roll back the years and look as young as some of those film stars who are actually older than you but look 30 years younger.

State Pension To Be Quadrupled

Well, even quadrupling it wouldn't mean it was a king's ransom but it would be a start.

Loud Car Stereo Systems To Be Outlawed

Them and piped music in shops and pubs, those irritating 'personal stereos', telephone 'hold' music and all the other so-called music you have to put up with all flipping day long.

Wrinkly Conquers Everest

Well, we need role models too you know. Surely it must be possible to build a stairlift up the north face somewhere.

A Wrinkly Page Three Model

If only to remind us that we're not the only people in the world with saggy bits.

The TV Guide In Large Print

By the time you've scoured through the tiny print with your magnifying glass and found out what time the Inspector Morse repeat is on he's already worked out whodunnit.

New Prime Minister Is Over 50!

If politicians get any younger they'll be sitting on high chairs in the House of Commons. Bring back politicians with grey hair and a bit of gravitas (even though Harold Wilson was only in his forties when he became PM and William Pitt the Younger was barely out of his teens.

Doctors Perfect Bladder Transplants

No more stumbling around in the middle of the night trying to get to the loo.

Public Hangings For Greedy Bankers

Well, let's face it, that would put a spring in anyone's step wouldn't it?

Automatic Custodial Sentences For Anyone Heard Swearing In A Public Place

About blooming time and all!

Are You Really A Wrinkly?

Statistically, you are quite likely to have received this book as a gift. There you were on your sixtieth (or perhaps even your fiftieth) birthday hoping for a present that would reflect your venerable status with its quiet dignity and good taste. Oh well...

So, somebody decided that you are now officially a wrinkly – but are you? Take this simple test to find out.

It's 10 o'clock in the evening, are you:
a)   Still out and about, completely oblivious to the time?
b)   Nodding off in front of the TV news?
c)   Tucked up in bed in your jimjams?

Do you wear:
a)   Designer clothes?
b)   Chain store clothes?
c)   It's so long since you last bought any clothes you can't remember where you got them?

Does the word 'apple' conjure up images of:
a)   A computer
b)   The Beatles' record label
c)   A nice pie with custard?

Is your pension something that you:
a)   Never think about?
b)   Have started to worry about?
c)   Try not to think about?

Do you drive:

a)   A fast sports car?

b)   A sensible, safe, and fuel-efficient car?

c)   You're not allowed to drive anything any more

Are you:

a)   Struggling to pay your mortgage?

b)   Just paying off your mortgage?

c)   Selling your house to pay for nursing care?

Do you:

a)   Zip up the stairs two at a time?

b)   Walk up the stairs carefully?

c)   Zip up the stairs at the push of a button?

Answers

Mostly a's: You have no right to be reading this book! Swap it for The Clubber's Guide to the UK or keep it under lock and key until you've got past the 'mature' stage and started to go rotten.

Mostly b's: You're a borderline case. Will you teeter over into full wrinklyhood or draw back just at the last moment and grow old disgracefully?

Mostly c's: Nice to have you on board! Yes, you have passed the test with flying (well, shuffling) colours. Award yourself the WBE (Wrinkly of the British Empire) medal.

Positive Thoughts For Grumpy Wrinklies About Tomorrow

- Look on the bright side! Tomorrow is going to be better than today! And if it isn't, look on the bright side! Today was a better day than tomorrow's going to be!

- Tomorrow is a new day! They keep sending them because you complained so much about the old one!

- Look forward to tomorrow! Surely those around you must have run out of new ways to annoy you by now!

- Good things come to those who wait although by your age it might be worth checking you're standing in the right queue.

- Tomorrow is a day of wonderful opportunities. It will bring a vast, fresh array of incredible new experiences for you to moan about!

- The good thing about tomorrow is seeing a lot of people's confident predictions proved completely wrong!

- Tomorrow is the day when you can enjoy looking back nostalgically on the rotten time you've had today.

- Every day you get older makes each individual day a smaller and smaller percentage of your life! So by that way of thinking you're getting slightly less old each day!

- Tomorrow won't be so bad. And if it is, you should be getting used to it by now!

- You've waited a long time but eventually there's got to be a day when things go according to plan.

(Grumbling) Appendix

How To Speak Wrinkly

If you are new to the wrinkly world, or perhaps you are an unwrinkly having a sneaky look at this book before you give it to someone else you may like to be au fait with a few wrinkly terms. Here goes…

- 'Youngster' – Anyone under the age of 50.
- 'Old person' – Anyone five minutes or more older than you are.
- 'A bit of peace and quiet' – An unearthly silence akin to sudden deafness.
- 'A nice cup of tea' – One made by somebody else.
- 'Feeling a bit peaky' – Call an ambulance!
- 'Godawful racket' – Someone else's taste in music.
- 'Typical!' – Something has gone wrong as usual. Strangely never used when something has gone right.
- 'Forty winks' – A two-hour daytime kip with mouth gaping open like the Mersey tunnel and a snore like a startled buffalo.
- 'A bit of what you fancy' – A lot of what you fancy in an orgy of self-indulgence and potential damage to one's vital organs.
- 'Proper music' – Something with a tune, and words that can be easily distinguished (i.e. anything released before 1970).

- 'A bit of a knees-up' – An embarrassing display of terpsichorean abandon after 'a bit of what you fancy'.
- 'A bit parky' – The temperature has dropped to a level that would make an Everest climber's nose drop off.
- 'Decent TV programme' – One with no sex, no swearing, no violence, and not too many people under the age of 50 in it.
- 'Mustn't grumble'/ 'Could be worse'/ 'Surviving' – The wrinkly's choice of responses to the enquiry 'How are you?'
- 'Incredibly expensive' – The price of everything.
- 'A bargain' – Something that isn't really needed and which will soon be put up in the attic for all eternity.
- 'Rather complicated' – The wrinkly's assessment of any technical device introduced since 1973.
- 'It didn't seem to agree with me' – The meal you have just served me was inedible muck which almost killed me .
- 'Very nice I'm sure' – It was really horrible.
- 'Very interesting' – Of no interest to me whatsoever.
- 'I've heard you've not been too good recently' – I heard you were dead.
- 'Lovely weather' – It isn't raining.
- 'Terrible weather' – It is raining.

Glossary

There are certain words and phrases used in this book and elsewhere in the wrinklyverse (ah, there we are, there's another one) which may not be easily understandable by the public at large. So to assist in your enjoyment of this book we have provided a short glossary as follows:

Bingo wings

There is a tale (probably apocryphal) of one old dear who tried to order these from her local Chinese takeaway, but no, bingo wings are the unsightly appendages of excess flesh that hang heavily from under the arms when one's pencil is hovering expectantly over one's bingo card.

Dalek years (the)

The point in a wrinkly's life when they are no longer able to get up the stairs.

Gazunder

Nothing to do with gazumping, the gazunder is the wrinklies' chamberpot of choice because it 'goes under' the bed.

Grubes

Intimate body hair that has turned grey leaving the area between a wrinkly's legs looking a bit like Tom Jones now he's stopped using Grecian 2000.

Moobs

A slightly quicker way of referring to your man boobs.

Muffin top

The ridge of fat spilling up and over the top of your pants is said to make you look a bit like a muffin. Well, as they say, you are what you eat.

Pharmaceutical advent calendar

Plastic box which organises all your pills and medication according to which day you must take them.

Silver surfers

Wrinklies who have discovered the internet and have thus somehow become associated with a Marvel Comics superhero in the process although the original Silver Surfer probably didn't spend quite so much time researching his family tree and sending emails to his children in Australia.

Sognobs

Biscuits that have been too liberally dunked in tea.

Wind tunnel effect

Not a reference to any sort of bowel disorder but the look achieved by wrinklies who have had a bit of cosmetic surgery. The wind tunnel is clearly going to get you at one end or the other.

Wrinkleati

Readers will be familiar with such terms as literati, glitterati and twitterati, meaning the cream of the worlds of literature, showbiz, and twits. The wrinkleati is of course our equivalent.

Good Night, Wrinklies

It's time to say good night, sweet wrinklies. Time to go up the wooden hill to Bedfordshire and slip away into the deep dark wrinkle of sleep.

However if reading this book still hasn't left you ready to drop off – although goodness knows, we've tried our best – then please take advantage of the additional sleep-inducing element contained in the volume.

Yes, this book has been sprinkled with magic wrinkly sleepy dust. Shake the book over your pillow before bedtime to release the magic sleepy dust and you should soon fall into a deep relaxing sleep (albeit after several minutes continuous sneezing from the cloud of dust now hanging over your headboard).

If this still doesn't make you drowsy, shake the book even more vigorously for about half an hour. You should then collapse sweating and exhausted into bed and, thanks to magic wrinkly sleepy dust, fall swiftly asleep.

If you're still not feeling tired, what in heaven's name have you been taking? Clearly you will need an elephant tranquilliser to get off to sleep.

You could try battering yourself insensible with the book. Your wrinkly partner might like to assist with this process particularly after all the time you've been keeping them awake. And also this should release an enormous amount of magic wrinkly sleepy dust at the same time.

Or you could just read the entire book again from the start. Well, your wrinkly memory will probably have forgotten most of it by now!

Night night!